Migrating to AWS:
A Manager's Guide
How to Foster Agility, Reduce Costs, and Bring a Competitive Edge to Your Business

Jeff Armstrong

Beijing · Boston · Farnham · Sebastopol · Tokyo

Migrating to AWS: A Manager's Guide

by Jeff Armstrong

Published by O'Reilly Media, Inc., 1005 Gravenstein Highway North, Sebastopol, CA 95472.

O'Reilly books may be purchased for educational, business, or sales promotional use. Online editions are also available for most titles (*http://oreilly.com*). For more information, contact our corporate/institutional sales department: 800-998-9938 or *corporate@oreilly.com*.

Acquisitions Editor: Jennifer Pollock	**Indexer:** nSight, Inc.
Development Editor: Amelia Blevins	**Interior Designer:** David Futato
Production Editor: Kate Galloway	**Cover Designer:** Karen Montgomery
Copyeditor: nSight, Inc.	**Illustrator:** Rebecca Demarest
Proofreader: Shannon Turlington	

July 2020:   First Edition

Revision History for the First Edition
2020-06-26:   First Release

See *http://oreilly.com/catalog/errata.csp?isbn=9781492074243* for release details.

978-1-492-07424-3

[LSI]

Table of Contents

Part II.   Phases of Migration

Foreword

I'm a golfer (thanks in advance for the sympathy)—I started playing as a teenager. As a kid, I played baseball and tennis. When it was time to play golf, I just picked up a club. How hard could it be? I already understood foot position, grip, weight shift, and follow-through. To suggest I wasn't very good for the first 15 years I played golf would grossly understate just how bad I was at the sport. What I came to realize was that, while there were numerous similarities, the subtleties of the swing in each sport were very different and appreciating the differences was important. We'll get back to this.

For the first 15 years of my professional career, I worked in IT. I managed large IT programs in the mid-late 1990s, during the boom of the large enterprise resource planning (ERP) transformations. There were several drivers for these transformations as the year 2000 approached. For some companies, significant growth over the past several years—including expansion from the "dot-com" explosion—led to the need for transformation and reengineering. Global companies needed to transform as well, but the scale and architectural constraints imposed by their geographic requirements often led to ERP instances in multiple geographic regions. Lastly, for companies with large legacy mainframe systems, the large ERP was a means of fixing the most famous Y2K problem: six-digit date mathematics.

By the time 2001 rolled around, many CIOs were challenged to quantify the value their recent large ERP programs delivered. In the early 2000s, many companies intended to transform by leveraging an ERP implementation, but the programs became so complex and costly that they dropped the transformative aspects of the effort and resorted to simply implementing the technology, failing to deliver many of the anticipated results. Then, a couple years later, many CIOs and their key business colleagues went through an ERP "second wave" effort. These programs were much less technology focused. Instead, the focus was on the transformational agenda: optimizing processes, reducing costs, standardizing operations and architectures around the globe, and getting products to market faster. Most companies recognized the needed benefits.

I would suggest that both analogies are relevant to the world in which we find ourselves today, migrating workloads to the cloud.

On one level, migrating to the cloud is like other significant IT activities, but it's important to look at the details. Like every good IT shop, there is a strategy, tightly linked to the business objectives, and a team of people with the right knowledge and skills to execute. Migrating to the cloud is no different; what is different is that the skills, knowledge, methods, and capabilities required to migrate, execute, and then operate migrated workloads are often different than those required in our traditional "on-prem" world.

In 2020, we find ourselves in an analogous situation, as many CIOs haven't realized the benefits for moving workloads to the cloud. There are several reasons. First, we see corporations start their cloud journey without defining why they plan to move workloads to the cloud. What's the strategy? Are you trying to close data centers? Reduce IT costs? Are you trying to move critical workloads to the cloud to take advantage of cloud native services? For those companies that do define these goals, there is inadequate governance that prioritizes investments to help guide the company toward achieving its strategy. As a result, workloads get to production with inconsistent architectures—perhaps on different clouds, inefficiently using cloud resources, and, frequently, without the necessary security to keep the information safe. It can be difficult to correct these issues quickly. Shifting to the cloud effectively and efficiently requires a thoughtful plan and a good deal of preparation from the business and IT.

Second, to migrate workloads to the cloud and operate them, a company needs cloud skills in many areas. Most of the skills categories resemble those categories required in their on-prem world. The topics are well known: infrastructure, security, development/programming skills, tools, DevOps, and much more. Some of these topics are reasonably easy to understand and appreciate—for example, the good migration tools available on the market are easy to review and score. However, the effort to transition from your traditional software development life cycle to DevOps takes time and practice from people in both IT and the business.

Just as the golfer with an awesome baseball and tennis swing needs to adjust to the nuances of golf, so must an organization transition from "on-prem" to cloud skill sets and processes.

Let's compare the golfer's skills to the shift toward cloud—we will evaluate the stance, the swing, and the grip. The *golf stance* is the cloud landing zone: it's the foundation on which everything is built. There are so many options that influence your workload performance, your backup and disaster recovery options, and your global data storage requirements. The company strategy will provide requirements that affect the landing zone design. Your migration *swing* is the set of tools used to execute the migration. The *swing* moves the objects from location A to B. There are tool sets that can be used to automate the movement of applications into their landing zones, including mission-critical mainframe workloads. The *grip* is the reliable set of hands that are required to execute the swing. Instead of holding a seven-iron, you're placing your hands on the AWS console, and you need the right skills and knowledge to execute successfully. Building a team with the required cloud skill sets to migrate and operate cloud workloads is frequently underestimated.

One of the guiding principles I've used throughout my career is this: it's very difficult to manage that which you've never done. When you don't have experience, your advice is more academic, and for large, complex technology projects, relevant experience is important. I met Jeff Armstrong two years ago at AWS. He's had an amazing technology career in numerous roles—from software engineer to technology executive to consultant—and he has never strayed far from the technology. For the past several years, he's helped customers migrate workloads to AWS and has firsthand experience with the many decisions companies have to make throughout the cloud migration journey.

This book is a result of those experiences. Successfully moving workloads to the cloud has strategy, technology, process, and human aspects to it. Documenting a thoughtful, coordinated, holistic approach up front will dramatically reduce the challenges a client encounters on this journey. Jeff shares an extensive discussion of the many levers a company can pull when embarking on a migration—you won't need them all on any given migration effort, but over time, you will pick and choose several of them depending on the specific situation. If you are newer to cloud migrations, you may find it beneficial to "power scan" the book to appreciate the multiple topics, and then go back and read it carefully.

With that, I'm off to hit a bucket of balls…

— Jonathan Bauer
Principal, Deloitte Consulting–US AWS Lead Alliance Partner
Chicago, IL
May 2020

Preface

Sam sits at her desk. It is late, but she doesn't know how late. The clock on the wall clicks away behind her. No reason to look at it; she has not gotten around to changing the battery for days. The second hand sits there one step forward, one step back. Sam feels the same way; how did she get here? She scans around the office. The only thing she sees is her reflection in the dark glass of her window. Pressing her palms against her eyes, she tries to relieve the stabbing pressure behind them. She saw this migration project as a way to boost her career, stand out as an innovator and leader, and clear a path from IT director to VP. Instead of receiving praise for the company's success, fear of termination sinks in.

Sam's company started its migration project four months ago, and it is now consuming her life. Project delays are driving up costs, and outages are affecting their customers' experience. The CIO is growing impatient with the issues and has begun to question Sam's capabilities. *I have worked hard to become the director of IT; I need this migration to go smoothly*, she thinks. Sam saw migrating to AWS as a catalyst to improve her company's agility and drive more ambitious changes. In the past couple of years, the competition from startups has become fierce, and as an enterprise company, they cannot keep up with their competitors' release cycles. By moving to AWS, they could gain agility and become competitive again. If this project were successful, it would gave her career a significant boost. With the unforeseen issues piling on, she now fears her decision to migrate was a mistake.

"Samantha, I like your migration plan, but do you expect that we can meet these timelines?" asks her VP. Sam snaps out of her flashback, planted back in the chair in her boss' office. It is 10 a.m., and the sun is shining through the windows, warming her feet.

"As long as the stakeholders meet with the migration team and give the information required," she affirms.

"And these costs, are these correct?" asks her VP, raising his brow. Sam replies, "There may be a change of plus or minus five percent, but I'm confident we are close." The

VP agrees to take her plan forward to the executive team for approval. Sam stands, proud and tall; she has won over the VP and is confident that executive management will follow. *One step closer*, she thinks with a smile as she walks out of the room.

If you are reading this book, you may have been in this situation before. A high-stakes opportunity is at your feet that will elevate your career, but fear, uncertainty, and doubt (FUD) seep into the situation and prevent you from moving forward with confidence. It is only natural, and I assure you I too have suffered this pain and can sympathize with you. However, this feeling is unnecessary and easy to allay. This book aims to deliver you the knowledge and information you need to obliterate FUD. This book supplies a comprehensive look at migrating to AWS and offers real-life insight into the things that work, the things that do not, and the things you should look out for. I want you to be like Sam, squash the FUD, stand proud, and take your career to the next level.

Who This Book Is For

This book is not a technical how-to book but addresses the process of migration through the lens of a manager. As we walk through the migration process, we will discuss not only the process itself but also risks, benefits, and potential roadblocks that may arise as you go through your migration. Any IT operations manager, development manager, migration project manager, CIO, or CTO will find value in this book. To help you understand the subjects deeply, we will walk through numerous scenarios and deconstruct what went right and what went wrong in each. These scenarios will allow you to draw similarities to your situation, company, and applications. This depth will prepare you and give you confidence to face these situations when you encounter them in your company.

What This Book Covers

This book covers the migration process from inception through final application planning. In my experience, the business and management aspects of migration easily account for 90% of the effort in a migration. Unfortunately, many overlook their importance and focus solely on the technical aspects. Following the techniques and insight in this book will ensure that you have a successful migration, and that you maximize your agility and cost savings along the way. We will cover:

- Why you should migrate to AWS
- The risks and how to mitigate them
- Discovering your workloads
- Building your business case
- Addressing your operational readiness

- Defining your landing zone and governance
- Planning your migration
- Refactoring, retooling, and final preparations

Each chapter will not only help you understand the process but will help you develop the necessary deliverables to ensure success. For instance, in Chapter 1, we will walk through creating a "why" narrative and FAQ for your migration to help communicate the business value to the rest of the management team. These deliverables significantly increase momentum and gain buy-in. The result is that you will not only gain valuable migration knowledge but also tangible processes and deliverables to increase success and decrease delays.

Conventions Used in This Book

The following typographical conventions are used in this book:

Italic
Indicates new terms, URLs, email addresses, filenames, and file extensions.

`Constant width`
Used for program listings, as well as within paragraphs to refer to program elements such as variable or function names, databases, data types, environment variables, statements, and keywords.

`Constant width bold`
Shows commands or other text that should be typed literally by the user.

`Constant width italic`
Shows text that should be replaced with user-supplied values or by values determined by context.

> This element signifies a tip or suggestion.

> This element signifies a general note.

This element indicates a warning or caution.

O'Reilly Online Learning

O'REILLY® For more than 40 years, *O'Reilly Media* has provided technology and business training, knowledge, and insight to help companies succeed.

Our unique network of experts and innovators share their knowledge and expertise through books, articles, and our online learning platform. O'Reilly's online learning platform gives you on-demand access to live training courses, in-depth learning paths, interactive coding environments, and a vast collection of text and video from O'Reilly and 200+ other publishers. For more information, visit *http://oreilly.com*.

How to Contact Us

Please address comments and questions concerning this book to the publisher:

O'Reilly Media, Inc.
1005 Gravenstein Highway North
Sebastopol, CA 95472
800-998-9938 (in the United States or Canada)
707-829-0515 (international or local)
707-829-0104 (fax)

We have a web page for this book, where we list errata, examples, and any additional information. You can access this page at *https://oreil.ly/migrating-to-AWS*.

Email *bookquestions@oreilly.com* to comment or ask technical questions about this book.

For more information about our books, courses, conferences, and news, see our website at *http://www.oreilly.com*.

Find us on Facebook: *http://facebook.com/oreilly*

Follow us on Twitter: *http://twitter.com/oreillymedia*

Watch us on YouTube: *http://www.youtube.com/oreillymedia*

Acknowledgments

Although my name might be on the cover, a book is by no means a one-person show. This book would not be possible without the endless support of a host of people. The first person that I want to thank is my wife, April Armstrong, for being super supportive and forgoing many morning conversations over coffee to allow me to write. Without her, I would not have been able to complete the project. I wouldn't be a particularly good dad if I didn't give a shout-out to my kids, Natalie and Hailey, for giving up some more time with me so I could work on the book. Whether they know it or not, my family gives me my relentless drive to be more tomorrow than I am today.

Special thanks also go out to my coworkers William Ying and Manas Srivastava, who provided feedback and inspiration, even if they weren't conscious of it. I would also like to thank Pi Zonooz, Danielle Adams, and Kamal Arora for guiding me on how to get my book approved through management, public relations, and legal.

The technological world is full of fast-paced changes and conflicting terminologies. If it weren't for my tech reviewers John Culkin and Mark Wilkins, this book wouldn't be as polished as it is. I want to take the time to thank you for reading and providing your detailed feedback.

Of course, this book wouldn't be a reality at all if it weren't for all the hard-working folks at O'Reilly Media. I want to thank Kathleen Carr, my acquisitions editor, who worked on getting my proposal approved so my idea could become a reality. My acquisitions editor Jennifer Pollock and my production editor Kate Galloway did an excellent job of ensuring that my book got over the finish line. Last but certainly not least, a huge thanks goes out to my development editor Amelia Blevins for putting up with me and my quirks as a first-time author. Amelia, without you, I don't know if I could have finished. You are a fountain of positive energy and inspiration.

PART I

Migration Foundation

Welcome to the first part of *Migrating to AWS: A Manager's Guide.* In this portion of the book, we will talk about the foundational aspects of migration. Chapters 1 and 2 discuss the benefits and the risks of AWS, and how to mitigate them. During these two chapters, we will build a detailed understanding of these concepts and create key deliverables that enable you to communicate this information effectively to other constituents throughout the company. Migration to AWS isn't a project that you tackle only with the IT department. Other migrations you may have done in the past, such as migrating from physical to virtual servers, or migration of one VMware-based data center to another, could remain compartmentalized within IT. Migrating to AWS allows your company to become more agile and increase business value. To facilitate these capabilities, you will need the cooperation of the entire organization. Compartmentalizing within IT should not occur while migrating to AWS, nor would it be advisable, because you will not reap the maximum benefit. We will cover agility and business value benefits in depth in Chapter 1.

I want to take this opportunity to clarify the use of some language used in the book. Throughout this book, there will be two words that I use extensively, *spend* and *compute.* They will, however, appear in a different context than you are familiar with seeing. Before the cloud, spend and compute were mostly used as verbs, as in *I have to compute how much my wife spends on kitchen carpets and hand towels for every holiday.* However, in the context of the cloud, these words are often used as a noun as well. You will see sentences such as *Storage tiering will reduce your cloud spend.* In this context, spend means the amount of money spent on your AWS bill. You will also see sentences such as *AWS Auto Scaling will reduce your overall compute usage.* Compute, in this case, is the servers that you will use to run your programs, rather than a calculation. The reason that compute is used rather than instance, virtual machine, or server is because the processing power in AWS is decoupled from storage and networking. Also, compute in AWS might refer to a serverless technology where you wouldn't use a server or instance. I am also kidding about the hand towels and carpets. She doesn't buy them for *every* holiday.

Before we get started, I want to cover some basic concepts on AWS pricing and how you can find this information. Throughout the book, I will refer to the current cost of services to help highlight the savings and costs associated with deploying specific solutions to AWS. When I do this, I will reference all prices from the *us-east-1* region. We will cover what regions are in Chapter 1. At this stage, what you need to know is that *regions* are where AWS deploys infrastructure throughout the globe, and they might have different pricing based on location. However, where your company is located may require you to look up pricing for a region other than us-east-1. It is also possible that AWS pricing might have decreased, and the costing listed in this book may no longer be accurate. I would suggest you research the latest costing directly from AWS for any analysis you perform.

Looking up the current pricing for AWS is easy. AWS has located all its pricing under the same URL structure on its website. The structure is *https://aws.amazon.com/ + service name + /pricing*. For instance, the URL to access EC2 pricing is *https://aws.amazon.com/ec2/pricing*. For ease of use, Table I-1 shows the most frequently used AWS services.

Table I-1. AWS pricing URLs

Service	URL
EC2	https://aws.amazon.com/ec2/pricing/
RDS	https://aws.amazon.com/rds/pricing/
Elastic Load Balancing	https://aws.amazon.com/elasticloadbalancing/pricing/
Lambda	https://aws.amazon.com/lambda/pricing/
Elastic Block Store (EBS)	https://aws.amazon.com/ebs/pricing/
Amazon S3	https://aws.amazon.com/s3/pricing/
DynamoDB	https://aws.amazon.com/dynamodb/pricing/

Now that we have covered the contents of Part I, and how to look up AWS pricing so you can directly relate it to your business and locality, let's move on to Chapter 1 and discuss the benefits of migrating to AWS.

Why Should I Migrate to Amazon Web Services?

I wondered whether putting such a loaded question as the first chapter of my book was a good idea. The actual list of reasons to migrate to AWS could be as long as this book, but like Simon Sinek says, "Always start with why."[1] Thus, I felt it prudent. The biggest roadblock you will encounter is people's reluctance toward change. Migrating to AWS from your current platform is a change to the way people operate and the skills required. A sound narrative around the *why* will allow you to inspire the people around you and deliver better results while removing reluctance. This chapter will delve into many technological and business benefits gained by migrating to the cloud. With this information, you can provide the *why* to the upper levels of management and staff.

As you read this chapter, I encourage you to think about the situations your company is experiencing and how these benefits relate.

A way that has worked well in the past for communicating the *why* to coworkers is through a set of frequently asked questions (FAQ). Later in this chapter, we will walk through building out your FAQ to communicate the *why* to upper management and staff. You can accomplish this by anticipating the questions they will be asking and constructing answers based on the benefits your company will realize. By completing this exercise, you will gain acceptance and lessen detractors. You are increasing the probability of success and efficacy of the transition.

---

1 Simon Sinek, *Start with Why: How Great Leaders Inspire Everyone to Take Action* (New York: Porfolio, 2011).

Cloud Technology Benefits

AWS offers several benefits with the latest cutting-edge technologies. However, not all these technologies and their benefits apply to every company. Instead of walking through every benefit, we will walk through the technical benefits that apply to every company. They may not be flashy, but they create a solid base on which you build your infrastructure. By taking advantage of these benefits while you migrate to AWS, you will reap enough capital and time savings to fund the testing of more advanced technologies. I have been able to save companies millions of dollars using these methods, which they can then reinvest in innovation. I agree that automatically transcribing customer support calls and analyzing for customer sentiment is an awesome and powerful tool for your business. However, I believe that migration is one of the crawl-before-you-walk situations. As a manager, your primary concern is to ensure that your migration meets your business needs and regulations. Implementing the latest cutting-edge AI is secondary; after all, the infrastructure you have today is what pays the bills and provides your current customer value.

Scalability and Dynamic Consumption

When you migrate to AWS, you need to focus on diverging your thinking from how you used to operate on-premises infrastructure. Many of the conventional design patterns and operational processes are anti-patterns in the cloud. For scalability and consumption, many of these anti-patterns show up early in your migration. It is best to identify and move past them quickly. Changing your existing thought process around on-premises scalability will immediately afford you cost savings and agility when comparing it to scalability in the cloud. Before we cover these new patterns and why the on-premises patterns are anti-patterns, we will walk through the scalability AWS offers you. Again, as you read, it might make sense to jot down some notes about your applications and how these scaling methods might improve your capabilities.

Vertical scaling

Vertical scaling is the practice of adding compute and memory to a server to increase the performance available to the workload. I liken it to being Amish and plowing my field. I am plowing a new row, but the soil gets hard. To complete my plowing, I unhitch my quarter horse, go to the barn, and get a bigger draft horse. Vertical scaling is not a novel idea for the cloud. It has been there the whole time in your data center, and in my experience, it is the go-to method of improving performance and increasing capacity. However, with migrating to AWS comes some key differences.

When you have your infrastructure running in AWS, you have a pay-as-you-go dynamic consumption model instead of a prepaid model. I like to explain it like the tides: the moon's gravity pulls on the earth and raises the water level of the ocean as it passes. This analogy mirrors the usage of your infrastructure throughout the day—

the pull on your resource load ebbs and flows. Just like the tide, you end up with a high and low watermark. The difference with the cloud is that you only pay for what you use; you only must buy at the low watermark. Then you incrementally pay for more consumption during the high usage times. On-premises, you have to prepurchase at the high watermark. To complicate the issue further, you must forecast your consumption for the life of the hardware, which will be over or under the actual consumption. Underutilized resources are a drain on your company's funding, and overutilized resources provide a poor user experience. The purchase of on-premises equipment in my analogy can be pictured like building a dock. If you place the dock too high, you will have to put in ladders for people to get to their boats. If you place the dock too low, they will be sloshing around in the water. AWS is a floating dock and eliminates both issues; it rises and lowers, providing optimal conditions. Figure 1-1 shows what prepaid purchasing and consumption looks like over its lifetime.

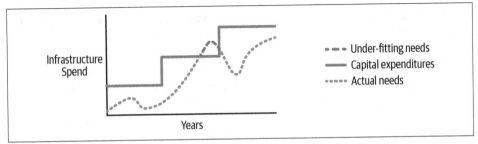

Figure 1-1. Infrastructure costs over time

Figure 1-1 does an excellent job of showing how the purchase of on-premises equipment under- or over-fits your company's needs. If you compare the dotted line, which stands for your need, and the solid line, which represents your capital expenditures, you will see how far the gap between them ebbs and flows. At one point, the demand exceeds the capacity of the infrastructure, indicated where the line is dashed, meaning that you do not have enough capacity to service customers. I would say not having enough capacity is not common. Most people, including me, buy more than they need, so a situation like that never arises. Having consistently underperforming IT resources is a good reason for your manager to ask you to empty your desk. The important thing this graph shows is how you must purchase not only for the high watermark, but also for well above it. The overage ensures enough capacity, and all the space between the dotted and solid lines is wasted capital. The dynamic ability of AWS eliminates this overage and lost capital, allowing you to use those funds for other business needs.

If you think back in your recent history, you may remember a conversation much like the following scenario.

Scenario 1-1

The server for Tom's meme generator is seeing a lot more traffic these days. He must address the performance. He has looked at the CPU and memory usage. It has two allocated CPUs, and Tom is seeing spikes of up to 100% usage multiple times throughout the day. The memory usage is within limits; it must be the rendering process for the graphics that is taking too much of the CPU. Tom has looked at the VMware cluster, and he has plenty of capacity. He considers adding just two more CPUs to compensate.

This is a prevalent scenario, both on-premises and in the cloud. There are a few things I would like to draw attention to that will change after you migrate to AWS. First, *instance* is AWS nomenclature for a server or virtual machine from the Elastic Compute Cloud (EC2) service, and these terms can be used interchangeably. However, I will use *instance* whenever I am talking about a server in AWS, and *server* or *virtual machine* to indicate a server on-premises. The second is the statement "memory usage is within limits." When working with instance sizing in AWS, you cannot adjust CPU and memory separately. You must find the smallest instance that meets the memory *or* CPU target, and whichever is not your target goes along for the ride. In this example, the CPU capacity is your target. When you increase by two more CPUs in AWS, your memory will increase as well. Third, it may be better to use horizontal scaling instead, to spin up more instances when needed to address the load instead of making a permanent vertical change. We will discuss horizontal scaling in the next section.

 AWS offers a capability called Optimize CPUs for Amazon EC2 instances. This capability allows you to set the number of CPUs when you launch an instance. The setting cannot be modified later and does not alter the run rate of the instance. These limitations may not be immediately evident when reading the documentation and make it appear that AWS operates like on-premises capabilities. The primary reason for the Optimize CPUs function is for the software licensing base on CPU count and edge-use cases when CPU is low while also requiring high RAM.

Let's take a look at another possible scenario.

Scenario 1-2

Mary is looking into some performance issues that have been affecting her company's end-of-the-month accounting process since the latest software service pack. It looks like the patch introduced more CPU load into the process. She will have to add more CPU power to the server to meet the deadline requirements of the month-end batch processing.

In this situation, AWS can shine by reducing your costs of operation. As mentioned before, while on-premises, you must purchase equipment to meet your high water-mark, so you have already committed funding to operate your environment. Allocating more CPU power to address batch processing is irrelevant to the costs of operation. However, in AWS, you are purchasing at the low watermark, and it is best to stay there.

You may be wondering how you address the performance issue. It is best to solve this scenario by using temporary vertical scaling. You know when this workload will come up, and you know it is only temporary. It would not make sense to increase the capacity to address the batch process permanently. Using scheduled events or third-party software, you can schedule the scaling up of this server before the workload and then scale it back down after it completes the work. Temporary scaling would give you the most cost-effective operation.

 You may wonder why we did not cover horizontal scaling for this situation. For an application like an accounting system, it is commercial off-the-shelf software (COTS) and not commonly engineered for horizontal scaling.

Horizontal scaling

Although vertical scaling adds more capacity to a single server, horizontal scaling allows you to add more servers to meet the load for your application. Using my Amish analogy again, if the soil got too hard, I would hitch a second horse to finish my plowing instead of getting a bigger horse. Again, with the AWS pay-as-you-go model, you can gain significant cost reduction by using horizontal scaling. To achieve horizontal scaling, AWS offers two crucial services, *Elastic Load Balancing* and *AWS Auto Scaling*.

Always start with horizontal scaling and work back from there to find technical reasons why it will not work. Only then revert to vertical scaling.

Windows servers that are attached to a domain require special consideration. These servers need special scripting to add and remove themselves to the domain during horizontal scaling events.

Elastic Load Balancing. You may remember I had said that vertical scaling was typically the go-to method of scaling on-premises. To implement horizontal scaling on-premises, you would have to buy a load balancer. The increased capital, maintenance, and care-and-feeding soft costs are a significant deterrent to using load balancers for capacity needs. Implementing on-premises load balancers is seen more often when there is a specific high-availability concern, or there is limited ability to scale vertically. With load balancing, the dynamic consumption in AWS again provides a considerable advantage. You only pay for the load balancing you need, so there are no up-front costs. You will also benefit from a serverless technology. The Elastic Load Balancing in AWS does not have any servers you need to maintain or patch, reducing your soft costs. As you can see, load balancing in AWS is more attractive, making horizontal scaling for performance more accessible.

The term *serverless* means a lot of things to different people and companies. In the context I use it, as represented in this book, it refers to any service that doesn't require you to manage servers or infrastructure. Obviously, there are servers somewhere doing the work; you just don't need to care about them.

AWS Auto Scaling. While the Elastic Load Balancing service provides the network connectivity between the users of your application and the servers, the AWS Auto Scaling service contains the needed logic to control the expansion and contraction of the server pool. Without this expansion and contraction, your costs would again be static and less efficient. Auto Scaling has multiple triggers available to add and remove capacity from your application server pool. You can use CPU usage, memory usage, and disk input/output operations per second (IOPS) for a needs-based option. Another option, if you know when your load will occur, is auto-scaling using a schedule. The AWS Auto Scaling service also allows you to set a minimum number of servers and can act as a high-availability orchestrator, ensuring that a minimum amount of compute is available to service your customers. The way you look at availability and disaster recovery (DR) also changes, but I will touch on that later in "Disaster Recovery/Business Continuity" on page 31.

Let us take a second to think back to the conversation with Tom about the CPU capacity needs for the meme generator application in "Scenario 1-1" on page 6. In this scenario, it makes perfect sense to switch from a vertical scaling solution used on-premises to horizontal scaling in the cloud. Using this method will produce the best experience for your customers while supplying your company with the best cost consumption available. When CPU usage rises as more people generate memes, the auto-scaling service adds a server to meet the load. When the server is online and available, auto-scaling will add it to the load balancer to service customers' requests. The process works in reverse when load drops, returning to your baseline settings. There are a few caveats to using horizontal scaling, though. Your servers need to be stateless. *Stateless* means that no specific configuration or data lives on the server, and the server can be deleted with no adverse effects on the overall operation. Another caveat might be that you need preconfigured instance images created to reduce instance launch time.

 You can use sticky sessions on a load balancer to ensure that the same server always services users as a potential workaround. However, if the server is removed from a load balancer, users will still experience adverse effects.

Geographic Diversity

Now that we have covered scalability, let us cover another key AWS benefit: geographic diversity. Think about your data center(s). Where are they? How far apart are they? How many are there? If you manage a smaller operation, then the answer is probably few, and if you have more than one, they are probably not far apart. I can tell you from my experience that my data centers at one company were only seven miles apart. Not exactly geographically diverse, but better than the solution was before, having a single data center. If you are a large enterprise, you probably have two or more data centers, and they are most likely farther apart. However, how close are they to your users? How is the remote office in Brazil connected to your data center in New York?

I have migrated many Fortune 500 companies and a few smaller companies to AWS. Throughout my experience, I can tell you that no matter what your configuration is, when you migrate to AWS, you can do it better. AWS has impressive geographic diversity, and you can use that to your advantage for high-availability and disaster recovery concerns and bring the services closer to your customers for a faster user experience. To highlight how you can take advantage of this capability, we will walk through how AWS deploys its infrastructure. There are regions and availability zone

(AZ) concepts, as shown in Figure 1-2. AWS provides a website (*https://infrastruc ture.aws*) with an interactive globe detailing its regions, network connectivity, and points of presence.

 Do not try to extend your company into many regions for the sake of diversity. There should be a compelling business reason, because there may be additional costs associated with it.

Regions

AWS regions are a collection of availability zones that have data centers in a geographic area. The concept of regions is very foreign when compared to on-premises operations. On-premises you don't have the ability to create a comparable infrastructure design. You don't have the economy of scale to create such a vast infrastructure.

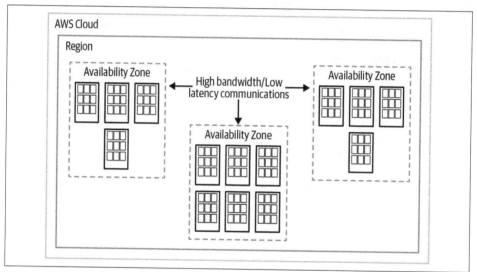

Figure 1-2. AWS region components

To help understand the concept, we can draw a similarity to how the United States is segmented. A region could represented by an individual state. Within a state there are counties (*parishes* if you live in Louisiana, or *boroughs* in Alaska), and they represent availability zones. The last aspect of a region in AWS is the data centers; you can think of these as the cities within a county. At the time of writing, the AWS infrastructure consists of the regions shown in Table 1-1.

Table 1-1. AWS regions

Region name	Region
US East (N. Virginia)	us-east-1
US East (Ohio)	us-east-2
US West (N. California)	us-west-1
US West (Oregon)	us-west-2
Africa (Cape Town)	af-south-1
Asia Pacific (Hong Kong)	ap-east-1
Asia Pacific (Mumbai)	ap-south-1
Asia Pacific (Osaka-Local)	ap-northeast-3
Asia Pacific (Seoul)	ap-northeast-2
Asia Pacific (Singapore)	ap-southeast-1
Asia Pacific (Sydney)	ap-southeast-2
Asia Pacific (Tokyo)	ap-northeast-1
Canada (Central)	ca-central-1
China (Beijing)	cn-north-1
China (Ningxia)	cn-northwest-1
EU (Frankfurt)	eu-west-1
EU (Ireland)	eu-central-1
EU (London)	eu-west-2
EU (Milan)	eu-south-1
EU (Paris)	eu-west-3
EU (Stockholm)	eu-north-1
Middle East (Bahrain)	me-south-1
South America (São Paulo)	sa-east-1

> AWS *does not* offer all services in every region. Refer to the AWS Region Table (*https://oreil.ly/18uh1*) to ensure that all the services you require are available before migration.

Data proximity. When you are getting ready to migrate to AWS, you will want to think about your users and their location, and select the region closest to them. These could be internal or external users, or both. The benefit AWS brings over conventional on-premises data centers is that you do not have to limit yourself to just one or two regions. You have at your disposal every AWS region across the globe. There are no sunk costs associated with launching a new region like there are with a data center. You do not have to lease space or purchase power conditioning, fire suppression, security, racks, and all the other things needed to launch a data center properly. AWS has taken care of this for you. Because of the multitenant and the pay-as-you-go models, you only need to pay for the infrastructure you use in that region. Let's look at a few scenarios to help you get an idea of how you might use regions in your migration.

Scenario 1-3

Sam's company is located in Washington, DC, and all of its corporate users are located in that office except for a few remote sales users. The largest customer using its online application—representing 90% of the consumption—is in Seattle, and the rest of the users are spread across the United States.

Let us take a second to walk through this scenario as if we were Sam. Most of the corporate users are in Washington, DC. The first thing you want to do is pick an AWS region with proximity to your staff to reduce latency. An obvious choice would be the us-east-1 region in Virginia. Selecting Virginia ensures that the bulk of the internal users have the lowest latency possible. The speed of light is fixed; there is not much we can do to make data transmission faster. Selecting something close like Virginia is not unique to the cloud; her data center is probably within a few hundred miles of the corporate headquarters already. However, when you think about the second statement, how the largest customer is in Seattle, this is where design planning in AWS shifts. AWS has regions all around the US; it would make sense to place some infrastructure to support her biggest client in Seattle. I would choose the us-west-2 region in Oregon as a second deployment location, specifically for her online application. The beautiful part is that Sam need not worry about all the components of a data center. She only has to concentrate on and pay for the servers required for her biggest customer. Deploying in two regions like this on-premises would be costly.

Scenario 1-4

Bill's company is located in Chicago and New York City. The offices are about equal in size. Bill's company has a website, but most of its infrastructure supports internal operations, and the company does not have to worry about external customer access. Bill has his servers in each office, and they serve most data to their respective offices. However, there is one internally built application in New York that the Chicago office also uses.

In Bill's situation, I would recommend starting with latency to find out how the base deployment would look. Since the servers in the offices only serve the local office in which they are located, there will not be much traffic crossing the country. I would recommend that Bill use the us-east-2 region in Ohio for the Chicago servers and us-east-1 for his New York servers. Using this configuration should give his users the lowest latency to their respective servers. Since his company has a website, but it is not an essential customer application, I would suggest that Bill place it in a single region in AWS. Bill can make his website faster for customers by using Amazon CloudFront, a content distribution network (CDN). Using CloudFront will increase performance without the complexity of more servers in other regions. Lastly, Bill has an internally developed application that both offices use. Since this application is privately built, Bill can take advantage of the two regions with some minor reprogramming. This design provides a multimaster (you can write data in both places) and multiregion solution, which would give the best performance and availability.

Scenario 1-5

Brittany has a similar situation to Bill. The servers in her company are only for internal staff. However, her company only has one office in Columbus, OH, and a third party hosts its website.

Brittany has the most straightforward selection process. Her entire user base is located in Columbus, OH. I would suggest she use the us-east-2 region in Ohio to host her infrastructure since a third party hosts her website. Where to locate their site does not affect her decision. Brittany may want to replicate her data to a second region for disaster recovery purposes, but I'll touch on that in the section "Disaster Recovery/ Business Continuity" on page 31.

Data locality and privacy regulations. There has been much talk about the General Data Protection Regulation (GDPR) in the European Union (EU). This regulation, along with others, has raised concerns with IT management on how to meet the data sovereignty requirements it imposes. Since AWS has regions located around the globe, it is easy to control data storage sovereignty according to the country where the regulations exist. Data locality is only part of the puzzle. You also may need to validate that the data does not cross borders during transactions. Just storing the data in the correct country does not rubber-stamp all your infrastructure and operations if you have processing outside of the designated region. However, having all the AWS regions available to you gives you a significant advantage over on-premises deployments where you may need to acquire new data centers to meet the regulations.

One important caveat that I want to point out for data sovereignty is that some countries don't have more than one region. For instance, if you have regulations in Canada that require data to be stored in the country, you will have limited options at this time for multiregion deployment. Currently, AWS only has the Canada central region (ca-central-1). AWS continues to add new regions all the time, and this may not always be the case for Canada, but it is essential to consider your DR requirements for sovereignty. AWS has sufficiently covered the US and EU, but areas like South America and Asia-Pacific may require added consideration. It is important to note that every region has at least two availability zones. For most companies, this may supply enough availability to cover your requirements for DR while maintaining sovereignty.

 AWS has a special region called GovCloud where government entities can host their infrastructure in AWS and meet strict guidelines at the federal, state, and local levels.

Availability zones

Thinking back to my state analogy, the cities represented the actual data centers; the counties were the availability zones (AZs) in an AWS region. AZs play a key role in high availability within a region. AWS connects AZs with low-latency fiber-optic networking, allowing data to move between them with ease. The zones are also geographically separated, so an event like a flood or tornado in one zone will not affect the others. To make it easier to visualize, you can think of an availability zone as a single data center. Most regions have three availability zones to choose from for the deployment of infrastructure. To help solidify the concept, let's walk through a hypothetical AWS region.

Scenario 1-6

One AZ in our region exists in Chicago, and this AZ has three data centers connected. The second AZ is located in Milwaukee, WI, and has three data centers connected at its location. Finally, the third AZ is in Rockford, IL, and it too has three data centers connected. That means there are three AZs and nine data centers in this hypothetical region. AWS does not publish the distance between AZs or where any of the existing AZs are located. Therefore, this example is an estimation. However, you should have a good understanding of the relationships between regions and AZs, and the importance of the geographic separation of the AZs.

The AZs and their separation are a significant benefit over conventional data centers. Many companies have the equivalent of two regions in their on-premises deployment but only a single AZ. A data center will typically be found close to the principal office and then a second in a distant location for disaster recovery purposes. The concept of *availability zones* rarely exists on-premises. Similar to the shift in thinking with scaling and regions, there also needs to be a shift in thinking on how you address availability in your infrastructure design. Shifting your thought process allows you to take advantage of the benefits of AZs. Let's look at a scenario to help you get an idea of how you might use AZs in your migration.

Scenario 1-7

Jim's company runs an application on the web that allows customers to transfer funds to friends and family in an instant. The primary data center for Jim's application is in New York, and the disaster recovery site is in California. Jim has been having issues with the Structured Query Language (SQL) server hardware, and there have been some outages that are unacceptable. He sees the potential to solve this problem by using SQL mirroring to create a second copy of the database. The mirror copy will allow Jim's SQL server to failover if the primary server's hardware fails, and to continue his application's operation. Jim located the second mirror server in New York because the latency to California was too high and would affect his users' experience. Before Jim migrates to AWS, he wants to better understand how he can use AZs to his maximum benefit.

Jim has increased his availability, but he has not improved his geographic diversity. If his primary data center goes offline, Jim will still have to failover to the disaster recovery site in California. I don't know about you, but thinking about DR used to give me heartburn. Our DR was all designed and verified, and we had done failover testing. However, testing is usually just one piece at a time, not an entire data center. Would it all work in the event of a disaster? *It should* is the answer. I dislike *it should*. I want sure things, and the best way to have a sure thing in a disaster is to shift your thinking from DR to business continuity (BC). On-premises, Jim would have a challenging time incorporating BC into his application and making it highly available. Business continuity is much easier to achieve in AWS thanks to AZs. Availability zones are geographically diverse within a region, giving them separate power and communication feeds. They are also far enough apart that a tornado would only affect one AZ. Jim could reconfigure his application when he migrates into AWS. He can use two AZs for his SQL server mirror and his web servers. His aim should be to create a highly available and continuous operation if one AZ were to go offline.

AZs and disaster recovery

The AWS AZs are one of the most critical changes that help businesses when they migrate to AWS. Disaster recovery on-premises is a hard problem to solve; it never gets the love, attention, and funding it should. It ends up being a drain on resources and a significant source of stress for management. I think back to my days in banking, where DR is critical. It would be so much easier to change the conversation to BC and add some years back onto my life. When you migrate to AWS, I encourage you to pay particular attention to how you can deploy your infrastructure in multiple AZs to achieve business continuity.

I want to bring attention to a design pattern that comes up many times with AZ deployment. You must not fall into the same trap. Many companies deploy and configure two AZs in a region and think they have all the availability they need. Who can fault their logic? They have two deployments; when one fails, the other takes over. I would encourage you to think long-term. What happens when an AZ fails, but it was because of a natural disaster? The failed AZ will not come back online soon. In this situation, you would have to redeploy the second set of infrastructure to another AZ. If you only have set up two AZs and one is now offline, you would have to construct a new AZ deployment. All the while, you are still feeling the pressures of being in a failed state. I recommend deploying at least three AZs from the start, to address any potential AZ failure.

Easy Access to Newer Technologies

With scalability and geographic diversity, we touched on the physical benefits of AWS; now, we are going to cover a logical benefit with easy access to newer technologies. In the early days of AWS, the services were limited to a few such as Simple Storage Service (S3) for object storage and Elastic Compute Cloud (EC2) for compute. AWS now offers dozens of services, from managed database platforms like Relational Database Service (RDS) to AI tools like SageMaker. Access to new technologies allows companies to adopt and expand their capabilities and innovate for their customers more readily. To highlight how access to these technologies can improve any company, I want to show it using a very drastic comparison. The addition of these more advanced services, coupled with the pay-as-you-go model, has changed the ability of small startups to compete with Fortune 500 organizations. Think of a boxing match. In one corner is the startup—small, but fast. In the other corner is the incumbent Fortune company—big, but slow. In this boxing match, the opponents are not evenly matched. The smaller, more agile company can outmaneuver the large incumbent, but its success depends on landing enough punches before the big company can wind up and knock them down.

To give an example of what this might look like, let us look at some technologies AWS can economically provide to startups. An example of a costly technology to implement on-premises is data warehousing and analytics. For a startup to get into analytics, it would have to generate a substantial amount of investment to buy the needed hardware to store and process massive amounts of data. The expenditure of this size takes funding away from vital company functions such as paying staff wages. Day-one operations of a startup doing analytics on-premises could cost tens or hundreds of thousands of dollars for initial hardware expenditures. The procurement of large amounts of hardware by a large incumbent company is easy. Paying hundreds of thousands is not hard; the difficulty for a large company is in the time to execute.

By launching in AWS, this same startup would have easier access to new technologies like analytics for two reasons. The first is that AWS has many advanced technology services available for a startup to choose from in the analytics space. There is Amazon S3 object storage for storing vast amounts of data in a way that is cost effective. Amazon QuickSight offers business intelligence tooling, and services like Amazon Athena and AWS Glue supply data processing and querying capabilities. Offering the services alone is not a special sauce. When you couple these advanced technology services with the pay-as-you-go model, you have the proper ingredients to incite competition by dropping the significant capital expenditure and removing the barrier to entry.

Inexpensive and easy access to these new technologies allows any company to test, experiment, and innovate in ways never before possible. The number one thing preventing companies from experimentation and innovation is the fear of failure. Failure on-premises is a very costly endeavor, leaving extra or specialized hardware and software sitting on shelves instead of cash in the bank. After migrating to AWS, the accessibility of technology and the low cost of failure can enable your company to innovate and deliver improved results for your customers. Let us look at what accessibility to new technologies might look like for your company.

Scenario 1-8

Amy works for a hospital, and someone from purchasing is asking the IT department to create an AI program to estimate supply need. Some supplies are expiring before they use them. However, sometimes if they order less, they run out. She is looking for a program to estimate when and how many to order based on historical patient data.

On-premises, Amy would have her work cut out for her to make this request happen. She would need to deploy some servers to do the AI model training. Depending on which machine learning algorithm is selected, Amy may need to buy some specialized hardware to run the computations. Amy will also have to solve the problem of who will program and maintain this AI application, which requires a specialized skill set. All these items create a significant roadblock to adoption. Amy does not have easy access to new technology. However, after Amy's company migrates to AWS, she would have a much simpler time implementing this request. AWS has a service called Amazon Forecast that does this AI computation. Amy would not have to worry about servers, hardware, or a specialized AI programming skill set to test this technology. Amy could use her current IT staff and programmers to implement a proof of concept (POC) and only pay for the training time in hours, data storage in gigabytes (GB), and generated forecasts ($0.238, $0.088, and $0.60 per 1,000, respectively).

Availability

We have already discussed geographic diversity and scaling and how they can increase your availability. However, these are not the only capabilities AWS offers to enhance your availability. There are many technological ways AWS increases availability, but let us focus on a select few that are most likely to be relevant to your needs.

If you look at the history of AWS, you can see that the offerings continue to be created serverless, like the elastic load balancers we discussed before. Since you are not deploying any servers, you do not control quantity or deployment location. AWS designs these services to be highly available for you, relieving this workload and stress from your life. I am sure you will appreciate less work and stress. You will not be sitting on the beach sipping piña coladas, but it is one less thing to worry about postmigration. The way AWS accomplishes this higher level of availability for these serverless offerings is by fully exploiting the availability zone concept to deliver them. Here are two scenarios detailing how you might use these services in your environment to gain higher availability as opposed to your on-premises configuration.

Scenario 1-9

Keith works for a financial services company that provides an online application to a host of banks throughout the US. The application generates and stores reports on a Windows file server where the web servers can access them. On-premises, Keith's team has deployed only one server. They had thought about replicating the files to a second server. However, they only have one active data center. They decided that the extra management of another server was not an efficient use of their resources. Keith is wondering whether there is a better way to deploy this solution when they migrate to AWS.

In Keith's deployment, there is a better way of architecting this solution in AWS to increase his availability. In this situation, my recommendation would be to move the report files to Amazon S3. S3 is an object store and is perfect for storing data that needs to be downloaded from the internet. S3 is also one of the serverless offerings from AWS and is designed for high availability. S3 replicates your files between all the AZs in a region automatically and provides 11 nines of durability. What are 11 nines of durability? It means there is a 99.999999999% probability your file still exists on the storage. I have heard it is probable that S3 data will outlive humanity. I am not a mathematician, so I cannot validate the claim. However, doing some napkin math, it sounds plausible. By making a few minor alterations to the application, Keith can achieve high availability, almost unimaginable durability, and confidence in the ongoing workload on his staff.

AWS provides 11 nines of durability, not availability. It is important to remember the difference. The AWS service-level agreement (SLA) guarantees that the data exists in storage, not that it is always available to be retrieved. Rest assured, their track record has been pretty darn good.

Scenario 1-10

Kathy is the manager of data management at a large insurance agency. They run a high-performance computing (HPC) cluster for actuarial computation. The servers themselves are stateless and do not store any data, but they access petabytes of data on a large storage device via the network file system (NFS) protocol. Kathy wants to migrate this application to AWS to take advantage of the vast scaling capabilities to run these computations faster and more cost-effectively. She needs to devise a way of storing the data that provides high availability. The storage device has redundant controllers to continue serving data if one fails. However, last year, there was a leak in the data center roof that disrupted the network, causing tens of thousands in lost revenue. Kathy wants to ensure that physical data center issues do not disturb the operation.

Kathy's situation is not unique. I based this scenario on my real-life experience with one of my data centers. Water raining down in a data center is not a good thing, and something you never thought about addressing. Come to think of it, this is the same data center that had part of the wall collapse. Construction workers were removing a pedestrian bridge next door. A crane slammed a massive piece of concrete into the wall. These are the situations when life is stranger than fiction. I could not make this stuff up, and neither can you—that is the point. You cannot think of all the things that can happen to your data center and, like Kathy, it is best to address this in your deployment. For Kathy's implementation, it would make sense to use the Amazon Elastic File System (EFS) to store the data for her HPC cluster. EFS supports the NFS protocol required for the operation of her cluster and offers redundant data storage across AZs. This service is a serverless offering and does not require any input for this availability.

Increased Security

In keeping with the trend of logical benefits, AWS offers another with increased security. A few years ago, people were fearful regarding the security of their data in the cloud. I can partially understand their reluctance. I say partially because large software as a service (SaaS) providers like Box had a booming business. People were not afraid to put their business data on those platforms. It is ironic to me that those same people feared placing the rest of their data on AWS. For most, the fear of moving their data to AWS has passed. After breaches, large companies have stated that if they were on AWS, the breach would not have happened, or it would have had less impact. Zero trust and least privilege are best practices in AWS. These two methodologies are quite effective in securing your environment. The benefit in AWS is that it makes the implementation of these principles quite easy.

Zero trust

Trust security on-premises has mostly remained unchanged for the past few decades. Most networks have a three-zone deployment. An internet zone exists for connecting to the internet and hosting other devices, like firewalls and virtual private network (VPN) controllers. Behind that, there is an edge zone or demilitarized zone (DMZ) that hosts the web servers and email servers.

Further into your network, there is an internal zone that hosts your private servers and data. Some companies deploy a fourth zone where printers and workstations exist, which allows further separation from the private servers. Having zones was a good security design for networks 20 years ago. The problem with this design is that there is a level of trust for each zone. You do not trust the internet, somewhat trust the edge, and fully trust the private zone. This concept sounds good when you think about it, but after all the recent corporate breaches that have occurred, you can see why it is dated. Once you pierce the veil of the edge or internal zones, you can skip around like Dorothy on the yellow brick road. This design implements perimeter security. Break through the perimeter, and there is little to stop you from poking and prodding the rest of the servers until you break into them.

Zero trust is when no server trusts any other server. If you can break into a server in the edge zone, you cannot communicate to any other servers in that zone unless allowed by design. Instead of happy Dorothy, you end up in a cold dark cell, like Al Capone, contemplating your rapidly declining health. Zero trust restricts your blast radius from any attacks, thus making your environment more secure. Nothing says you cannot do this on-premises. I implemented this security for a bank I worked for. It took a long time to implement, and it cost tens of thousands of dollars for the technology and tens of thousands more in employee effort.

AWS Security Groups are a significant benefit to zero trust security and do not cost tens of thousands of dollars. Security groups cost nothing. Security groups are how AWS implements firewalls in AWS. A security group provides an external firewall to your instance or group of instances; it is not a piece of software running on the instance itself. Like a firewall, it controls all the traffic flowing into your instance and blocks anything that you have not explicitly permitted. To make management even easier, you do not have to control traffic by just IP addresses either. Security groups allow you to reference other security groups. This referenceability makes managing security even less burdensome than it is on-premises. When you assign or unassign instances from a security group, the security group automatically adjusts without manual intervention, whereas changing servers and IP addresses on-premises becomes an issue if firewall rules are not updated and become stale. By referencing a security group as a source when a server is added or removed, it is automatically inserted or removed from the security group. This automation ensures that there are no old, static references.

 Make sure your team breaks the habit of using IP addresses for AWS resources and switches to security group references.

Let us look at a scenario where this would happen on-premises.

Scenario 1-11

John runs a web server in his edge zone, and it reaches back into a database back end. John needs a lot of performance for the database, so he has set up three servers in the internal zone. The web server needs to talk to these three servers, so John adds a fire-wall rule referencing the three database server IP addresses. Later, John gets new servers with more processing power, and he decides that he only needs two servers when he rebuilds them. A few months later, John's web server was hacked because of a missing patch on the operating system. It was discovered during forensics that the hacker was able to log on to six other web servers in the edge zone. The damage did not end there. The hacker could also get into the payroll system because John never removed the third IP address from the firewall rule when the server was decommissioned. The IP address ended up being repurposed to the database server for the payroll system, granting access from the web server. After the incident, upper management asked John to be successful at another company.

If John's servers had been in AWS, most of this attack would have been blocked. The web server compromise would have still occurred—John did not effectively manage the security and remove the vulnerability. However, once the attacker had gotten into the web server, they would not have been able to jump from the server to another server so easily. By implementing zero-trust security group rules, the hacker could not have moved to the other servers in the edge zone. They would not have a way of getting there, and the second that John removed the third database server, it would no longer be in the security group. Therefore, access to the payroll database server would have been blocked as well.

Least privilege

Least privilege is controlling authorization to the smallest level of access to do the work required. You can think of it as security at an airport. As a passenger, you can get through the security checkpoint, but you cannot get on the wrong plane or enter a storage room. The woman who works the counter at Starbucks can get through the security checkpoint and enter the storage room, but she cannot get on any plane or the tarmac. A baggage handler can get on the tarmac and into the baggage processing rooms, but he cannot get onto a plane or into a storage room. This is least privilege: everyone gets the access they need to do their job, nothing more.

AWS considers security *job zero*, by which they mean that it's even more important than priority number one. A lot of thought has gone into how access controls work. AWS offers very fine-grained control over the capabilities of each service through a service called Identity and Access Management (IAM). This control allows you, like the airport, to give only the access needed to operate a particular service. The countless permissions AWS services offer are segmented into *list*, *read*, *tagging*, and *write*. Table 1-2 details the capabilities associated with these permissions.

Table 1-2. AWS IAM permissions

Permission	Access
List	Allows access to list components for a service, such as instances or security groups
Read	Allows access to read the properties of components like the configuration of an instance
Tagging	Allows access to add or remove descriptive tags to resources
Write	Allows the changing of properties of a resource like adding another disk to an instance

By using these individual access controls, you can grant access to a minimal subset of actions. Why would you want to do this, and why is it a benefit to security in AWS? It boils back down to blast radius. If an attacker were to gain access to a set of credentials, you want to limit the actions they can perform to limit the amount of damage they can do. Let us look at a scenario without least privilege set up and see what can happen.

Scenario 1-12

Rob is migrating to AWS and needs to set up access for his performance monitoring team to log on to the AWS console to look at server performance. Rob is in a rush and does not implement least privilege. Instead, he grants admin-level rights to the performance support desk. He will have more time to take care of limiting the permissions in a week or two. A few weeks pass, and Rob has forgotten to update the security. Someone on the performance team left their credentials on their desk on a sticky note. Late one night, a malicious security guard found the sticky note. Feeling slighted for not getting a raise, he logged on to the company's AWS account and started clicking around and deleting things. By the time Rob and his team had figured out what had happened, the malicious actor had removed half of their infrastructure.

A situation like Rob's is not unique to the cloud. Just like scaling on-premises is possible, so is least privilege. It is just more difficult to implement on-premises. When you are working on-premises, there are dozens of places where you need to implement security: firewalls, switches, hypervisors, and the list continues. It is like an office full of desks, and you need to go around to each desk and lock the drawers. After you migrate and start using AWS services, your task of securing becomes a lot easier. Instead of focusing on securing every desk in the office, you just need to secure the office. IAM works as the door to your infrastructure. Every user passing through that door gets their authorization as they pass through. IAM allows you to assign the list, read, tagging, and write permissions as your users enter, to give you granular control.

Cloud Business Benefits

Although there are significant technical benefits in migrating to AWS, there are a number of business benefits as well. I consider the business benefits significantly more attractive than the technical ones. It is a bit like beginning a relationship. The technical benefits attract you in the first place, whereas the business aspects are the mental attractions that keep the relationship growing and interesting. Although the technical benefits might be a *why* when you start migrating to AWS, they will quickly become a *how* after the technical hurdles are resolved. Just like the world of love, the physical side of the equation can wane as it becomes ordinary and expected. Sure, AWS will come out with new services and capabilities to spice up the technical side; however, it all comes back to the business side of the house. You do not implement technology for technology's sake—there is always a business driver behind it. That is why I want to bring to the forefront the business benefits that migrating to AWS will offer you.

The business benefits are going to have staying power as a *why*-driver in your business for far longer than any technical driver. Because of the longevity of these motivations, it makes sense to attribute extra time to evaluating and thinking about how they relate directly to your company. Crafting a great why around these benefits will provide a compelling story to drive and maintain motivation in stakeholders and staff for your migration.

Reduced Expenditures and Support

We have already covered the concept of *pay as you go* and purchasing your infrastructure at the low watermark, so we don't want to dive into those waters any deeper (pun intended). However, these are not the only ways that AWS can help to reduce your costs relating to IT expenditures. When discussing the benefits of AWS regarding costs, I like to break them down into two buckets. In the first bucket, we have the hard costs associated with running your environment. These are the costs for equipment, software, services, power, fire suppression, and the like. They are very tangible and easy to measure. On the other side of the question, the second bucket contains the soft costs associated with your estate. These costs, such as staff time for patching, racking equipment, performing backups, and others, are tough to measure. These soft costs are the parasite attached to your IT budget that sucks the life out of it. These costs, if saved, would provide your company with more IT funding for innovation and delivering value to your customers.

Hard costs

I just said that hard costs are easy to measure, but now I'm going to qualify that heavily. They are easy to measure *if you measure them*. When you talk about hardware like servers and switches, I am sure that you have an accurate measure. You purchased them, they are on your books as a depreciating asset, and you can probably tell me exactly how much that costs you. Once you step beyond hardware, things might get a bit trickier. For instance, if you do not have a colocated or dedicated off-site data center, accounting for individual costs becomes difficult. I have detailed two examples here that show just how drastic the difference in cost allocation can be.

Scenario 1-13

Andrea works for an advertising company that does ad placement in magazines and newspapers. As the VP of IT, she is responsible for the entire IT budget for her company and is keen on knowing where her expenditures are year over year. Andrea's company is midsized and has a decent-sized infrastructure estate. Several years ago, they moved their equipment out of their office building and into a colocation facility. Andrea buys equipment new from Dell and has it shipped directly to the facility and racked by their staff. Andrea pays for a single rack at the facility that has 8KvA of electricity. The facility takes care of all power, internet feeds, generator, fire suppression, and battery backup power.

Andrea has a pretty easy job. Everything that Andrea needs to run a data center is sold to her with a cute little bow on top. She knows exactly what all these items cost her, and she does not have to worry about accounting for them. AWS does not offer any simplification to Andrea in terms of how she accounts for costs. The cost of running her systems in AWS will also be delivered in one bill with a nice bow on it. Andrea might have some unused capacity in her rack if it is not chock-full of equipment. She may benefit from AWS because she would not have to pay for that extra capacity. When comparing the cost-benefit to AWS, Andrea will have an easy time performing the analysis.

Scenario 1-14

The medical software company that Jim works for has an extensive infrastructure that is located in two data centers in its central office location. Jim wants to analyze how much his data center is costing him compared to what it would cost to run it in AWS. Jim starts to dig into his costs but is having a hard time breaking things out. Since the data centers are on-site, the power bill is for the full facility, and he does not know how much the equipment uses. He ran into the same issue when he went to cost out the HVAC expenses. The contract for the service includes the whole building, so he cannot allocate that either. To make matters even more frustrating, he ran into the same issue with the generator and fire suppression. The only item that Jim could adequately account for besides the equipment was the battery backup system. That system is only used in the data centers.

Believe it or not, I run into Jim's situation all the time. Many companies have no idea what the actual costs are to run their infrastructure. Like Jim, things just grew organically on-premises, and there was no real separation from an accounting perspective. It will be difficult for Jim to make a cost comparison between on-premises expenses and AWS. Since his costs are not attributed directly, Jim will have to make some assumptions. He can base them on the square footage of these data centers or use an industry standard as a baseline. AWS can help in this area by using the total cost of ownership (TCO) tool available online. I have found that the estimates AWS provides are not viewed favorably by some management. They feel it is more marketing material than qualitative data, and would prefer data from an unbiased third party. If you would like to build your estimations by hand, you can use the AWS Pricing Calculator (*https://calculator.aws*).

 The AWS Pricing Calculator does not support costing on all AWS services, but its capabilities continue to grow over time.

The economy of scale that AWS offers businesses in hard costs is a substantial benefit. It has more servers than any one company could have. It uses specialized equipment and can drive down acquisition and operational costs. These savings are then transferred to its customers. Even the largest companies in the world, ones with large-scale infrastructures themselves, choose to migrate to AWS and shut down their data centers. The reason is quite simple: they are not in the data center business. Their business is offering some other service or product to their customers. Since data centers are not their business, they cannot have the scale of AWS and thus the cost savings. If these massive companies cannot do it as effectively as AWS, imagine what migration can do for your company.

Soft costs

One of the most exciting benefits of AWS is related to soft costs. When you migrate to AWS, there are a lot of services available to help reduce the soft costs of operating your environment. In addition to eliminating the costs, the services can also help to reduce risk. One of the best services for reducing soft costs postmigration is RDS, a managed database service. This management means that AWS handles patching of the operating system, backup of the databases, and patching the database engine. This automation eliminates much of the effort needed from your staff to perform these functions. Many hours a year of staff time would be dedicated to installing the patches and checking to ensure that backups were occurring. Operations like these are a time suck and provide no value to customers. Customers want their data backed up, but they do not care how it happens, nor are they willing to pay for it. They see it as unavoidable and part of your problem, not theirs. Customers are looking for product capabilities, updates, and bugs fixed. AWS helps you with these non-value-adding functions, like database patching, and frees up the time for your staff to work on those value-adding items that customers want.

This form of soft cost savings is prevalent throughout the platform. If you think about all the items required to run a data center, you will start to see these savings. For instance, running a data center involves battery backup systems. These systems need maintenance and testing. If you run your own data center, these tasks fall on your shoulders to complete. Depending on your risk profile, you could be testing your backup systems every year, quarter, or month. Again, this provides no value to your customers besides them expecting your systems to be online when they need them. You can take this a layer deeper and think about the time required to negotiate contracts for your communications lines and HVAC support contracts. All these items consume your time and effort, and the real cost of this time is tough to quantify. When I think back to my data centers and the time required to manage them, I would have preferred to outsource all of that and worry about running my software. If you are using a colocation data center, many of these are already outsourced for you, and you don't have to worry about them.

If we take one step above the operational requirements for a data center and start looking at things like network and hypervisors, you'll see a trend where AWS can save you even more time. For instance, in AWS, you do not need to worry about managing the hypervisor. Patching your VMware environment or Microsoft Hyper-V becomes outdated. The hypervisor is part of the EC2 product you do not have to think about anymore. You consume the EC2 instances. AWS worries about the underlying hardware and operating system and patching. The same holds for elastic load balancing.

In your on-premises environment, you would have to patch your load balancer and maintain all security and updating of the hardware when it expires. The same holds for your storage subsystem, because AWS manages the storage subsystem for you. You consume the elastic block store (EBS) volumes. You do not have to worry about managing how much disk capacity is available, how much storage will be needed, or how much maintenance contracts cost.

 Reduction of soft costs can easily surpass hard cost savings. Employee salaries are most likely your company's greatest expenditure. Now this doesn't meant that you should be handing out pink slips like candy at Halloween, but it does mean that your staff will have more time to add business value.

The last major component we will cover that reduces operations soft costs is the firewall. Firewalls are another critical network communication device that you must manage, patch, and update. By using AWS Security Groups, you eliminate a significant amount of soft costs related to maintaining your environment. In addition, AWS has a networking service called Network ACLs that offers a second layer of security by implementing a Layer 3 firewall.

I could go on about all the capabilities AWS has that can save you these costs. I wanted to highlight a few of the important ones to get you thinking about other areas where your employees use a lot of their time to do mundane tasks—tasks that you can outsource and have managed by somebody else. Your product or service is what your company does best; it is what makes it unique. That is why you are in business. I will repeat that multiple times throughout the book. It is an essential concept, one I want ingrained in your being. It will help you with detractors later. Some staff will be reluctant to make changes, and fearful of obsolescence and additional workload. You will be able to show how their working life will improve by working on more interesting duties that will lessen their reluctance to move forward. I like to say it like this: nobody went to college or training classes to learn to perform monotonous tasks. They learned for another reason—to build a product, to create magnificent databases, or to make good money. I assure you, none of them were dreaming about work a robot could do.

There are many more services available in AWS to help reduce your workload on soft cost tasks that we will not review. There are tools to back up your data, there are tools to apply patches, and there are even tools to manage licenses. When used together, they are a formidable weapon against wasted time and effort. You will have to determine where your company has significant waste in operational tasks and determine whether there is a service or capability that will help to lessen it. Table 1-3 is a list of some additional services that could lessen your soft cost postmigration.

Table 1-3. Cost-reducing services

Service	Capability	Service information
AWS Backup	Provides automated backup for a number of AWS services	*https://aws.amazon.com/backup/*
AWS Systems Manager	Provides systems management automation such as software installation and patching	*https://aws.amazon.com/systems-manager/*
AWS License Manager	Automates and manages software licensing in AWS	*https://aws.amazon.com/license-manager/?nc2=h_m1*

 Do not use soft costs in your business justification unless you can absolutely quantify them. Failure to do so could lead to them being thrown out and possibly jeopardizing your migration. I have seen managers get into sticky situations where upper management thought they were pushing an agenda by providing "fluff" numbers.

No Commitment

When you are building on-premises, it is a lot like buying a new car. You put much effort into the evaluation to make sure it is a good fit. You will be together for the next three to five years, and you'd better make the best of it. It is the second-largest expense you will have after your house. It is a significant commitment that has a major impact on your life. Like with your car, the commitment is what makes businesses apprehensive about trying new things. It is a lot scarier to fail fast when failing costs hard dollars that are hard to recoup. Let's face it—computer hardware depreciates faster than your last car. A car will at least bottom out somewhere along the curve because it still performs the function of driving from A to B. Not the case with computer hardware; the value can continue to travel right down to zero because the software designed to run on it can no longer run. This depreciation leads to much fear of failing fast. Failing fast means that hardware you buy today might not work as expected with the concept you were testing, and now you have this hardware sitting around collecting dust. Do this a few times, and you have tens or hundreds or thousands of pieces of equipment lying around. What happens? You do not fail fast. You do not want to fail at all, so you do not innovate, and your company gets its lunch handed to it by a startup.

Do not tell my wife of 17 years this, but commitment is bad. At least when it comes to IT. AWS does not have any commitments. You can spin up a server, or test out a business concept or product enhancement. If it does not work out, destroy it and stop paying. Now your ability to test and fail takes a much smaller bite out of your budget. Failing fast means that you spend insignificant amounts of money multiple times until you find something that works and delivers on the product or feature that your customers want. It is like a fresh new product you see on the web that you want to try, but you are afraid it might not deliver on its promises. However, then you see that there is a money-back guarantee if you are not satisfied. Now your fear of failure is gone, so you move forward with your purchase. The no-commitment aspect of AWS is the same warm safety blanket you like to wrap yourself in before trying that new product.

One of the benefits you can take advantage of is around employee testing. Throughout my career, I have had many staff members that loved to tinker and try things out. I see this as an excellent business advantage. People can solve problems in ways never expected or thought of through experimentation. However, it would be best if you put some guardrails around experimentation. You must make sure your data is secure and your costs do not get out of hand. In AWS, you can set up a sandbox account that allows your staff to try new things, learn, and experiment in a controlled manner. You can set spending limits and alarms for this account to keep costs low. From a security aspect, you can prevent access to production data to limit data leakage.

Furthermore, you can run automated cleanup scripts to purge deployed infrastructure to keep costs low and shadow IT to a minimum. All these items provide a safe place where your staff can help you deliver better value to your customers while challenging themselves and staying mentally engaged with their work. It is a win–win all around.

Although AWS is typically no-commitment, you can have situations where there that require commitment. They are typically tied to discount programs in which you guarantee a specific spend to receive a discount. This is known as the Enterprise Discount Program (EDP).

Business Agility

Another business benefit you can leverage when you migrate is business agility, which is exceptionally critical for long-term survival. If you look at the companies that have struggled and failed recently—Sears, Kodak, Toys R Us, and Blockbuster, to name a few—their inability to adapt and change is what sped up their demise. The bottom line is that business agility translates into increased competitiveness, increased ability to adapt to changing market conditions, and increased revenue.

Agility is the number one benefit of migration. Make sure that you address this in your *why* FAQ.

I've noticed that in all the companies I have helped migrate to AWS, gaining business agility was the most challenging benefit to achieve, yet the most fruitful. It is difficult because there are many people involved—usually different departments, and different teams within departments. They need to cooperate as a cohesive whole to reap the benefits of agility. These teams are traditionally very siloed in a company. Unfortunately, when working with people and these silos, change does not come quickly. Many times, the reluctance to change leads to considerable roadblocks. One reason I find it vital to come up with the *why* narratives is that it will help move the process along and drive synergies between the silos.

If you were to go back about five years, you would not hear the words *business agility* mentioned within the context of IT. IT was there to provide the technology services the business required. Typically, you had long cycles for development using waterfall design methodologies, or you were running commercial off-the-shelf software. However, things have changed in recent years. The combination of Agile software development methodology and automated deployment pipelines has changed how the business looks at IT. It is not unheard of today for companies to release ten production updates every day. When you compare that to your on-premises system, you will see the dramatic difference these tools facilitate. AWS has created a suite of products for the automation of the building and deployment of infrastructure and software. However, these services on their own are not especially useful. For instance, AWS CodePipeline allows you to automate the building and deployment of software. Unfortunately, if the software cannot be automatically installed and requires user intervention, an automated deployment pipeline is not extremely useful.

Put another way, agility is the combination of tooling and people process. Unfortunately, as an IT manager, the responsibility will fall to you to address this disconnect. IT will be the central point of contact between all the other teams, divisions, and business units within an organization. This centralization gives the IT manager a unique perspective to create a uniform mode of operation across the entire company. Let's dive into the following scenario, which shows how agility can affect a company.

Scenario 1-15

Judy works for a large firm that manufactures pet supplies. The software that Judy's company uses for sales, logistics, and the manufacturing floor is built in-house. The software works well for this unique business and has been evolving over the last 20 years. It was last updated about two years ago, although the development team has been working on new features. In the previous year, a new competitor came into the market and is applying much pressure to Judy's company. Her competitor is also running custom in-house software for its operations, but it is much more advanced. Its software has real-time analytics and AI that aids the logistics and warehousing functions. Judy's management has also heard that the competitor's software does real-time pricing updates based on current stock and production. This capability ensures that product does not sit in the warehouse for extended periods. The sales team got the scoop from a long-term client who also buys from that company. They told the sales team that the competition has a much better purchasing website and a streamlined return process that is done online rather than over the phone. The customer also said that within the next week, the other company is offering an API that will allow its system to hook in automatically to reorder everyday products like dog food. Also, last week, their competitor released an update to forecast order quantity based on past purchases.

I have seen some exceptionally large and successful companies in a comparable situation to Judy's. They created their internal tooling long before the current wave of technologies. Their competition is newer and was built in a cloud-native state, which gives them several advantages. In Judy's case, the competitor is using analytics and AI and can push out updates at least weekly. For her company to compete on a level playing field, it will have to implement quite a few changes:

- Implement a continuous integration and continuous development (CI/CD) pipeline
- Regression-test two years of changes before updating the production environment
- Train staff and customers on the two years of changes

Once the update is pushed out to production, they can think about switching to an agile development methodology. All the while, Judy will need to ensure that the mentoring, training, and motivation of the staff is in place to ensure the successful outcome.

Disaster Recovery/Business Continuity

When I started my career, DR was not thought about by many companies. For many years, the extent of my DR plans was a tape backup that was stored in a fireproof safe. The term *proof* should not have even been used–it was more of a fire *delay* and did not guarantee that the temperature of the fire would not melt my tapes. As the years progressed, so did the importance of DR. IT moved from just running an accounting system to become a critical part of the business. Today, IT might be your business, and without it, you won't be in business long. DR is a large part of your current budget and a critical part of your processes.

When companies migrate to AWS, they should try to move the focus from DR to BC. Business continuity is more concerned with operations continuing than recovering from a complete failure. I am sure you will agree with me that continuity is better than recovery. Who wants to recover when it is so much easier to continue? With the capabilities of the AWS infrastructure behind you, it is easier to create a BC plan that can meet your required objectives. Those objectives are the recovery point objective (RPO) and recovery time objective (RTO). To help remember these concepts, I always think about the RPO objective as the sell-by date on my milk. How old can it (the data) get before it is of no use to me? I remember the RTO as how long I take to get to the store to get more milk, or how long I can be offline.

Using AWS AZs in your design allows you to meet near-zero RTO and near-zero RPO by deploying your applications in an active/active or active/passive configuration. Active/active means that your applications are running on at least two servers at the same time. You could do this with a load balancer in front of the servers. Active/passive is similar, but one of the servers is replying to requests at any given time. In case of a failure in an active/passive deployment, the second server takes over for the primary. Congratulations, you now have a near-zero RPO/RTO BC design in AWS. This design will allow you to survive the failure of one AZ and continue operations without interruption. The question you must ask yourself is whether this is enough protection for your business. What if an entire region goes down? If you ask that question and the answer is, *That is unacceptable*, then there is more BC/DR work to be done.

Using the benefits of AWS regions, you can expand your infrastructure to account for an entire region failure. However, depending on your implementation and your requirements, there can be a significant difference in cost, depending on your implementation. You will need to decide whether your company wants cross-region DR or BC. Cross-region DR is less expensive but has a much higher RTO and RPO, whereas cross-region BC costs more because there must be more active infrastructure running to accommodate the lower RTO/RPO. Let us walk through two scenarios to show how your DR/BC might look after migrating to AWS.

Scenario 1-16

Kevin works for a local school district and is thinking about migrating to AWS. The school runs all 12 servers in an on-site data center in the district office. They connect the schools to the head office via VPN tunnels over the internet. Kevin's systems do not have remarkably high RPO or RTO requirements. The district requires all systems to be online within 24 hours, a typical RTO. The district is less concerned with RPO, because all the data in the systems is stored on hard copy for at least a week. In the event of data loss, grades and attendance can be reentered from the hard copy. To accommodate the RPO, tape backups are taken every Friday and removed from the site. Even though it is not expected, Kevin would like to improve upon the RPO.

Meeting the district requirements will not be a difficult task to achieve, given the capabilities of AWS. Since there is such a high RTO and RPO, it makes little sense to deploy BC and continue with a DR strategy. Kevin will be able to snapshot (take a copy of the data at the block level) the servers using an automated system called Data Lifecycle Manager (DLM). DLM supports an RPO as low as 2 hours, which is better than the requirement of 168 hours. Since Kevin only has 12 servers, it would not be that hard for him to manually redeploy instances to another AZ within the required RTO of 24 hours. If an AZ failed, Kevin could start up new servers and attach the latest snapshots to them in about six hours, leaving plenty of time to spare. It would be best if Kevin deployed his 12 servers in three AZs. This configuration ensures that only 4 servers could go down at a time instead of 12. Deploying in this configuration would save him four more hours in redeploying instances.

Scenario 1-17

The local restaurant chain that Amelia works for runs 52 servers in a colocation facility. The servers run the website, online ordering, and restaurant point-of-sale systems. Her company has set an RTO of only four hours. It has not analyzed how much downtime costs and thinks four hours is acceptable. Amelia disagrees and wants her servers to stay online. Having their website down for four hours is unacceptable.

Amelia should look at changing from a DR to a BC thought process. She has enough systems with high business criticality to call for it. By using some of the benefits of AWS, Amelia can deploy her applications to three AZs and use load balancing and auto-scaling to provide availability. By moving her database backend to Amazon RDS, she can benefit from active/passive database availability. With this configuration, Amelia will reduce her RTO/RPO to virtually instantaneous. To add another layer of protection, she can implement DLM with four-hour snapshots and replicate them to another region for DR capability. She can restore her servers if an entire region goes down for an extended period.

BC is not a concept you associate with cost savings, but with AWS and the regions with three AZs, you can cut 25% of your costs while still providing the same level of availability. It depends on the capabilities of your application, but if your applications can support it, you can save a considerable amount. This savings is another benefit of AWS regarding BC.

Scenario 1-18

Jimmy works for an advertising company that runs a critical application on the web. To meet the RPO/RTO requirement of his application, he deployed an active/passive cluster. Each half of the cluster is in a separate data center to supply redundancy for a regional outage. Jimmy is moving his company to AWS and needs to replicate this level of availability.

Jimmy will save some money moving his application to AWS. Let us say that Jimmy's production server costs $100 a month to run. To meet his availability and BC requirements, Jimmy has a second server in another data center. This server also costs $100 a month to have online to receive database updates and be prepared to serve traffic. Jimmy is paying 200% for his application: 100% to serve the application, and 100% to be available for failover. Since Jimmy is in the United States, he has at least three AZs available to him. When he migrates his servers, he can use auto-scaling and a load balancer to change his application to an active/active cluster instead. In this configuration, Jimmy can deploy three servers that serve 50% of the load, meaning that he will pay $50 a month for each server, bringing his total to $150 instead of $200. In this configuration, Jimmy can have one server or AZ fail and still be able to serve all of his load, even while saving 25% of his ongoing costs.

 Determine whether your company needs more than one region to meet its availability requirements. Many executives *want* more than one, but the business does not justify the expense. They want the Lamborghini when a Dodge Hellcat is just fine.

Decreased Vendor Lock-in

Whenever I hear the words *vendor lock-in* regarding migrating to AWS, I have to scratch my head. If anything, migrating to AWS opens more options rather than restricting them. When you built out your infrastructure on-premises, you accepted a lot of vendor lock-in. You could change your storage area network (SAN) vendor or server hardware vendor, but you would do that when you had to refresh hardware. When you bought that hardware, you were locked into it for three to five years. It was not like you could buy a SAN from Dell EMC and then a year later buy disk capacity from Hewlett-Packard to expand it. It just does not work that way, and the same goes for your hypervisor. Sure, you can change from VMware to Hyper-V, but the level of effort to accomplish that is high.

When you migrate to AWS, you exchange your hardware for bits and bytes. If you were to upload my server to AWS and have it run there, you could take that server the next day and move it to Azure. By moving to the cloud, you cut the strings to your hardware. There are some costs for outbound data from the cloud providers generating a small cost to move, but those movement costs exist everywhere, even on-premises, so I consider them moot. Converting your systems to purely data makes them more mobile than ever before. Running instances in AWS offers you more mobility benefits than you could ever have on-premises; it all ties back to the pay-as-you-go model and the lack of commitments.

Real vendor lock-in comes into play when you use proprietary services that are only offered by one vendor. I have heard many managers state that they only want to use services available in all the clouds so they have mobility and can change vendors. This mentality does not bode well for your career long-term. Keeping your infrastructure in lockstep with the lowest common denominator ensures that you will never have a competitive advantage in your marketplace. Your competition will move forward with adopting lock-in technologies to add value to their businesses. It is like buying a Corvette and then never leaving first gear. Some amount of lock-in is unavoidable, and when a lock-in situation arises, it is important to ask yourself whether it is good for your business.

 Be leery when discussions shift to multicloud. It is the surest way to see your costs skyrocket. You have to start paying for everything twice. Twice the security tooling, twice the audits, and potentially twice the staff, depending on skill sets.

Change to Operational Expenditures

A benefit of migrating to AWS and adopting a pay-as-you-go model is that you switch from a capital expenditure to an operating expenditure. On the surface, it is not immediately visible why this is a benefit, and some see it as a negative. If you purchased a server on-premises and depreciate it, meaning to expense the wear and tear of the asset over several years, you end up with a fixed monthly expense for that hardware. After migration, you exchange this form of accounting for a variable operating cost. This change does not seem like a good thing from an accounting perspective; you are going from a fixed monthly expense to a variable expense. Many people prefer a fixed, known variable for expenses, and the addition of a variable expense makes them uneasy.

Even though the expense is variable, I still see it as a benefit over on-premises. To have the benefit of a fixed monthly server expense, you must buy it. The purchase of hardware means that you are drawing down on your cash account, which you then create an asset account for in my accounting system. Once you have the asset account set up, you can divide the total cost of the server by the number of months you plan to keep it. Many companies use 36 months or 3 years as their depreciation schedule. You have to draw down your cash account. That money is gone, and it is not available to do other things like pay staff or buy more advertising. This is not the case in AWS—you do not have that drawdown, and your cash is still available to drive the business forward.

You still may be asking about the variable cost and its unpredictability. I see this as a benefit. It is not always the easiest construct to understand how it is a benefit, so let's look at the following scenario to get a better understanding.

Scenario 1-19

Duke works for an online application company that helps users park in the Chicago area. The company still has not launched the application, so it does not have a user base yet. It migrated a year ago to AWS, and the bill has been around $850. The CFO asked Duke what the bill will be when the site goes live, and the user base ramps up. Unfortunately, Duke cannot provide those exact numbers, but he has created a *scientific wild-ass guess* (SWAG). Duke knows from the application testing and data footprint that an individual user has a cost of $0.55 a month, plus or minus 10%. With this knowledge, Duke can say that for every 100,000 users, the costs will be $49,500 to $60,500. What Duke does not know is how successful the launch campaign will be and how many users they will gain.

To explain how Duke's situation and variable cost is a benefit, let's break down some numbers. Duke's platform is running in a steady state with no users at around $850 a month. This cost translates into Duke's fixed cost for his product. No matter how many users are on the platform, it will cost around $850 a month to produce the product for them to consume. The variable cost is the per-user cost of $0.55. The sum of the variable cost goes up for every user added linearly. Now for the best part: since the cost is based on consumption—the users—the revenue scales linearly as well. These numbers help Duke's company create predictions about how much it will cost and how much they will make. It will not tell them anything about their market penetration, or how many users did not like the application and canceled the service. However, Duke's CFO will feel a lot more comfortable with a variable cost knowing that it is tied to their user base. If you were to compare this scenario to Duke running his application on-premises, he would have to buy a large amount of hardware for his expected demand. The cost would be fixed, but it would also be more costly and fixed, even if the company only obtained ten thousand users at launch instead of one hundred thousand.

If you want more predictability in your bill and have a relatively static consumption, you can purchase AWS reserved instances. A reserved instance is a prepaid EC2 instance rather than the pay-as-you-go model and offers you a discounted price. You pay for a reserved instance up front and then amortize the cost over the year. It forms a function remarkably similar to deprecation because you pay up front and then expense back 1/12th of that cost every month. AWS also offers three-year reserved instances, but I frown on those for many reasons I will get to in "Run Rate Modeling" on page 114.

Sometimes the pay-as-you-go model does not work for everyone; it limits some capabilities for small and medium businesses to speed up deprecation. Your accountant might want to reduce your tax burden, using IRS Section 179. Before migrating, it will be essential to talk to your account or CFO and determine the right course of action in these circumstances and how to address the issue.

Converting Your Why into an FAQ

In this chapter, we have covered much ground regarding how, with a little change, you can reap a significant number of technical and business benefits by migrating to AWS. I hope that as you read the various scenarios explaining some of these changes, you were able to reflect on your personal experience and draw similarities. You should have a good baseline to build out your FAQ for migrating to AWS, using your notes as a guide.

Why are we building out an FAQ for migration? Well, people will ask questions; it is a given. I like to build out an FAQ ahead of time with answers to questions I feel people are most likely to ask. For one, it shows you have spent much time looking at the project through their eyes. This connection gives them the sense that you feel their pain and understand their viewpoint. Empathy will gain you support quickly. The fact is that, by doing this exercise, you will understand their perspective! The next thing the FAQ does is get the general concerns off the table right away and allow you to get to work faster. I am sure that you do not want to be in more meetings discussing the same detractions repeatedly. As you work and communicate with teams, you may find that you did not capture all the thoughts and ideas that people have. That is OK. It is all part of the process. It will be important to capture their questions and answer those questions as well. The chances are high that someone else in your organization will ask it again.

How to Build the FAQ

The first step to building out your FAQ is to decide on the audience. This audience may be management, a development team, your staff, or a business unit. You will go through this exercise multiple times using a different audience to flush out your FAQ. For the purpose of this exercise, we will use upper management. Now that we have our audience, you need to put yourself in their shoes and think of questions or objections that they might have about migrating to AWS. Let's step through two questions that you might get from upper management and think about how we would craft a response based on the knowledge we have gained from this chapter.

How much more is AWS going to cost us?

—CIO

You can bet you will get asked this question, and it is a very fair question. The problem with this question is that they have a predisposed attitude to think AWS will be more instead of less. It would be an excellent idea to rewrite this question in a more neutral stance. You want people to decide on their own and not be influenced either way by the questions in your FAQ. "How will our infrastructure costs change after migration?" would be a better way to phrase this question.

To answer this question, it would be important to focus on the high- and low-watermark buying aspects of your infrastructure. For added support, you can also include any applications that can save costs through an updated BC model and save 25% of those costs. It is important to draw vision from your company's inner workings as much as possible to personalize it and make it real for them.

> How will this migration affect our staff and operational expenses?
>
> —CFO

This is another very common question that comes from upper management. It's trickier to answer. Technically, your operational costs will go up from an accounting perspective because of the shift from a capex to an opex model for your infrastructure. It might be an excellent idea to separate that into another question and answer for the FAQ. Then you can reword this question into "How will this migration affect our staff's productivity?" Now you can answer this question with all the soft-cost savings that you have thought about earlier.

The next step in the process is to continue iterating to all the teams and departments your migration to AWS will affect. It will be a time-consuming process, but it will help overall by reducing the friction to change. As you go through more teams, the number of net new questions will decrease because many of the groups will have the same concerns. The viewpoints and motivations for their questions will change depending on their position. Based on this different viewpoint, you might not add another item to the FAQ but add more to the answer to address the additional concern instead.

Wrapping It Up

We covered much ground in this chapter, reviewing the technology and business benefits of migrating to AWS. The fact of the matter is that we just scratched the surface, and there are many more ways to benefit from migration. Again, these are the benefits that universally apply to anyone migrating and were the most important to cover. Every company that I have migrated to the cloud has leveraged AWS to benefit its unique aspect and scenario. AWS could be looked at as the largest Erector Set in the world. It allows you to build a *Shannon number* of possible solutions.

Claude Shannon was a mathematician who theorized the lower bound of the game tree complexity in chess, which results in about 10^{120} possible unique games. This number is known as the *Shannon number*.

By now, you should have a solid understanding of how your company can uniquely leverage the benefits of AWS by relating the scenarios and explanations to your experience. You should have a solid FAQ built that helps to address users' concerns and move the conversation forward. Lastly, you might have some ideas for what the future holds for additional benefits postmigration.

CHAPTER 2

What Are the Risks and Their Mitigation?

A ship in harbour is safe, but that is not what ships are built for.

—John A. Shedd, *Salt from My Attic*

Risk is unavoidable; your job as management is to mitigate those risks as much as possible and accept the rest. I have seen many people try to remove all risk from their migration, and this is impossible. You can spend hours and hours analyzing the situation, trying to account for every permutation of risk, start your migration, and get hit with an outage you had never even thought of. Just like in my story from Chapter 1 about the concrete crashing through the data center wall, you cannot account for everything.

What you do not want to run into with your migration is analysis paralysis. One of the unfortunate truths of any migration is that you are running portions of your infrastructure in two places at the same time. Double infrastructure means doubling some amount of cost. There are no magic migration fairies that come down and sprinkle migration dust and *poof*, you are in the cloud. Analysis paralysis elongates this period and puts your migration and company budget at risk. You want to address and mitigate the most significant risks to your migration. Then remind yourself that there will be some bumps along the road that you need to address on the fly.

This chapter aims to help you understand the significant risks to be mitigated. Many of these items require retooling in your thought process, such as the benefits in Chapter 1. Like before, I will walk you through different scenarios to help you relate to your situation so you can mitigate your risks and implement a successful migration.

The output that this chapter will help you build is a list of guiding principles. Having a set of guiding principles for cloud operation will help create a solid foundation for your company to operate in the cloud and reduce your technological and business risks. You can create this set of principles and always follow them unless there is a good business reason to deviate. One guiding principle might be that you always design for multi-AZ deployment in AWS. Another might be that you always have stateless application servers. These standards ensure that every department and team follows best practices and designs and builds toward standards that meet your business and regulatory goals.

Technology Risks

Technology risks are what everyone defaults to when they think about risk while migrating a workload. I define a *technology risk* as a risk that is directly affected by implementing technology or technology processes. Most technology risks manifest because people are not aware of the changes in security and the way systems run. They try to apply the design patterns they used on-premises in the cloud, which are many times anti-patterns. Lack of understanding creates confusion, poor migrations, failures, unneeded expenditures, and potentially an inability to migrate. This chapter aims to help you understand these differences in technology and the way security works. It is better to revamp your process and get people on your team to realize that they need to change their security processes. It also would be an excellent idea to create some common design patterns you see in your environment as a blueprint to follow. The blueprints will help create a baseline understanding with the teams of what good looks like.

Security

For security risks associated with migrating your workloads to the cloud, it boils down to four significant concepts:

- Implementation of a proper landing zone
- Implementation of the practice of least privilege
- Understanding of the shared responsibility model
- Use of contemporary and legacy security patterns in AWS

If you can address these four fundamental concepts before migration, you reduce the risk of your workloads in AWS. If you look at many of the security events that have happened related to AWS and other clouds, such as the Capital One breach, they all have boiled down to a lack of proper controls on the resources in the environment. The breaches were not due to the failure of the cloud provider to secure its service. If you can follow these four concepts, you will have a more secure environment than you ever had on-premises.

Landing zone implementation

Starting with a good security foundation is critical to ensuring the security of your workloads. In AWS, foundational security, compliance, and the base deployment of your infrastructure are called a *landing zone*. The landing zone provides baseline security controls and guardrails, account structure to segment environments, and last, security notifications. AWS has a service to automate the deployment of a landing zone for you called AWS Control Tower. The landing zone gives your company a baseline from a security and compliance standpoint. There may be additional requirements based on your environment and regulations to meet your company-specific needs. However, by using Control Tower, you can address many of your needs and requirements with a low effort from your engineering team. The landing zone deployed by Control Tower is not for every company. AWS gears the service toward enterprises, and not necessarily small and medium businesses.

AWS Control Tower requires the AWS Organizations service, which allows for central management and governance of your AWS accounts.

There are several important items that you want to address in your landing zone. By targeting these items, you ensure that you have a solid baseline for security and compliance. Ensuring that they are correct from the start saves you significant amounts of effort later, trying to rectify an improper deployment. I have had a few clients who did not start with the correct landing zone. This oversight created significant security issues, cost overruns, and shadow IT (servers and applications that fall outside of a known state yet are still running). I have detailed these essential items, as follows:

- Account structure
- Baseline security compliance monitoring
- Baseline logging for security groups
- Baseline security roles
- Configuration of crucial AWS services
- Protected logging

You may notice that I call some *baseline*. The reason for this is that you set them up across the entire environment and accounts uniformly. However, you can build on them for each account to meet specific needs, such as tighter control in the production account.

Account structure. A key advantage in how you can segment your infrastructure and reduce risk in AWS is to use separate accounts for environments and logging. Each account is separate just like individual customers in AWS; you have access to them, unlike other customer accounts like Netflix, because you set them up and have root access. Each account has its own unique security roles and configurations. An account compartmentalizes your blast radius from attacks and issues that might arise from service limits. By segmenting your account into development, testing, and production accounts, you can compartmentalize access for each use case. For example, in the development account, you can enable access for developers to create AWS resources without using infrastructure as code (IaC). However, in the testing and production accounts, you want to enforce best practices, only deploy by IaC, and lock down those accounts. Locking down is quite easy when using separate accounts. Using separate accounts also gives you more control over data leakage and enables you to ensure that developers use only anonymized data. Having a distributed account structure also affords you fine-grained network control and command over who is allowed to make those connections, enabling you to dictate which subnets can even communicate with one another.

Baseline security and compliance monitoring. By using services such as AWS Config rules, Amazon GuardDuty, and Amazon CloudWatch, you can configure a set of baseline compliance and security monitoring in your entire AWS estate. With these tools, you can scan your entire AWS environment for items such as EBS volumes that are not encrypted, root accounts without multi-factor authentication (MFA) activated, root account logins, and more. These controls help you reduce security risks by notifying you when these items do not comply or an action was taken. Another critical takeaway when you migrate to AWS is automation. Try to automate everything—this is a crucial point. By using these security and compliance monitoring alerts, you prevent someone from having to check manually, and you reduce errors and decrease response time.

Baseline logging for security groups. AWS allows you to log the ACCEPT and REJECT notifications for instances running in your VPC, or Virtual Private Cloud (a per-customer segmented network). These notifications are generated by the security groups attached to your instances based on the rules you have established. You can set up a VPC flow log to capture these notifications in Amazon CloudWatch, which allows you to investigate any blocked communications quickly. The Amazon CloudWatch service offers a managed logging solution. Typically, packets are blocked because of improper security group configuration. Another side benefit of this configuration is that you can set up CloudWatch metric filters and create alarms to send notifications for items such as high packet drop count and other proactive security measures.

Baseline security roles. It is best practice to establish security roles throughout the accounts to segment authorization between teams. A role establishes the level of access users have to your AWS environment. You should establish these roles with least privilege and allow multiple levels of access. Common suggested levels are a read-only role for audit and a role for system admins to start and stop instances. A full administrator role should be used sparingly.

Configuration of crucial AWS services. As part of your landing zone deployment, you should be configuring some key AWS services regarding security. These services help to protect your environment and are very cost-effective to implement. Many services can be enabled, but I will focus on the ones I like the best. The reason I love these services is that they provide a critical security function but have a minimal cost associated with them:

CloudTrail
AWS can log API calls in the environment by using a service called CloudTrail. Programs not only log these API calls, but also every time someone uses the AWS command-line interface (CLI) tools and the AWS console. CloudTrail is a vital part of your forensic toolkit and should be enabled in every account and every region.

 Although AWS enables the CloudTrail service by default, it only stores seven days of activity. This retention period is not sufficient to secure your environment properly. CloudTrail should be implemented fully with at least a 90-day retention. I recommend a retention period of one year for CloudTrail.

Config
The Config service from AWS allows AWS to track the state of configuration in your environment. Think of it as a photographic memory of how things were configured in the past. This tool serves a dual purpose in your environment. It is a tool for forensic investigation but also for debugging issues that arise from a change in the environment. You can see how that server was configured before an outage and restore the changes made to the security group.

Inspector
On-premises, you might use a vulnerability scanner like Nessus or Qualys, but AWS has a service called AWS Inspector. A vulnerability scanner is a specialized security tooling that looks at all the servers in your environment and identifies unpatched security flaws. Inspector is not as fully featured as the tools mentioned above, but it will meet the vulnerability scanning needs of many organizations at a significantly lower cost. It would be a good idea to investigate its capabilities

and supported operating systems to see whether it makes sense for your company and lowers your cost.

GuardDuty

GuardDuty is an AI-powered malicious-activity scanner in AWS. It is purpose-built to test and notify you of the risks in your AWS environment by monitoring VPC flow logs, Domain Name Service (DNS) logs, and CloudTrail logs that we discussed earlier. It aggregates all this information and looks at your environment as a cohesive whole. You can find more information about the threats that GuardDuty recognizes online (*https://oreil.ly/dCn40*).

An example of a GuardDuty finding might indicate that a known bad host was performing a port scan of your web server. GuardDuty would notify you of this scan, which host was performing the scan, and the AWS instance that was affected. By using this information, you could validate that the host is still running properly and that no breach was performed by the bad actor.

Protected logging. With CloudTrail enabled to log your API calls, the next step is to reduce your risks, and forensic capabilities are designed to ensure that these logs are protected from modification. The best way to accomplish this is to create another AWS account for logging and auditing so these critical logs can be sent there for protection. This protection prevents a malicious actor from changing your environment and then editing the records to remove their API calls.

For a recap, here is a scenario to help build on the items discussed here.

Scenario 2-1

Hanna has recently started working for a large grocery chain in the Midwest. They are currently about six months into their migration to AWS and have moved 10 workloads into production. Hanna's predecessor decided to leave after the migration project had mixed results. There were many issues with cost, and someone on the development team accidentally terminated a production server. This oversight caused an outage with 10 stores' point-of-sale systems and cost the company tens of thousands in lost revenue. They were never able to track down who it was because Cloud-Trail was not active. The CEO was excited for Hanna to come on board with her previous experience with AWS migration. He is hoping that she can get the company back on track and resolve the issues. Hanna performed an in-depth discovery on the AWS infrastructure and design, and deduced that there was no preplanning put into place before migrating systems. There was not a landing zone or any of the recommended baseline security. Hanna is recommending that they build out a new landing zone and move the instances to the new landing zone before migrating any new workloads.

Hanna has her work cut out for her. From the sounds of it, they have one account set up, which is going to make segmenting security between environments more difficult. It also sounds like they have not implemented least privilege, because someone in the development team deleted a protection server. This error should never have been possible with adequately implemented security. Without CloudTrail, Config, and VPC flow logs activated, it will be hard to do any forensics if a security event does occur. Hanna's situation is an excellent example of how not to migrate to AWS.

Unfortunately, I have seen a scenario like Hanna's before. In a rush to save money or get out of a data center with an expiring contract, people jump headfirst into migrating without thoughtful planning. In the end, it costs the company even more money. The cost overrun happens because you must stop migrating to get the baseline configuration and landing zone correct before you can move and jeopardize your operations and security. A little preplanning goes a long way with mitigating security and operational risk in AWS.

When we started this chapter, I stated that it would be a good idea to create some guiding principles for your operation in the cloud. When it comes to the landing zone, a guiding principle is not prudent because your landing zone is a one-time design and deployment. In the future, you might add new accounts, but they follow the original design pattern that incorporates all the features used in the current accounts. When creating a guiding principle, it is essential to evaluate whether it is against a set or variable pattern. You only want to create guiding principles for variable patterns. Ensuring that guiding principles are created for variable patterns ensures that best practice is maintained, and you mitigate risks. The next section on least privilege implementation is an excellent example of a variable pattern.

Least privilege implementation

When you migrate to AWS, one risk with least privilege is that most companies do not have a full understanding of how their systems interface on-premises or who owns them. I have been guilty of saying, "Don't turn that server off—we don't know what it does, but things break if we turn it off." There is much churn in IT staff, and I have walked into this situation more times than I would like to admit. With a situation such as this, it is hard to set up roles to manage said systems when you do not have all the information about the server. The more servers you have on-premises, the higher the probability of this situation. In a perfect world, I could tell you who owns a server, how it should be deployed, and the level of access their development team and support team need to do their jobs. The lack of information around this tribal, unwritten knowledge—only passed on by storytellers around the water cooler—is a real threat to your implementation of least privilege.

This lack of knowledge leads to the second risk of least privilege implementation in AWS: giving up. Least privilege is not easy. Sometimes it can take a considerable amount of work if you are doing something advanced. Once I was building a server-less application using the Serverless Framework. Wanting to implement least privilege down to the lowest level by granting every read, write, and tag function, I went through 36 iterations of the AWS role during its development to achieve that. Your roles will not be that complicated for general use and limited to EC2 and other core services, but it is essential not to give up, throw your hands in the air, and assign admin-level privileges to get the ball rolling. The probability of you coming back and fixing it later is low; you will not remember it until there is a breach, and then it will be too late.

A guiding principle that would be logical for the implementation of least privilege could be that you review all security for least privilege before the application goes live in AWS. This forethought would ensure that every application that is ever launched in AWS has the proper security review performed and validated before customers and employees begin using it. This evaluation ensures that you properly mitigate the risks associated with the erroneous privileges that have plagued companies and landed them in the press or testifying before Congress.

Shared responsibility model

The shared responsibility model is a concept that often confuses people when they first migrate to the cloud. This confusion is what can lead to security holes in the environment. When you move your workloads to AWS, you are giving up some control of the components in your environment. These are things like the physical data center, the networking equipment, HVAC, fire suppression, network stack, and fire-walls. You are also giving up control over your hypervisor. AWS manages and maintains the hypervisor. When you give up control over these items, you also give up responsibility. Since you do not own the data center and the equipment in it, you are not responsible for its management and security. That is Amazon's responsibility and seems self-explanatory, but these are the lower tiers of the responsibility model. Once you move up the responsibility model, it can become confusing.

An excellent example of this potential confusion would be Amazon S3. As I stated before, Amazon S3 is an object storage service that allows you to store files and serve them to the web or an application. Amazon handles the servers and storage back end. AWS handles all the security of those components for you. However, you handle the security of individual files and buckets (a storage location you created). A sizable number of breaches you hear about that are tied to S3 are caused by faulty access control. Customers put the files out in an S3 bucket, and then they improperly secure them. They grant access to it publicly when it should not be, or they do not remove access when employees leave.

There are many different security consumption models in AWS based on different services and technologies. Knowing where the responsibility lies amid so many services is often challenging. Amazon has recently added more security information in its documentation that does a respectable job of addressing this. You can locate the specific security documentation in each service's developers guide. This documentation covers data protection, identity access management, logging, monitoring, compliance validation, resilience, infrastructure security, and security best practices. Amazon designed this documentation to address the confusion over securing the service and to clarify where responsibility falls. Here are a few scenarios to help show the shared responsibility model.

Scenario 2-2

The bank where Kim works is migrating to AWS. Kim's team operates the data center on-premises in the head office and is responsible for the infrastructure, information security, and help desk. Kim's team operates on VMware and Cisco equipment in the data center that runs Windows workloads primarily. About three years ago, the bank replaced the aging storage with a unit from EMC. The Security Officer has asked her to update the Responsibility assignment, or RACI, matrix for their servers postmigration. RACI stands for *responsible, accountable, consulted,* and *informed.* The RACI covers:

- Patching of servers
- Patching of the firewalls
- Maintenance of firewall rules
- Patching of the hypervisor
- Patching of the switches
- Patching of the software
- Patching of the storage subsystem
- Monitoring of system performance
- Monitoring of system availability
- Testing of the backup generator
- Testing of fire suppression
- Testing of the battery backup system

In Kim's situation, there will be many changes to the items listed in the RACI. However, since Kim is still running servers on EC2, many responsibilities again fall to her team. Let us step through each of these to understand better how the responsibility shifts and why:

Patching of servers

In AWS, patching of the servers does not change, and Kim's team will still handle them. The reason for this is that AWS does not have access to your servers and could not update them if it wanted to. Only you can log on to your servers. AWS offers the Systems Manager service to aid you with patch management. It will still be the responsibility of Kim's team to manage this service and the approval of patches.

Patching of firewalls

By using the security groups in AWS, Kim's team will no longer have to patch any firewalls, because AWS maintains them.

Maintenance of firewall rules

AWS doesn't manage the security group rules for your server. AWS does not have any idea what software is running on your server, so it cannot decide what traffic to allow in and out. Kim's team needs to create and manage the rule set. Also, since Kim should switch to a zero-trust model, her team will need to research all the communications between the servers and create the corresponding rules.

Patching of the hypervisor

The hypervisor is another item that Kim's team need not worry about going forward. AWS maintains the hypervisor; Kim's team will have no access to it.

Patching of the switches

AWS delivers the networking layer as the VPC and is a managed service. Kim's team will not have to patch switches.

Patching of the software

Patching of the software on servers falls on the shoulders of Kim's team. Just like patching servers, AWS has no access to your EC2 instances.

Patching of the storage subsystem

Unlike her on-premises storage, Kim will not need to worry about patching the operating system of her subsystem. In AWS, Kim's team will use EBS to store data for the servers, and EBS is a managed service. Kim's team will only need to manage the space allocated to servers to ensure that they have enough storage. Kim's team will need to monitor the free space of the disks themselves. AWS has no access to the contents of the drive to evaluate free space.

Monitoring of system performance

AWS has a service called Amazon CloudWatch. CloudWatch is a metric and monitoring tool that captures some aspects of system performance. Since AWS does not have access to the system, not all the performance metrics you may need are available by default. The most common ones AWS cannot report natively are disk usage, as previously stated, and memory usage. These can be monitored in

CloudWatch only if you enable an agent on your operating system to report them. AWS also does not monitor any usage metrics by default. Kim's team will need to create CloudWatch alarms to track and send notifications if they are out of tolerance.

Monitoring of system availability

Like the monitoring of system performance, AWS offers metrics that monitor system availability. The system and instance status checks monitor your system and report positive or negative status information to CloudWatch. It will be Kim's team's responsibility to create alarms on these if they wish to be notified. The system status checks monitor for items such as a power failure and hardware issues, whereas the instance status checks monitor the network of your instance by sending an address resolution protocol (ARP) request to the network interface.

Testing of the backup generator, fire suppression, and battery backup system

These items are all provided as part of the AWS region and availability zones, and Kim's team need not worry about any of these items. Since Kim works at a bank, compliance audits might require proof of these items taking place along with other audit checks. AWS provides comprehensive, third-party audit and compliance reports to customers in the AWS Artifact service. From Artifact, customers can access audit reports such as Payment Card Industry (PCI), Service Organization Control (SOC), ISO, FFIEC, and more. You can find the complete list online (*https://aws.amazon.com/compliance/programs*).

Here is a scenario that will demonstrate the changes necessary when refactoring your application from an EC2 server-based technology to a managed serverless technology. Refactoring to serverless has a dramatic effect on your company's responsibilities.

Scenario 2-3

Margot's company is migrating to AWS and wants to move a large data store from the NFS server on-premises to Amazon S3. It serves the data to mobile application users via web servers. The NFS server has both public and private customer files. Margo wants to explain the reduction-of-management benefits of moving this data to S3. She wants to compare the security responsibilities between the two designs regarding:

- Web server patching
- Web server security controls
- Storage server patching
- Storage server security controls

Since Margo is changing from a server-based solution on-premises to a serverless technology on AWS, she must be mindful of how her team's role in securing the environment changes. Failure to understand the responsibility model and overstating the responsibility of AWS can have severe repercussions. Let us walk through these items to get a clear understanding of how her team's role changes:

Web server patching

When Margo's team moves the data from an NFS server to S3, new capabilities will be available over a standard file share. S3 can serve files to the web. This hosting allows Margo's team to eliminate the servers required to serve this data to the internet. Her customers' mobile application instance fetches the data from S3. S3 hosting ends her need for patching the web servers.

Web server security controls

Since there are no web servers, people would probably think there are no servers to apply security controls. This perception is only partially correct; because Margo's NFS server has both public and private files, there needs to be security controls on S3 to protect those files. Margo's team might want to implement signed URLs for those private files to ensure that other parties do not access them.

Storage server patching

Since there are no more NFS servers to serve the data to the web servers, Margo's team will not have to patch the server, and she can show that this is an additional soft cost saving.

Storage server security controls

The storage server security controls are like the web server controls. Even though there will not be an NFS server anymore, Margo needs to make sure that only the proper users have access to the data. She would not want to have a rogue employee with access steal or damage confidential customer data.

By now, you should understand how the changes in responsibility can lead to risks and unintended circumstances if not adequately understood before and during migration. A guiding principle that makes sense for the shared responsibility model is that you create a RACI for each class of application you are migrating. For example, this would mean that you would establish a RACI for COTS applications, internally developed conventionally designed applications, and internally developed cloud native applications.

Legacy security patterns

Using legacy security patterns in AWS affects not only your security posture but also performance. The legacy security patterns that cause the most critical issues are the ones that create a choke point in the infrastructure. There are many ways to create choke points. However, the most common one I see is trying to implement zoned security by using contemporary firewalls rather than relying on security groups. Another issue I see is when there is an implementation of a network intrusion prevention system (IPS).

These choke points also cause a commingling of application environments. Your development, testing, and production environments will all be traversing the same security equipment. The shared communication pathway leads to the possibility that a malfunctioning development application can negatively affect your production workloads, whereas, if you shift your thought process on security to better align with cloud technology, these issues can be avoided.

Contemporary zoning. Using contemporary zoning and firewalls versus using security groups and zero trust affects both security and performance. As we discussed earlier, zero trust gives the smallest attack surface possible, allowing only the required communications to pass between machines. Implementing zoned security with a firewall ditches zero trust. Zero trust is like locking all the rooms in your house; a burglar would not only need to break into the front door but then also every other door to steal anything. In contrast, using zoned security is like only locking your front door and allowing a burglar easy access to find your prized TV and computer, and be long gone before the police arrive.

Not only does the contemporary zoning design pattern not have the best security available in AWS, but it also can cause performance issues. To run a contemporary firewall in AWS, it needs to run on an EC2 instance, which creates a scaling issue in terms of CPU and network performance. A firewall is not a type of technology that can scale horizontally, because it is stateful. A firewall holds the state and session of every inbound and outbound communication. Because of this capturing of state, it cannot scale out because it would drop connections when it scaled back down. Since you cannot scale horizontally, you must scale vertically, and it must have enough capacity to meet your high watermark. Vertical scaling unnecessarily adds costs to your infrastructure. I hope it is clear why using this contemporary pattern is a bad idea.

Network IDS/IPS. Similar to using a contemporary firewall in AWS, using a contemporary network intrusion detection system/intrusion prevention system (IDS/IPS) causes many of the same issues. It creates a single point of failure and a scaling issue. The best design pattern for applications in AWS is using the horizontal scaling method. When your horizontally scaling applications scale out to meet your needs and the network IDS/IPS is a static size, you run into performance issues. A better solution than this contemporary design is to use a host-based IDS/IPS, which ensures that your IDS/IPS capabilities scale out at the same rate as your application. Host-based IDS/IPS removes the bottleneck and ensures that your environment stays secure.

Legacy security patterns are another concept where a guiding principle does not always make sense. For many companies, the designs around these concepts are a *set it and forget it* item. However, if your company does many mergers and acquisitions, it may make sense to have a guiding principle to address these concerns long-term. When undergoing mergers and acquisitions, you don't know the state of the purchased environment, and it would be essential to ensure a proper review to mitigate the risk.

Application Connectivity

As you migrate your workloads, there may be potential risks involved regarding the interconnectivity of applications on-premises and the cloud. Latency and bandwidth are the two primary concerns, but security group misconfiguration can also be a potential issue. When you are assessing risks regarding network connectivity in this stage of your migration, you will not have any data on how much bandwidth you need. However, you probably have a good idea about latency requirements based on the design of the application. To help illuminate how your applications might be impacted, we will cover some scenarios. First, it makes sense to talk about the connectivity available in AWS for a solid understanding of the options available and which fits your scenario.

Virtual private network

A site-to-site virtual private network (VPN) is a popular option for connectivity in small and potentially medium businesses. I would not recommend VPN for larger organizations because of performance limitations and potential costs due to the number of required connections. VPN is an internet-based communication method to encrypt your data between two locations. The downfall of using a VPN is that the path is at the mercy of the internet. It may not be the same every time because of things like a rogue backhoe digging up a fiber optic line. Potentially different paths mean potentially different latency. If you are migrating an application that needs to communicate back to an on-premises location that is latency sensitive, this can be an issue. The second issue with VPN is that there is a limited amount of bandwidth available, and once you reach the threshold, look at other connectivity methods. Often, a hidden risk of using a VPN is that it is sharing bandwidth with all your other internet traffic. This traffic is often inconsistent and unpredictable. If you are using a VPN, it would be an excellent idea to implement quality of service (QoS) on your networking equipment. QoS ensures that the VPN has priority over other traffic so that your back-end operations operate unhindered.

VPNs are not capable of transitive routing between accounts or VPCs. Transitive routing is the ability to use AWS as an intermediary router between two sites. For instance, data center A cannot connect to AWS and then route traffic to data center B. There is an advanced service from AWS called Transit Gateway that has this capability, but that is outside the scope of this book. Figure 2-1 visualizes this concept for you.

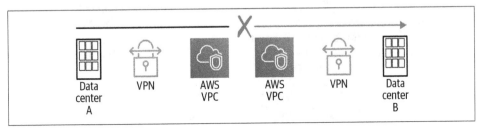

Figure 2-1. Transitive routing

Direct connect

AWS Direct Connect offers a dedicated link between your data center and the AWS region that you are migrating your infrastructure to. To connect with Direct Connect, you work with a telecom provider to establish a point of presence on that network, which connects to the Direct Connect termination point in the AWS region. This form of communication ensures dedicated and constant bandwidth and latency. Direct Connect does not traverse the internet, so you do not have the issues associated with a VPN. Direct Connect can also provide a significant amount of bandwidth by aggregating multiple 10 GB connections. Direct Connect is the less risky choice, but it costs more than a VPN. If you already have a multiprotocol label switching (MPLS) network set up, then the use of Direct Connect would be appropriate. Many MPLS network providers, such as Verizon and AT&T, already have connectivity to AWS regions. MPLS would provide connectivity at a smaller incremental cost since they already brought the circuit into your locations.

Internet

It does not happen often, but some companies can migrate to AWS and use an internet connection. It is limited most of the time to newer startups that use applications that are internet hosted and have internet-based internal applications. Companies that can operate this way use a bastion host in AWS to connect to the back-end systems. A bastion host is a hardened instance that can withstand attacks and allows IT staff access to backend servers by using the Secure Shell (SSH) protocol for Linux servers and Remote Desktop protocol (RDP) for Windows servers. Using the bastion allows them to perform maintenance and support, eliminating the need for a VPN or Direct Connect altogether.

Now that we have covered the connectivity to AWS, we can dive into a few scenarios to highlight the decision process. These will help you feel more comfortable making a decision to reduce your company's exposure to connectivity issues.

Scenario 2-4

Emma works for a small advertising firm that has been in business for 20 years. The company hosts several applications in an on-site data center that Emma's team needs to migrate to AWS. There are seven applications that serve multiple functions, including file server, accounting, and collaborative design platforms. Emma's company has about 100 users, of whom 50 are designers who work from home. The files the company creates are typically 2–20 MB in size.

From the sound of it, Emma has a lot of COTS applications that potentially have been in use for many years. The potential age of these applications shows that most, if not all, require network connectivity of some sort and are not internet-enabled. Since the total application count is low and the size of the working documents is small, VPN appears to be a satisfactory solution for Emma's company. Since half of the company's staff works remotely, it makes sense for Emma to deploy a client VPN in AWS for those uses. That would mean that much of the available bandwidth for communication will be distributed over 51 points of presence because each user would have their internet connection.

One potential issue for Emma is the accounting system. A system like that would run on a relational database for data storage. A database might introduce a latency issue, depending on how the application is programmed. If it makes many individual queries to the database, all the round-trip requests and answers, although small individually, could add up to large delays. For instance, if one query has a round trip of 10 milliseconds and a single screen has 100 queries on it, it would take one second to load the screen. A one-second refresh time is not bad, but what happens if the latency of the VPN is 100 milliseconds? Now the screen is taking 10 seconds to refresh, and this would make the application unusable. It is improbable that Emma's application is written that poorly, but it is essential to think about this when assessing connectivity risk.

Scenario 2-5

The consulting firm where Steve works is a nationwide provider of management consulting for small and medium businesses. It has several hundred employees who work out of the New York and San Francisco offices. Besides the office staff, there are several thousand traveling consultants that are located across the US. Steve's team maintains all the applications across the organization. Except for the expense tracking

---

application, the rest of the applications are not internet accessible. The company has 256 applications in total and a backbone between the two offices provided by Verizon MPLS. All the remote consultants connect to the network via client VPN.

Steve, like Emma, has many older and non-internet-enabled applications that require direct network connectivity. Most of the staff connect through the VPN, so it would make sense for Steve to move or set up a new client VPN in AWS to address the remote users' connectivity. Moving the VPN would ensure the shortest route to the applications and the highest redundancy for his users. Based on the volume of users who are still left in the offices, set at several hundred, VPN will not be a good option. That high of a user count requires significant bandwidth, and Direct Connect would be a better option. Since Steve has already established MPLS connections to his offices through Verizon, it would make sense to talk to Verizon about AWS connectivity. Direct Connect would offer Steve the bandwidth and low latency that would perform best.

Let us look at another scenario of how using only internet connectivity might look for a company.

Scenario 2-6

Scott's company is still in startup mode and just finished its first round of series B funding. It provides an application that does AI business analytics. Because of the rapid growth, the company wants to migrate to AWS so it can scale the application better. The application is web-based, and the company is integrating the prototype admin interface from an internally facing web application to the externally facing client application. Scott deployed Google G Suite for its document editing and storage, and purchased several online applications, like monday.com and FreshBooks, for internal admin functions. There are 23 people at the company, and now, since the series B is closed, they expect to hire 10 more in the next 6 months.

It sounds like Scott has only a few systems on-premises, and they only run the client-facing application. Because they have not completed integrating the admin interface into the main application, Scott might need to run a VPN temporarily to allow admins to control the application. However, in the long term, it sounds like Scott will not need a VPN at all. If the development team uses CI/CD to deploy servers and has proper log aggregation from the servers to CloudWatch, Scott might not even need a bastion host. The lack of a bastion host would provide the least cost and best performance scenario for his company.

A guiding principle that makes sense for application connectivity could be that you analyze any application for connectivity concerns during the development and testing environment migration. Evaluating the application performance in the early phases ensures that you thoroughly test and resolve risks before migrating the production environment where users would be affected. Some risk will remain because the development and testing environments may not see as much load as production, but the risk will be significantly diminished. An important point to remember is that as an IT manager, your job is to mitigate risks, not eliminate them.

Technology Diversity

Operating in AWS is a significant divergence from running on-premises. The interfaces and capabilities differ significantly from VMware or Hyper-V. Virtualization and the legacy hypervisors were the next step in technology evolution from bare metal servers. With it, they brought the latest advancements in technology and propelled the world into a new and more effective operating pattern. No matter what they do, they can never truly compete with the cloud. AWS evolved from Amazon's knowledge of virtualization. It is this new paradigm shift that has allowed the capabilities to reach further than virtualization. AWS now brings with it the latest advancements in technology and is propelling the world forward just as virtualization did a decade earlier.

Whenever you move from one technology to another, you run into the risk of technology diversity. The risk usually manifests as a lack of knowledge and experience in modern technology compared to the platform being replaced. Another way that this can manifest is more of a split-brain situation, where one staff member has the experience with the older platform and another has the experience with the new, and they need to operate together to complete the task. When migrating to AWS, you have the potential to experience both situations. It could be in the stakeholder's business unit, the development teams, or the operations and support departments. There are many ways to address this risk; I will focus on staff assessment and training, and contractors and consulting. Throughout my experience, these have been the most effective ways to address technology diversity risk.

Staff assessment and training

AWS diverges from on-premises technology because it takes the approach that everything should be code, even your infrastructure. The primary interface is API based, and everything else branches off from there. The web console, CloudFormation templates, and the AWS CLI all communicate back to the AWS API. To harness the power of AWS fully, you need staff capable of using more programmatic interfaces rather than using a web console. Most of your staff are still using the consoles of your hypervisor with little automation. Pointing and clicking while manually performing operations repeatedly is not efficient. You need to train your staff on a new skill set. Your engineering teams need to learn more about infrastructure and compute capabilities. Your infrastructure staff must learn more about programming and markup languages like JSON and YAML. While operating in AWS, your development teams and operations teams merge—this is where the term *DevOps* originates.

To assess the current state of capabilities in your staff, I would suggest doing a simple skills gap analysis by using a survey. I would not overthink this step and get too complicated with the questions and what capabilities you are gauging. The critical part of this process is not the questions, but how staff receives the survey. You do not want to create an environment where a skills assessment may threaten your team. It is essential to frame the subject as training for upcoming changes and enhancement of their capabilities. You do not want your staff to think it is a threat to their job or position. If that were to occur, then you would not get back results conducive to their real capabilities, which doesn't help your company or them.

Once your gap analysis survey is complete, you will have a good idea of what kind of training ramp-up you need for a successful migration. As an added byproduct, you identify your first cloud champions who already possess skill sets between infrastructure and development. If properly motivated and energized, this staff can help other staff with the transition, by both leading by example and coaching.

Training for your staff should follow many paths. First, your staff should learn Python, which is a prevalent language in the cloud that many people use to perform automated management tasks. There are many projects on sites like GitHub (*https:// github.com*) that can help you automate or give you a baseline to build on for your needs. To do this, you need staff who can understand the language. There are many trainings available online, and at local community colleges and universities. A favorite of mine is Codecademy (*https://www.codecademy.com*); it offers many programs for free and has a paid program for more advanced classes.

 AWS also writes most of its examples in Python, so learning Python is a good choice.

Another vital skill set for AWS is operations. There are many training sites and programs available on the internet to train your staff. However, I believe the best way to learn AWS is by doing. AWS offers a free tier for most services. The free tier allows your staff to test the platform without running up their bill. The low cost continues if they stay within the constraints of the free tier. As far as AWS training, I have two go-to training sites that I recommend to companies migrating to AWS. The first is Linux Academy (*https://linuxacademy.com*), which provides a solid training platform for learning how to do things in AWS and perform daily duties. The second site I recommend is A Cloud Guru (*https://acloud.guru*); this site is an excellent resource for people looking to pass the AWS certification exams. There are many more sites out there, and more continue to be added every day.

Training your existing staff on AWS is a great approach to take for employee morale and job satisfaction. However, it is not the best for your migration timeline. It takes time for your staff to receive training, experiment, and then gain proficiency through experience. It is essential to take this timeline into account when you are doing your migration planning. We will discuss this in more depth in Chapter 6.

Contractors and consulting

> There is no compression algorithm for experience.
>
> —Andy Jassy, *CEO Amazon Web Services*

When evaluating your staffing requirements for your migration, it is important not to forget about the use of contractors and consultants. Using them can seem expensive. However, their expertise helps you meet your migration timeline and reduce not only your technical risk but also business risks. Consultants and contractors have been working with AWS and doing migrations for some time and have gained not only technical experience, but also implementation experience. One of the greatest advantages of contractors and consultants is that they work for many companies in many industries. This experience gives them a very diverse set of views that typical employees do not have an opportunity to gain. Together these forms of experience reduce your risk by knowing how to do something and what works in practice. They can also act as mentors to your staff, providing an additional training resource. It would be important to combine the experience for your staff, the project timeline, and your budget before deciding on consultants and contractors.

Although consultants and contractors are valuable for their expertise, they are not without their issues. It is important to ensure that you set the expectations that your staff is to be involved as part of the process, and that the consultants create proper documentation and runbooks. Integration can be a concern with consultants as they are not as entrenched with your team as a contractor would be.

Having been in IT leadership and getting bitten by this myself, I know what kind of long-term pain improper documentation can cause. Some consulting companies can be unscrupulous about enabling clients to be self-supporting in the long term. Their primary drive can be to run up billings and keep you on the hook. I experienced this firsthand with a backup solution. My predecessor needed a backup system and contracted with a consulting company for design and implementation. The setup was so complicated that even slight changes required the firm to come back on-site and implement the changes. We were spending upwards of $8,000 in a year just on maintaining the system. When I asked for documentation so my team could take over, I ended up with a two-page document. It was more of a high-level design overview, and the firm wanted dozens of consulting hours to document the solution properly. Lack of knowledge transfer is a form of vendor lock-in that many people overlook.

The guiding principles around technology diversity will be very specific to your company's needs. The principles will depend on your staff's level of experience and the company's appetite for consultant and contractor fees. An excellent way to frame the guiding principles for technology diversity is around triggers based on thresholds. For instance, a technology diversity guiding principle could state that consultants or contractors will be acquired if the training timeline for staff disrupts the migration of an application for more than two weeks. This principle ensures that the company is willing to accept some risk to train staff and keep knowledge inside the company while establishing a mitigating factor.

Perception of Increased Technical Complexity

When you first migrate to AWS, you will do much lifting and shifting for your workloads, that is, to pick them up as they are and move them into AWS without modification. Lift and shift is the fastest and most efficient way to migrate. Moving your workloads in this fashion produces the shortest timeline and lowers your period of duplicate spending. However, there may be a few workloads that need to be rebuilt during migration due to the legacy technology that is not supported on AWS. Unsupported technology might be a mainframe, and after you are migrated and have shut down your on-premises resources, you will want to refactor your applications.

Refactoring is converting from a legacy design to a more efficient cloud design. On-premises, your applications are most likely monolithic, running on a single server or a cluster of servers if they are large enough. These applications were built as separate entities with all functions clumped together. After migration, you can take advantage of new services and create a distributed application environment. In a distributed application, you split the individual functions of the applications into their components. Instead of running a single server with a single application, you could run dozens of AWS services running dozens or even hundreds of functions.

When some people look at the design of a distributed application, they see much complexity that was not part of the application before. They get apprehensive about adopting the new model. I can understand this apprehension and perception. It differs significantly from the designs they would have seen in the past. Figure 2-2 details the design of a three-tier web application.

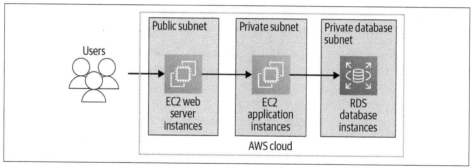

Figure 2-2. Three-tier application design

This design is a good representation of the contemporary on-premises design as a monolith. It has three layers and three servers, but other than that, it is a relatively simple design. In Figure 2-3, I have converted the three-tier web application to a serverless design.

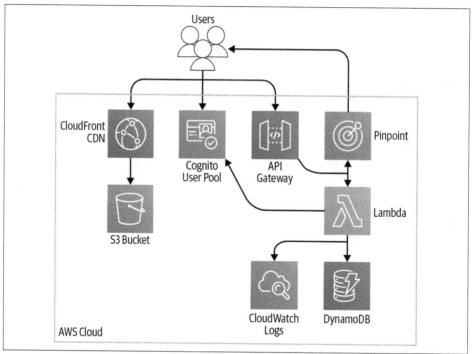

Figure 2-3. Serverless application design

As you can see at first glance, it looks a lot more complicated than the original design. However, when you operate in a distributed design mode, you do not have to develop, test, and deploy the components at once. You can focus on and update the individual parts that need attention. It may look complicated at the macro-level, but when working on an application, you do not work at the macro-level; you work at the micro-level, with only a small part of your code, and this significantly decreases the complexity. The propensities to disrupt the rest of the application's code is minimized. The perception of complexity is just that, perception. In practice, the distributed nature of the application decreases risk, rather than increasing it.

When establishing a guiding principle around technology complexity, it makes sense to focus on education. After all, what you are working against with this risk is a perception of complexity. The best way to combat an incorrect perception is through knowledge. A solid guiding principle for your company might focus on training any new business units on a high-level overview of these changes in design concepts. This principle will lay a good foundation and curb any confusion before the design discussions later in the process.

Business Risks

When you migrate workloads, there are a host of potential business risks. I define a *business risk* as a risk with causality driven by situational events and planning rather than directly influenced by technology. Except for a significant security breach, a lot of technical risks can be swept under the carpet and become invisible to customers and investors. This level of visibility is not the case with business risks. Risks such as reputational and contractual obligations and expertise loss can have a much more public impact. We will walk through these risks, and discuss how they might manifest in your migration and how you can properly mitigate them.

Reputation

The worst business risk to me is the reputational risk, and when you migrate a workload, this risk is hard to avoid but should be easy to mitigate. I want to say I have never seen this kind of risk play out in the real world, but that is not true; I have seen it happen to companies. What I can say is that it is avoidable, and the tarnish to those companies' reputations should never have occurred. However, I will give you the secret to mitigating this risk. The recipe is straightforward: one part proper planning, one part proper testing, and one part proper security review. It may seem like a simple cocktail, but just like Bond's Vesper martini, it is a recipe for success. It sort of sounds like something that you would read in a fortune cookie. You might think to yourself, *well duh*, and you would be correct. The problem is that your project managers, developers, and engineers all have good intentions. No one wants your company to be in the news; they did not make a mistake on purpose. Good intentions do not prevent issues; the correct process does. This recipe ensures success.

When talking about risk and planning, we are not discussing your overall migration plan. It is the planning that is done around the actual migration process itself on an application-by-application basis. This plan will capture the caveats and uniqueness of each application. It ensures that your team accounts for all the aspects of the workload migration. Some people think this level of detail is overkill and unnecessary. I agree with them, too, in one circumstance: when everything goes right. For those who know of Murphy and his law, may I suggest having this level of detail. We will cover these planning processes in depth in Chapter 8. However, it is essential to highlight them here because they are directly responsible for the mitigation of reputational risk. A good application migration plan will have at a minimum:

Application discovery
> Ensures that all the components of an application and its history are collected for evaluation. That you know as many *known* variables as possible. This information leaves you only the *unknown* variables as the residual risk.

A technical migration plan
> Covers the technology used in the actual migration process for the individual application and addresses its particular needs.

A testing process
> It is as simple as it sounds, to plan to test the application and its functions properly before cutover.

A cutover process
> The cutover processes for each application are somewhat different from each other, and a cutover plan ensures that all the nuances are captured before the actual cutover.

A rollback process
> Things go wrong, and they go wrong in unexpected ways. The best way to address this in a migration is to have a preplanned rollback process. Often the path to migrate to and the path to migrate from are not the same as one would expect.

Planning ensures that you minimize reputational risks by limiting the amount of surface area that leads to outages during migration. In my experience, having the right level of planning ensures that even when things go wrong, you still end up with a good result. Yes, you still might be running on-premises with a failed migration, but you are not offline in a failed state.

Building a guiding principle for addressing proper planning is straightforward. It should ensure that all levels of planning are put in place for all application migration. This mitigating factor ensures that you would not be caught in a state where your users or customers need your application and find it unavailable.

Staffing and Expertise Loss

As we have discussed before, change and people do not often mix. When you migrate to AWS, a few people might become uncomfortable with the change, or the potential change in their duties. When your company works in the cloud, things are not compartmentalized into beautiful little silos like storage, compute, backup, and the like. With the move from conventional infrastructure to code-based deployment, the blending of these technologies comes into play. One possible way you might see staffing risk is through attrition. Typically, two things happen that cause employee attrition when you are working toward migration to AWS. The main items to be concerned about are employees feeling like they have little value in your future state and employees who don't want to expand their tool set.

People's fear of being replaced or becoming inadequate can quickly be addressed through open lines of communication and training. People fear uncertainty and insecurity, and it is your responsibility to ensure that your staff is aware of their place in the future version of your company. Depending on your current structure and how your teams are laid out, this change could be as disruptive to your company as a merger or acquisition. As we discussed before, migrating to AWS and adopting a more DevOps agile model will change the structure of your company. For small and medium-sized businesses, this is not as much of an issue because people wear more hats and have cross-functional duties. However, large enterprises that have silos for functions like backup and storage will exhibit this issue more often. Let us look at how this might be exhibited in a large company.

Scenario 2-7

Stan has been employed as a backup engineer at a retail company for the last 15 years. He has been a devoted employee, has had three promotions in that time, and is now a senior engineer. This past year, Stan's company has been looking at migrating to AWS, and Stan is getting concerned. He does not know much about networking or servers and has primarily been focused on backup software, technology, and processes. As he understands it, much of his workload will be replaced by automated snapshots and AWS Backup. A substantial portion of the corporate data footprint that will be moving to Amazon S3 will not require backup. Over the last few months, Stan has tried to talk to his manager about how he feels like he might be phased out. Unfortunately, his manager has been too busy to meet. He wants to learn new skills but does not even know where to start. After a few months more, the uncertainty was too much for Stan to handle, and he got a new job at another company.

I urge you to please not let a situation like Stan's arise at your company. Stan was a dedicated employee with a long tenure and a deep understanding of the company. There is no doubt that he had a significant amount of tribal knowledge that will be irreplaceable given his tenure. With some training and shifting into a different type of role, Stan could have provided the company with many more years of experience. He also could potentially save the company thousands of dollars of wasted effort because of his expertise in company operations. Stan would have known precisely where data existed in every nook and cranny of the company infrastructure to ensure that it was adequately protected in AWS. Let us look at another situation on how you can experience staffing risk.

The following is another scenario with a different twist to highlight expertise loss.

Scenario 2-8

In the last six months, Bette's company has started moving some workloads to AWS. Her manager has provided training materials online so that Bette can learn new skills and expand her capabilities. Currently, Bette is an engineer on the VMware team, and she has doubts about learning a new set of tools. Bette feels that she spent much time learning VMware over the years, and she does not want to switch. She thinks that the cloud is a fad, like grid computing, and does not think it has long-term staying power. After her manager assigned additional training, Bette quit and walked out the door.

If I am honest, it is not an undesirable thing that Bette walked out the door. She is not the kind of employee that you want around for the long term because she will not adapt to the changes required to make your company successful. This fact will be increasingly true as we see accelerated change in IT as time goes on. The problem lies with the tribal knowledge that she had, which just walked out the door. You would not have prepared for her departure by capturing as much information as possible. Someone who exhibits Bette's mentality probably does not play well with others and hordes information as well, compounding the issue. This book is not about the managing process or people, so I will not get into ways of resolving this issue. However, I want to make you aware that a change such as migration to AWS can be an impetus to people with Bette's mindset. Since you are migrating to AWS and must perform analysis of the infrastructure and systems, you can use this as an opportunity to document your infrastructure and systems. This updated documentation will decrease the amount of tribal knowledge in your company, reducing your risk.

I would not create a guiding principle around staffing risk as part of the migration plan. It might come across as contrived and impersonal. That is not to say that I do not think it is an important principle to develop. However, I would not openly advertise it along with the other principles. As a manager, I would discuss the risks with other leaders and develop it as a part of the overall management strategy.

Contractual Obligations

A risk that many companies run into is existing contractual obligations. This kind of risk can manifest itself in a few ways. One that you probably think of right away is your data center contracts. When you are moving into AWS, you will not need all that space in your data center anymore. You might not need it at all, depending on the type of business you are in. However, there are other types of contracts you might uncover as well, such as third-party support and software licensing. Let us cover these three types in these scenarios to get a better understanding of those risks and how to mitigate them.

Scenario 2-9

Bob works for a media company that is looking to migrate to AWS out of its colocation data center. The vendor had locked the company into a 5-year contract that will expire in 18 months. Bob has decided to close the racks in the data center and move everything to AWS. The contract allows for a month-to-month lease at a 25% upcharge on the 5-year contract monthly fee. If Bob continues with a month-to-month contract, he will need to give a 60-day notice of termination.

Based on this scenario, I would say that Bob has it easy. He has 18 months left on his contract, and they will even allow him to keep his racks on a month-to-month basis. Having the ability to stay in the colocation after the initial contract relieves some stress around the migration plan and timeline, in case something goes wrong and the project sees delays. On the other side, he does have a 60-day notice period and a 25% upcharge that will drastically affect his budget. As far as data center contracts go, I would say that Bob is in a rather good spot. It is not uncommon for colocation data centers to require an entire year's extension. This length of extension can put companies in a bind with migration timelines if the contract end date doesn't line up with the migration timeline.

Let's take a look at a data center's scenario for a third-party support contract.

Scenario 2-10

The financial services company that Ben works for has a vast Oracle application estate. It has hundreds of servers running Oracle products and databases. To reduce costs a few years ago, it stopped paying Oracle for support, and instead went with a third-party company and limited the Oracle contract to licensing. About three months into the migration, the team ran into an issue with a workload that they had migrated to AWS. Upon calling the support company and disclosing that the

---

workload was in AWS, they refused to support the issue until it was reproduced with on-premises hardware.

Unfortunately, this kind of scenario happens when there is no technical reason for it. The cloud is just another form of virtualization and does not have any impact on software running on the instances themselves. When I first started using VMware in my companies, I had the same issue, with some vendors unwilling to support it. Running into a support issue like this can cause many headaches around having to reproduce the issue, taking valuable time away from your migration efforts. It would make sense to do a cursory review of the software support contracts as part of your application discovery. The review will ensure that you do not run into this issue while under pressure and constraints. If caught ahead of time, the possibility exists to negotiate an addendum to the contract before moving the workload.

Lastly, we will review the following scenario to cover software licensing.

Scenario 2-11

Mike is migrating some IBM workloads to AWS for his bank. One of the workloads he needs to evaluate is an IBM Connect:Direct middleware product. IBM bases its software licensing on CPU power, called a processor value unit (PVU). PVUs are based on the type of CPU, as well as how many cores are available. Mike is concerned about his licensing costs going up with migrating to AWS; the server Connect:Direct is running on is quite old and does not have as much power. His current on-premises server has 50 PVU per core, and AWS EC2 is 70 PVU per core. At first, Mike thought he would have to pay more for AWS EC2 licensing. When Mike was reviewing his application discovery information, he noticed that his server was only running at a 10% CPU location, and the server was grossly over-provisioned. By properly sizing his system, Mike was able to reduce his licensing costs during his migration.

While moving workloads to different hosting options in Mike's scenario, it does not matter whether it is on-premises or AWS due to the IBM licensing model. However, other vendors have licensing concerns based on how they count licenses for CPUs and cores. To minimize your risks for license compliance, it is important to review it as part of your application discovery and ensure that you address any discrepancies. Companies like Oracle and Microsoft have taken a very hostile stance to software noncompliance and have remarkably high penalties.

When considering a guiding principle for contractual obligations, I suggest that you review all the licensing for the applications as part of the application discovery process. This principle will ensure that any contractual risk is identified and mitigated before migration. To wait may put you in a difficult spot with a lack of support in the cloud or inability to continue your on-premises data center after migration delays.

Cost Regulation

One area where risks change significantly with migrating to AWS is cost regulation. Since AWS is a pay-as-you-go model based on consumption, your cost is based on your consumption. The problem arises when there are no proper controls around finances and spending in AWS. When operating on-premises, you have a hard stop on spending. You purchased the hardware, and you cannot consume any more than what you have available. The fact that you can scale on demand and use a nearly infinite amount of compute power can be a double-edged sword without proper preparation.

The key to mitigating this risk is through properly tagging AWS resources and chargeback or showback. By implementing these processes, you will have a way to track who or what is causing increased spending in AWS and resolve the issue before it gets out of hand. These processes will also ensure that you keep shadow IT to a minimum. It will be important that someone from finance is involved in your migration planning process to understand and offer input into the financial aspects of infrastructure in AWS. This tight integration of IT and accounting will be a new concept for both business units but is essential for proper cost controls.

AWS can also set billing alerts through the CloudWatch service. Billing alerts are very effective at watching your overall bill, but since they operate at the macro level, they are not effective at minimizing costs.

Resource tagging

AWS allows the tagging of resources to help identify and control them across your infrastructure. Tags can be used for identification, cost tracking, automation, and even access controls. Unfortunately, when many companies start, they do not understand the power of tagging and do not implement a good tagging strategy. Proper tagging will eliminate not only your cost risk but also much manual work, overall. There are several items that I suggest adding to the tags for your infrastructure. Right now, we will focus on EC2 tagging, but you can use most of these tags for other types of infrastructure as well. By using tags, you can see costs related to applications, business units, or financial cost centers based on your tagging scheme. The AWS Cost Explorer and Billing and Cost Management console both support cost allocation by tag. As a starting point, I would recommend using the tags in Table 2-1 as a baseline and modifying them as necessary to address your individual company's needs. The key items necessary for reducing cost risk are the department, the cost center, and the environment.

Table 2-1. Recommended tagging

Tag	Value
OS	Operating system
OS Version	Operating system major version
Department	The department that the resource belongs to
Cost Center	The cost center for this resource
Backup	Indicate whether Data Lifecycle Manager should target the instance backup
Inspect	Indicate whether AWS Inspector should inspect the instance for vulnerabilities
Environment	To distinguish between development, test, load test, and production
Owner	The person responsible for the resource
Data Classification	The classification of the data stored on the server
Compliance	The level of compliance for the resource such as PCI or FedRAMP
Patch	Indicate whether AWS Systems Manager or other tooling should apply patches

Tagging can be as straightforward or as complex and detailed as you would like, based on your company's needs. Currently, AWS allows up to 50 tags for EC2. Tag keys can have a maximum length of 128 characters and values of 256 in length. These tagging limits allow for much flexibility to address a plethora of applications, including configuration, backups, and even email addresses.

Chargeback and showback

Once your tagging is in place, the next place to look to reduce your cost risk is chargeback or showback. Many companies in the small and medium business space do not do chargebacks. The IT budget is lumped into a big bucket that you, as a manager, must claw and borrow to get. Then business units keep showing up at the tap like it is two-dollar Tuesday. At least on-premises, the tap would eventually run dry, and you could not provide any more resources. Unfortunately, this is not the case with AWS, because the tap never runs dry. To control costs, you will need to charge, or at least show, back costs, so business units drink responsibly. I have had a development team tell me that they need their development servers to have 16 CPUs and 64 GB of random access memory (RAM), even though they were using less than 5% of the capacity. Once chargebacks went into place and they could see that severe cost hitting their budget, they magically only needed 2 CPUs and 16 GB of RAM. Without teeth, your costs can grow uncontrollably.

Tagging enforcement

You have implemented tagging and chargebacks, everyone is on board with the strategy, and the CFO is happy. The only problem is that your bill keeps growing, and you are having trouble tracking it down. When you review your Cost Management console, you identify resources that are not tagged. You are probably thinking about how you can address people in your organization about not properly tagging resources. Thankfully, AWS has a feature called Config Rules, which allows you to create rules to enforce compliance in your organization. Config Rules enable you to set up a rule that will stop, terminate, or notify you of tagging noncompliance based on a configuration specific to your needs. Tagging enforcement is the last step in closing the loop on mitigating your risk of cost overruns in AWS. Because of the capabilities of AWS Config Rules, a guiding principle around cost regulation is not necessary. I would instead suggest creating a tagging policy as part of your landing zone design and implementing AWS Config Rules to enforce the policy.

Building Your Guiding Principles

Throughout this chapter, we went through multiple scenarios and ideas for guiding principles that will assist you in mitigating the technical and business risks associated with migrating your workloads to AWS. As part of your initial preparation for migration, it would be vital to thoroughly flesh out these principles so that they are relevant to your situation and needs. I also want to point out that there is no rule or reason to limit yourself to only one guiding principle per risk. Any additional principles will help to flesh out additional mitigating factors and further reduce risk. You may also identify additional risks that are relevant to your situation that were not outlined in this chapter. The purpose of focusing on the risks in this chapter was to identify the situations and risks that will affect most companies universally.

Wrapping It Up

Chapters 1 and 2 are designed to help you lay a solid foundation for your migration to AWS. Now that you have completed the exercise of creating your why FAQ and your guiding principles, we are ready to start diving into how to start preparing and planning for your migration. By creating these constructs, you have ensured that you can answer detractors' questions and risk concerns identified by management and business unit leaders. Being able to address these concerns quickly and with confidence will assure colleagues of your capabilities and boost confidence in the ability of your organization to navigate the migration successfully.

PART II

Phases of Migration

Before we get any deeper into the discussion about migration, I think it is vital that we review the actual migration process. We will detail what the phases of migration look like from a high level. This review will help paint a picture of what that process looks like long-term and what endpoint you are aiming for. There is no set rule on what migration should look like. Figure II-1 illustrates my process, which has been curated by years of experience. I designed it as a blueprint to show you a path, but it is not a recipe to be followed word for word. You and your company's unique needs could require some adjustments. That is perfectly OK and encouraged; this should be an agile process.

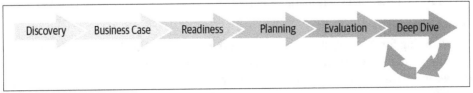

Figure II-1. Phases of migration

Let's walk through the phases and discuss at a high level what each entails. We are drawing a map of where we are, and where we need to be:

Discovering your workloads
    The first phase in the migration process is the discovery phase. In this phase, you will probably use tooling to discover your applications and servers. This phase must come first. Without it, you cannot do any of the work in the later phases.

Executing a well-crafted discovery phase provides a solid foundation for all the rest of your migration efforts.

Building the business case

Once you have discovered everything in your environment, the next phase in the process is to build your business case. The business case shows the value of migration to AWS and delivers it in a format that upper management and the board of directors can understand. It tells the story of your migration for the next few years and details key business drivers for the migration. Often the business case will come from the *why* FAQ that you developed as part of Chapter 1, with components from the discovery phase.

Addressing operational readiness

Once you have the approval from the executive team to move forward with migration, the next phase in the process is to address your operational readiness. As we discussed in Chapters 1 and 2, the cloud offers many benefits regarding agility and cost optimization, but it requires a retooling of staff and processes. The purpose of addressing your operational readiness is to ensure that major operational changes are addressed prior to migration.

Defining your landing zone and governance

One of the items that I like to place a little further up in the migration is the design of the landing zone and cloud governance. Some like to leave this phase until after migration planning is done, but by including it earlier in the process, you can have a team start to work on the deployment of your landing zone and governance controls while you are still planning your migration. This parallel planning will save a month or two in the overall process. In this phase, you will define your account structure and controls to ensure that the safety and security of AWS infrastructure is maintained.

Planning the migration

Planning for the migration entails using the data from the discovery phase to lay out your migration in waves of servers and applications. You will base these waves on the dependency between the applications and the availability of the business units responsible for the applications. The business units are the staff members who will need to test the applications for migration, or possibly to develop new code.

Evaluating for refactoring

After all the previous steps have taken place, your team might have identified some applications that would benefit from refactoring—that is, changing the application to use more cloud native resources to drive down costs or deliver better customer value. In this phase of migration, you will dive deeply into those applications to determine whether you should refactor them. You are looking for indicators of whether you should refactor as part of the main migration or if you should move them as is and refactor postmigration.

Application deep dive and planning

Application deep dive and planning is a repetitive phase that takes place before migrating each application. This phase ensures that you capture every possible piece of known information and that proper migration and rollback planning have taken place. The deep-dive phase is specifically designed to mitigate business risk and ensure a smooth migration and cutover.

This was just a short introduction to the phases, and we will talk about them in much more depth in the following chapters. I felt it prudent to give a snapshot of the whole process so you will not have to guess what comes next and can see how the phases link as you read. In Chapter 3, we will review the discovery phase in depth.

Discovering Your Workloads

Now that we have built the foundation for why you should migrate and the risks that you should avoid, it is time to get into the real meat of migration. The first step in any migration is to assess what you have in your environment. You need to determine how many servers you have, how much storage you use, and what the components of your network are, such as load balancers. In Chapter 8, we will talk about application discovery and planning. That is when you need to capture rules from the firewalls, but they are OK to skip for now. Right now, we will concentrate on the major components.

The reason you need to perform an in-depth discovery of your workloads is so you can assess costing, create a business justification, and conduct migration planning. You cannot plan and cost for servers and applications that you do not know about. Your natural reaction will probably be to assume that you know all about your infrastructure. Alternatively, you have an elaborate configuration management database (CMDB) that contains all the information you need. That may be true. In my experience, the level of knowledge and documentation about a company's environment for medium and large enterprises is about 70% correct. Seventy percent rivals house odds in Vegas. I do not know about you, but I will not bet my career on those odds. There are processes and tooling available that make the discovery effort easier and more efficient.

This chapter will walk through the various tooling requirements to ease your discovery. From there, we will dive deeply into compute, storage, and network, respectively. We will highlight things that you should look out for and ways to optimize your spend postmigration to AWS.

Discovery and Assessment Tooling

There are several tools that you can use for discovery. AWS has tooling for application discovery, server discovery, and cost analysis, but this tooling is geared for medium- and large-sized companies with hundreds or thousands of servers. For smaller companies, I would suggest a more manual method. The time it takes to set up and configure the assessment software for smaller companies might not make sense compared to the time spent entering data.

For medium- and larger-sized organizations, the use of tooling makes sense. The bigger your organization, the higher the probability that you are unaware of the state of your infrastructure. More teams mean more cracks for information to fall through and get lost. This lost information will affect your costs and timelines during migration. Missing information could also lead to unexpected outages when servers that were not identified are subsequently left off the migration plan. This oversight costs dearly when tightly coupled ancillary servers are left on-premises and cause outages or poor performance.

A lot of third-party tools can perform discovery, but there is much flux in the market, and capabilities and limitations often change. For instance, in the past two years, ATADATA, Movere, and TSO Logic were all purchased by different firms. Deloitte purchased ATADATA in 2018; it can no longer be purchased by consumers and is offered in tandem with services. Microsoft purchased Movere in 2019, and I am sure that it will limit the capabilities to only Azure. AWS purchased its own discovery tool called TSO Logic in early 2019. Providers continue to seek competitive advantages by purchasing these tools and limiting the capabilities to enhance that competitive edge.

Besides the flux caused by mergers and acquisitions in the market, there is an additional amount of flux added by the advancement of the tools themselves. The migration tooling market still is not mature. Many features can still be added to tooling to optimize it and add more value, such as features around cost management, reserved instance recommendation, business case development, license optimization, and others that are being added all the time.

Since many changes are happening around migration tooling, we will not focus on any specific tools. Instead, we will cover the capabilities that you should look for in your discovery tooling. I want to ensure that you get the most value and the capabilities necessary to ensure a successful migration. I consider these capabilities the minimum required to assess for migration accurately. There are many more capabilities that may be appropriate for your company, and you should take those into account when evaluating tooling.

Server Discovery

When looking for a discovery tool, there are several baseline features that you need to have to migrate to the cloud. Without these key items, you cannot plan and evaluate costs for your environment. The key items your discovery tooling should have are:

Server identification
> The type of server, operating system, operating system version, operating system patch level, CPU type, CPU speed, number of CPUs, number of CPU cores, and amount of memory

CPU and memory utilization
> The amount of actual CPU and memory usage by the server over a period of weeks

Disk capacity
> The disk capacity and disk space used for all disks in the system

IOPS usage
> The usage of input/output per second for disk read and write operations over a period of weeks

There are two kinds of server discovery collector methodologies: agent-based and agentless. They both have pros and cons, and both will have to be approved by your information security team, which will need to ensure that the tool meets internal security and any regulatory requirements. The tooling will scan and touch all the servers in your environment to find what you have. The methodologies have different security profiles, and it is essential to understand the difference.

Agent-based collector

The agent-based collector is the more secure method of assessing your environment. An *agent* is a piece of software that is deployed to every server and relays important server telemetry back to a central repository. By installing an agent, you allow the tool to collect the data locally without the need for inbound network connectivity. The agent then sends that information back to the discovery tool for aggregation via an outbound channel. Since the agent is only communicating with the discovery tool, it will communicate on a limited number of ports, usually standard HTTPS over port 443. Most security teams like this: it has a small compute footprint and is encrypted to ensure that traffic is not intercepted. Since you locate the agent on the server, it has unfettered access and can see the applications, performance, and network connectivity with a high level of detail and precision.

Agent-based collectors add a number of compute and memory capacity requirements. These capacity requirements are typically small, but when you have thousands of servers, it is something to be aware of. Anything multiplied by thousands can add up to a large number quickly. I have never run into a capacity issue in any of the migrations I have done. However, if your hardware is near max capacity, it would be necessary to factor the usage into your decision.

Another issue regarding agent-based collectors is that you must deploy them to all your servers. Doing this manually makes little sense. Most companies use some existing tooling like Windows Group Policy or Chef to install the agents across the infrastructure. This method works well and allows your staff to work on an exception basis on servers that had issues rather than having to touch all of them to install the agent.

Agentless collector

Agentless collectors use a host of technologies to access data on the servers from a central location. Typically, they need some form of administrative access, allowing them to log on to servers and retrieve information. Also, some types of access, such as Windows Management Instrumentation (WMI), require many ports on the servers to be opened to allow the collector to probe the instrumentation. This opening of ports significantly increases a server's attack surface and makes it more susceptible to attack. Because of the access to the environment that an agentless collector uses, many security departments are uncomfortable with this style of deployment and won't approve its use.

Since agentless collectors are not located on the system themselves, they might not have access to as much information as an agent-based collector. They should be able to provide the minimum amount of data required to achieve a proper discovery, but they may not have access to provide advanced features. It would be essential to evaluate which type of collector you need before purchasing your tooling to ensure that you can use the entire feature set; otherwise, you might pay for features you will not be able to use.

Instance right-sizing

Discovering your servers and capturing the details about them is the bare minimum. From there, the tooling should analyze the performance data to evaluate the actual system usage and perform *right-sizing*. Right-sizing is when you take a server's on-premises usage into account and factor that usage into the instance selection process. This adjustment will provide an instance that optimizes your spend in AWS. It is important to right-size your instances in AWS due to a few features of modern hypervisors. These features are:

- Sharing and deduplication of memory
- Sharing of CPU resources
- Thin provisioning of disk

When you migrate to AWS, these capabilities are not available. AWS grants you precisely the amount of resources per instance that you pay for, and those resources are not shared with other customers or instances. In my experience, all of the companies I have migrated have over-allocated resources because of this sharing. This fact means that every company can benefit from right-sizing instances in AWS to save costs.

I have seen over-allocation of at least 50% in the estates I have migrated. Some have gone as high as 90%. These are not small numbers and could cost large companies millions or tens of millions in additional and unnecessary AWS costs. It is vital to ensure that the tooling you select for your discovery can perform right-sizing calculations and adequately optimize the instance types.

Another item that should be evaluated with right-sizing capabilities is CPU aging. A 2 GHz CPU that was released five years ago will not have the same capabilities as a 2 GHz CPU that was just released. CPU power continues to increase even though clock rates remain the same. The tool that is evaluating your estate should be able to take this into account and adjust the recommended instance size as necessary. Failure to make these adjustments will, again, overinflate your AWS spend.

Disk right-sizing

Right-sizing your disks is another important feature your tooling should have. Because of thin provisioning on hypervisors like VMware and SANs themselves, many disks are larger on-premises than they need to be. Just like over-allocating CPU and memory, this leads to additional spend for resources you do not need. There are two things that I like to see regarding right-sizing disks.

First, I like to see that the tool adds an amount of free space to the disk. Using this method ensures that you remove unnecessary space and minimizes costs. The second item I look for is a tool that can optimize disks for IOPS requirements. In AWS, you get a certain number of IOPS per gigabyte of storage. For standard solid state drive (SSD) disks called gp2, you get three IOPS per gigabyte. This allocation means that a 1 TB disk will have 3,000 IOPS allocated to it. When you right-size a disk, both size used and IOPS requirement should be taken into account to ensure optimal performance and cost.

One additional item I like to see but is not a requirement is that the right-sizing algorithm includes free-space decay. This decay should be based on disk size rather than on a flat percentage or number of gigabytes to add. If you were to add 30% of free space to a 10 GB drive as a buffer, you would end up with 13 GB of storage. This 3 GB of space makes sense to have available to the system as free space. If you were to take 1,000 GB of space and add 30%, you would allocate 300 GB of free space. That number is starting to be out of line with typical data growth rates. Three hundred gigabytes is about enough space to hold six feature-length movies in 4K format. The problem compounds itself as you increase the space used. By implementing a decay into the calculation, the free space will go down by percentage as the space used goes up. This decay ensures that you don't over-allocate free space and, again, drive up your costs in AWS unnecessarily.

Application discovery

Knowing what servers you have and how much CPU and memory they need is a big piece of the migration puzzle but is not the only one. Another vital piece is knowing what applications you have installed on those servers. When it comes down to it, moving a server is easy. AWS has a tool called CloudEndure that can copy the blocks on the disk of an on-premises server to AWS. The tool is super easy to use. I say that if I had enough bananas, I could train a monkey to do it; it is that easy. The more difficult part of a migration is knowing what is on the server. The applications on the server determine what other servers it has to talk to, what business unit is in charge of it, and which customers access it.

Since what is running on the servers has more impact than the server itself, your tool should discover what applications you installed. I recommend that it capture not only what is installed, but also what version is installed. This information helps you later during application discovery and planning around what needs to be done to migrate. The version is relevant because vendors do not certify some software on the cloud except for more current releases. Having this information will allow you to assess the risk associated with support for that application and mitigate it before migration. If your tool cannot collect this information, you will have to collect it manually, which will increase the manual effort and your timeline.

Dependency mapping

The last piece that a discovery tool should include is dependency mapping, which looks at the traffic between servers and maps out which servers communicate with one another for you. When an application is first deployed, your team will be familiar with the state and the other systems it communicates with. However, as we have covered before, attrition, continual evolution, and poor documentation move you further and further from a known state. With migration, knowing these interconnections is vital to the success of your migration. As we mentioned in Chapter 2, not knowing enough about the estate is a business risk that we all want to avoid. Dependency mapping is an important part of mitigating this risk. It also helps you later when planning out your migration waves.

One item I like to see but is not completely necessary is the ability to blacklist servers from the dependency mapping. It is common to have servers in your infrastructure that every other server communicates with. An excellent example of this would be servers for Microsoft Active Directory (AD). Since AD performs all your authentication and authorization, it is obvious that nearly every server will communicate with it. These types of servers introduce a level of noise to the dependency mapping that is unnecessary. The ability to blacklist servers like AD, security, and logging servers will significantly reduce the level of noise and make the dependency tree more understandable.

If you can find a tool that has these features, you will have optimized the discovery and assessment phase of your migration. Unfortunately, that may not be as easy as it sounds. Your company might have some specific needs that you would like to address during your assessment. For instance, you might have some specific needs around licensing information and have found a tool that meets that need for you. However, the tool does not have IOPS optimization for disks. Since it cannot adjust disk space for IOPS, this is something that your engineering team will have to review by hand.

Compute

After you have selected your discovery tool and you have run it against your environment, you will end up with a list of all of your servers and the corresponding instances that the tool recommends you use in AWS. I would love to say you are all set and ready to move on to the next phase of the process. Unfortunately, this is not the case. All the tooling currently on the market needs a little polish to yield the best result. The fact of the matter is that some of the benefits you can get from the cloud are items that require human intervention to determine whether they can be used. For instance, a tool cannot tell whether or not your deployment of a custom web application can support horizontal scaling. These types of decisions will have to be addressed by someone on your team. This section aims to educate you on the items that you and your team should address after discovery to refine your run rate numbers.

An important point to remember is the amount of estimation that needs to occur. You are trying to make a reasonable estimate of what it will take to migrate and run in AWS, but you are not looking for *to the penny* accuracy. Until you reach the application deep-dive phase, some items, such as the capability to scale horizontally, will be assumptions. I liken it to blasting a rocket into space versus landing on the moon. Right now, you are just blasting into space. You can add more thrust to get it there, and if you overshoot a little, it is not a big deal. Later on, the deep-dive and planning phase is when you will need precision to land on the moon.

Latest Instances

Once your tool discovers all your servers and attempts to right-size your instances, there may be some additional massaging required. Many tools on the market load all of the available systems on AWS into their tool and then scan this list to find suitable matches. What I have found is that not all the tools are good at weeding out the older instance types. Amazon names its instance types, starting with a letter to signify the class. The class designates what type of workloads or capabilities the instance has. Table 3-1 shows the current instance family available in AWS.

Table 3-1. Instance families

Class	Class name	Use case
C	CPU Optimized	Instances that favor higher-performance CPUs
M	General Purpose	Balanced compute, memory, and networking performance
T	Burstable Instance	Lower-cost instances that consume CPU credits over a baseline CPU allotment
A	General Purpose ARM	Custom AWS CPUs supporting advanced RISC machine (ARM) workloads
R, X, Z	Memory Optimized	Instances that favor large memory capacity
P, G, F	Accelerated Computing (GPU)	Use hardware accelerators (GPU/FPGAs) to accelerate floating point and graphics calculations.
I, D, H	Storage Optimized	Favor high sequential read/write access to high-performance local storage

After the letter comes a number that signifies the generation of the instance. The higher the number, the newer the generation. So an M5 is newer than an M4, and a T3 is newer than a T2 instance type. After the generation there is a period, followed by instance size: *small*, *medium*, *large*, and so on. I have included the current instance sizes in Table 3-2.

Table 3-2. Instance sizes

Size	Instance ratio
nano	0.25
micro	0.5
small	1
medium	2
large	4
xlarge	8
2xlarge	16
3xlarge	24
4xlarge	32

Size	Instance ratio
6xlarge	48
8xlarge	64
9xlarge	72
10xlarge	80
12xlarge	96
16xlarge	128
18xlarge	144
24xlarge	192
32xlarge	256

Instance ratios are used as a way to know how instances *stack* from an AWS Reserved Instance (RI) perspective. We will cover RIs and their cost savings in depth in "Reserved instances" on page 124. Amazon Linux reserved instances can be stacked or split if there is no exact match for the purchased instance type. For example, two t3.large reserved instances can be stacked and cover a single t3.xlarge running instance.

The issue that comes into play with some tools is that they are always looking for the lowest price. Unfortunately, the lowest price does not always equal the best performance. Typically, the latest-generation instances are slightly less expensive than the previous ones, but that is not always true. Here your tooling may pick an older instance type based on that cost. However, newer instances will provide better performance that would offset that small difference in price and be cheaper overall.

An excellent example of this is the latest T3 instances. AWS builds the T3 instances on the new Nitro engine; they are 30% more performant than the T2 instances per dollar. If your tool were to select a T2 instance because it was two cents cheaper per hour, this recommendation could cost you much more because the system performance is 30% lower. Therefore, I recommend that you have your team review all of the instances selected and ensure that they are the latest generation available.

CPU Type

One of the newer additions to AWS is the ability to choose instance types that have different CPU manufacturers and capabilities. Before AWS released these options, the only processors available were from Intel. Today AWS offers Intel, ARM, and AMD CPUs. Switching your CPU type can save you some additional money over the standard Intel instances. However, there are some caveats. ARM instances will not run all software. To use the ARM-based instances, you will need to be running a Linux OS running software that is compiled for ARM CPU instruction sets. This CPU change works great for web servers and Java applications but will not work for Windows workloads or COTS software.

The story is different for AMD CPUs. AMD is compatible with the x86 instruction set. This point means that you can use AMD and Windows and all the COTS applications you have in your estate without issue. The AMD CPU instances are about 10% cheaper than Intel, and that can lead to many cost savings for large companies. Not all instance classes have AMD counterparts; it will not be a question of AMD versus Intel but rather how much AMD.

However, this is another area where many discovery tools fall short by not offering you a way to select CPU types when they are making instance recommendations. Unfortunately, your team will most likely have to review all the instance types and manually select AMD or ARM equivalents.

Relational Database Service

We mentioned in "Soft costs" on page 26 that AWS offers a service called RDS. To recap, RDS is a service that manages several types of relational database management system (RDBMS) platforms for you. It offloads applying OS patches, RDBMS patches, storage capacity expansion, and backups from your staff as part of its integrated management, thus freeing your team to not worry about those items. The RDS service offers you significant soft-cost savings for your company. Most discovery tooling cannot map the servers running RDBMS to RDS. The tooling will map what you have and make an EC2 recommendation. If you were to migrate your databases directly to EC2 in this way, you would be leaving a major benefit of migration off the table.

Like CPU types and using the latest instances, the onus will fall to your team to ensure that your servers on-premises are appropriately mapped to RDS instances where applicable. Making this change won't save you hard costs or make an impact on your run rate, but it will save you cost, time, and headaches in the long run.

Partial Run Rate

An area where discovery tooling needs some human assistance is with instances that have a partial run rate. With AWS, you pay only for what you use, so it makes sense to turn off certain types of servers so that you do not have to pay for them. This makes sense in development and testing environments. Your development and testing teams probably do not work around the clock as your customers do. This timing means that instead of running those servers 24/7, you can turn them off at night and turn them back on in the morning before people start working. Say you run your development and test servers for 10 hours a day to address teams coming in early and leaving later in the day. That would mean that those servers will run for only 50 hours a week as opposed to 168 hours. Performing shutdown and startup means that you will save

70% of the run rate for those systems. That is significant savings and one that most companies can take advantage of.

It would be a good idea to have your team review your development and testing servers to see whether you can benefit from this type of savings. You may have to adjust some manual calculations to compensate if your tool cannot set a partial run rate.

Auto Scaling

You might have noticed that quite a few items need human intelligence to make adjustments to your discovery. Auto scaling is no different. Your chosen discovery tool will not be able to determine whether your application is stateless or not. Your team might not have that level of detail at this stage of the process, because they haven't dived deeply enough. What we are looking for here is an educated guess about whether the application can use auto scaling so that you can build it into the costing model. It is a safe bet to assume that most web applications are stateless. Making this assumption allows you to adjust the run rate for servers that are part of a web server farm to compensate for auto scaling. Let us look at this scenario for more clarity.

Scenario 3-1

Robert's company has a web farm that runs its main website. The website is a business-to-business platform that is used mostly Monday through Friday, with some intermittent weekend usage. The high point of weekday usage occurs on Wednesday, when most customers are putting in their orders for the following week. Robert's team has noted that 12 servers are running in the farm currently.

Let us break down Robert's scenario and determine what his run rates should look like after migration to AWS for this web farm. First, Robert's team should ensure that they have the best availability they can have. That means that three of the servers in the web farm should be running 100% of the time. Having three servers, each one in a different AZ, ensures the best uptime for Robert's customers. The three servers will also provide the baseline performance that the company needs on the weekends and low points during the week. We also know that usage reaches the peak on Wednesday, so that day we know we need all 12 servers online. What we can do now is apply a normal distribution curve to the 9 remaining servers with the high point at 12 on Wednesday. What we end up with is three servers set to 100% of the time, four servers running for 71% of the time, nine servers running for 43% of the time, and two servers running 14% of the time. This distribution is visualized in Figure 3-1.

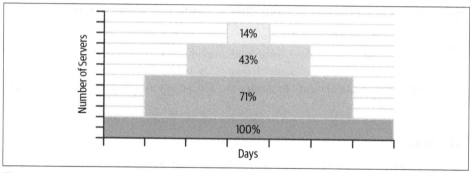

Figure 3-1. Server distribution

When Robert sees the usage in real life, the numbers will not line up with what we have calculated here. Robert's company will see an ebb and flow throughout the day, and servers will spin up and down to compensate. The important thing to focus on for the cost model is that Robert's team approximated a more realistic run rate for 12 servers that were running all the time. Ultimately, we are creating another SWAG. The resolution for the data that Robert has is in days, and his customer usage and auto scaling has a resolution of minutes. It would be impossible to model any more precisely with the limited data at Robert's disposal. Remember the mantra, blasting into space.

License Model

We have covered run rates, CPU types, and auto scaling, and now we are headed for the homestretch for compute. There are a couple of ways to purchase licenses in AWS when it comes to operating systems and RDBMS engines. You can bring your own license (BYOL) or purchase it as part of the service. Both RDS and EC2 offer this capability, and both models have their benefits and drawbacks.

License included, or bring your own

BYOL can offer some benefits in AWS. It depends on the software, the type of license, and the type of instance required in AWS. To be up-front, this is a bit of a moving target. Companies like Oracle and Microsoft are changing their license agreements often, and it can be a bit of an obstacle to navigate. Microsoft licensing can be so complex that some consulting companies have staff dedicated to evaluating it for customers and making recommendations on how to comply prior to an audit.

My biggest issue with BYOL is that some require you to use dedicated instances, dedicated hosts, or possibly bare-metal instances. Using these instance types requires more work on your end, and you take a step toward looking more like an on-premises data center. For instance, when you use dedicated hosts, you purchase a host in a single AZ. To add high-availability (HA) and BC capabilities, you need to extend them into another AZ, which means purchasing another host. You also must be aware of which applications and instances you place on a dedicated host and balance out the load. As you can see, this looks less like the cloud and more like a management hassle.

 My recommendation on BYOL: Just say no.

The license-included model allows you to purchase the license for Windows, SQL Server, or Red Hat as part of the EC2 service. I prefer the license-included model. There are a couple of benefits to using it over the BYOL model. The first benefit is that you eliminate that licensing risk. You know that your instances are covered from a licensing perspective. Thus, you do not have to worry about them in an audit. Companies like Oracle and Microsoft are making a business of going after companies for using software that is not licensed. The worst part about this scheme is that often you are out of compliance because the licensing models are so convoluted. You can get hit with huge fines just because there was a misunderstanding. They don't care whether there was intent to steal licensing or not—you still get the fines. The penalties allowed by law are up to $150,000 per title infringed. According to The Software Alliance (*http://bsa.org*), underreporting of licenses used is the largest and most common infraction.

The second benefit to using the license-included model is that, because you are aiming to be more agile and dynamic in the cloud, you are only paying for the licenses that you are using. If you BYOL and are running an auto scaling group, you will have to purchase licensing for the high-water mark. Eliminating this cost is yet another way to save capital by migrating to AWS from on-premises. This savings is not just concerning auto scaling either: you can see this benefit when you try out some new capabilities in a sandbox.

You might be asking yourself why you should forgo the licenses that you already have. Well, that is a good point and one I want to call out. About 90% of the companies I have migrated have chosen to scrap their on-premises licensing based on the risk associated with license compliance and the cost of managing those licenses by staff. The fines for noncompliance reach into the hundreds of thousands of dollars. The management and internal auditing of licenses have costs in the tens of thousands. Putting these costs together, these companies felt that it was a better investment to retire the licenses they had.

When you are working on your discovery, your team should be validating that your tooling is using the license model properly. Evaluating licensing ensures that license costs are included in your run rate. Most discovery software allows for the configuration of licensing, and this should not be a significant area of concern.

We have covered a lot of ground regarding discovery and compute resources. Your tooling will help you a lot by reducing the manual work required to detail your environment. However, as you have seen, your team still needs to do a lot of manual work to complete the discovery process properly and to ensure that the optimal state is attained. Doing more work on the up-front processes will provide a smoother migration later.

Storage

Now that we have covered the additional items to manually review for migration, it is time to move on to storage. Not as many items need manual review when it comes to storage. For most instances, having the standard SSD storage known as gp2 is the best choice for most servers. However, there are a few options that make sense some of the time. In this section, we will review those types and some places you might want to implement them. In addition, we will also cover some special instances that offer benefits by modifying standard storage for database servers and NFS servers.

As long as the tooling you selected to perform your discovery supports right-sizing disks, most of the storage work will have been done for you. If it doesn't, your team will have to put in quite a bit of effort to verify that the disk sizing is correct so that you minimize your costs. EBS does offer dynamic storage increases after volume deployment. This feature enables you to increase your capacity (not decrease) if your free space is becoming low. This ability reduces risk when sizing disks too small. You can always go back and make them larger later. The same cannot be said when making volumes too large. They cannot be made smaller. Thus it's better to err on the smaller side.

EBS Volume Types

Most of your servers in AWS will use EBS volumes for storage. EBS is similar in use to SAN storage that you would use on-premises. It is connected to the instance by a network and is not connected directly to the host server by a disk controller. EBS offers redundancy like a Redundant Array of Inexpensive Disks (RAID) in a conventional SAN. AWS handles this redundancy for you. Therefore, you do not have to configure it on your servers.

> EBS volumes are only redundant in a single AZ. If an AZ goes offline, the volume will be offline as well. EBS volumes are not replicated outside of the AZ. For redundancy, snapshots of EBS volumes should be taken to recover the volume to another AZ.

AWS offers four types of EBS volumes. These four storage types cover virtually every type of use case you could have. The four types are gp2, io1, st1, and sc1. For 95% of workloads, gp2 will probably be your volume of choice. The other 5% will be made up of a mix of the rest of the volume types:

gp2

The gp2 SSD disk offers remarkably high input/output (I/O) at 3 IOPS per GB and decent throughput as well. It works well for everyday workloads like web servers and database servers. It is also very cost-effective at only $0.10 per GB in the us-east-1 region as of this writing.

io1

You would use the io1 storage when you need extremely high IOPS for performance workloads. I have not seen io1 used as often as you would think. You might also think that you would see it in situations like database servers where I/O is high. In my experience, I have found that the ratio of storage to I/O requirement matches quite well with the gp2 volume type. For instance, you might have an Oracle server that needs 30,000 IOPS. But that same server needs 10 TB of disk capacity. Well, 10 TB of disk gives you 30,000 IOPS. There is no reason to stray from gp2 for that use case. I have found io1 to be useful when you need a high amount of IOPS but little storage. A workload where you needed 30,000 IOPS but only 100 GB of storage would be an ideal case for io1 storage.

st1 and sc1

I lump sc1 and st1 together because they are similar. These storage types are magnetic disks, not SSD. You know, those things the Flintstones used that went *clickity-click-click* and tended to crash, taking all your family photos with it. This storage does not have a lot of I/O capability, but it does have a high throughput. The throughput is well above gp2 at 500 megabytes per second. This type of disk works well with consecutive read/write data, such as database backups.

 Sc1 and st1 disks have a minimum size of 500 GB. Keep this in mind, because it might inflate costs over gp2, depending on the original disk size.

Although AWS offers you these four options, you will probably only need gp2 storage for your instances. Some people think they will save money by using the magnetic storage types but forget that they need a minimum of 500 GB. This oversight quickly elevates the cost. Start with gp2 and work down from there if you think you have a special use case.

Network File System Replacement

An item that should be addressed as part of the manual review and polishing for storage is the replacement of network file system (NFS) servers in your environment. AWS offers a service called Elastic File System (EFS) that manages NFSs. This service allows you to forget managing and patching any NFS server instances, saving you soft costs. As a bonus, EFS is a cross-AZ service. This service offers multi-AZ redundancy as a native feature. Having this prevents you from having to create an HA solution for NFS yourself, saving even more engineering time. I have not seen a discovery tool to date that can make a judgment call on replacing NFS servers. Since this decision will not be made for you, I would suggest that you have your team do a review for any NFS servers in your environment and adjust accordingly.

I want to point out that the cost at first looks high. EFS in us-east-1 costs $0.30 per consumed gigabyte at the time of writing. This price is three times the cost of EBS storage, because the EFS service replicates data two more times for a total of three AZs. Two things to keep in mind are that the service probably provides greater availability over your original on-premises design and you do not have the costs of servers with EFS. These features might make EFS more palatable when you consider these capabilities.

 Very large data footprints can become very costly in EFS. AWS introduced EFS life cycle management and an infrequently accessed storage tier, which has a lower price point. However, for exceptionally large data sets, it may make sense to use a combination of EFS and S3 to minimize expenditures.

Windows Server Replacement

EFS is not the only service that offers the ability to decrease soft costs for storage management. AWS launched Amazon FSx in 2018. FSx is a managed file server service that provides Windows and Lustre network file system support. The FSx service provides the ability to replace Windows file servers in your environment with a managed service, easing their management after you migrate them to AWS. Like RDS and other services, AWS manages the operating system (OS), backups, and patching, allowing you and your team to focus on delivering customer value.

In late 2019, AWS released multi-AZ capabilities for FSx for Windows. Unlike EFS, which is always redundant across AZs, you must select the multi-AZ deployment option with FSx. Also, the pricing is different based on whether you choose multi-AZ or single-AZ deployment. During discovery, you should establish if your file servers that are migrated to FSx require the availability of multi-AZ to maximize storage savings.

Instance Store Volumes

There is one last type of storage that AWS offers that may be of use for certain workloads. Instance store volumes are disks that are available on certain instance types. These instance store volumes are local to the host and offer very high I/O and throughput. These high-performant volumes work very well for intense I/O workloads. A critical concern with instance store volumes is that they are ephemeral. This means that when a server is stopped, the disk is wiped out, and the data is no longer available. This erasure limits this storage to a particular use case and is not for general server storage. Ephemeral storage works great for high-speed processing applications where the data can be re-created with ease, such as for video transcoding, image manipulation, or HPC.

Like most items we have talked about in this chapter, flagging disks for instance store volumes is not something that any discovery tool will be able to do. It is not aware of the software and storage patterns on the disk that would allow this kind of decision to be automated. In fact, your team may not be aware of the applicability of the application for instance stores. Like we discussed with auto scaling, this is an item for which your team may be able to hypothesize which servers could use or benefit from this type of disk and adjust later in the process.

Network

Since you must manually review for auto scaling, it makes sense that you also must manually account for load balancers in AWS. I have not seen a discovery tool that can scan load balancers and paths. However, since you are probably changing from vertical scaling to horizontal scaling, there would be nothing to discover. Load balancers can add a modicum of cost, making it important to review and ensure that it accurately represents them in your discovery and costing.

The other item that we will touch on is the costs for outbound bandwidth. AWS does not charge for data coming into the estate, but it does charge for data that is leaving. There are several costs per gigabyte, depending on what service is reporting that data usage. Typically, data is not a huge expense, but it is important to understand the circumstances of when you will be charged.

Overall Outbound Bandwidth

Many companies get nervous when they hear that AWS charges for outbound bandwidth. The number one reason I think this fear exists is that no one knows how much data they are pushing outside of their network. They imagine this huge number of gigabytes, and at the base rate of $0.09 a gigabyte, that can be scary. If you are not accounting for bandwidth today on-premises, then it will not be substantial enough to concern yourself about it in AWS either. For example, media companies like Getty

Images or *The Wall Street Journal* would account for data on-premises. For a media company, outbound data is the bulk of its business, and outbound traffic would be a sizable expense in AWS. But then again, it was on-premises as well.

For every other company that does not track its outgoing bandwidth, I typically add an uplift onto the expense of EC2 to accommodate outbound bandwidth. I have found that adding 8–10% is more than adequate to accommodate for outbound data charges. This uplift should be added to the EC2 expense only, and should not include EBS, S3, and load balancers. If you were to have an EC2 spend of $10,000 a month, the estimated data charge would be $800–$1,000.

Data out is another situation where you are strapping on more rocket power to get into space. The costing for data out is very complex. There are different charges in regions, between regions, over Direct Connect, EC2 to CloudFront, and CloudFront to the internet. It would be much more effort than I would want to spend to calculate it for landing on the moon. Using the 8–10% uplift will give you a worst-case scenario since all the other data out charges are less than EC2 to the internet.

Elastic Load Balancers

When your team went through and decided which applications would use auto scaling, they accounted for changes to spend based on the changes in instance count and run time. However, this does not consider the additional spend for elastic load balancers (ELBs) in AWS. ELBs in AWS have three consumption models. There is a baseline cost for activating and running an ELB. You then add to that unique charges based on the type of load balancer you are using.

An ELB also gives you the ability to offload Secure Socket Layer/Transport Layer Security (SSL/TLS) encryption from your servers: the load balancers do that work and decrease the load on your servers. The ELB, in this case, would talk to the back-end servers over unencrypted HTTP. Typically, I recommend against this design because I believe it is too cheap to run SSL/TLS not to use it. I would rather have the extra layer of encryption and be able to tell any auditors that everything is encrypted in transit. I use ELBs to offload the SSL/TLS from the client connection and then configure the ELB to create an SSL/TLS session to the source servers. This design offers another layer of protection for your servers, with the load balancers working as an intermediary rather than passing traffic directly through. Your team might not have gotten to this level of granularity with your EC2 costing adjustments for auto scaling. However, it might be a good topic of discussion to ensure that this is not the case.

An added benefit of using SSL/TLS on the AWS load balancers is that you get SSL certificates for free from the AWS Certificate Manager (ACM) service. On-premises SSL certificates are an additional cost of around $100 a year for a single host/subdomain certificate. You can get wildcard certificates to help drive down costs, but then you forsake security. ACM offers you free host/subdomain certificates, and you do not have to sacrifice security. AWS has three load balancer types: classic ELB (not to be confused with the generic ELB acronym for all the services), Application Load Balancer (ALB), and Network Load Balancer (NLB).

 ACM certificates are only free for AWS load balancers and Cloud-Front. You cannot use them for non-AWS services and servers.

Classic Elastic Load Balancer

The classic ELB is a holdover from the days before VPCs existed in AWS. It works fine with VPCs, but the NLB has supplanted it. The classic ELB is a Layer 4 network device, meaning that it cannot see inside protocols to do advanced routing. It accepts traffic and can route it based on ports. The ELB cannot do much more than that. For many instances, this is just fine. However, I typically see ALBs being deployed today instead, for reasons we will cover shortly.

Ultimately, I would suggest not deploying classic ELB anymore, since the new NLB service has outdone it. If you do use a classic ELB, then keep in mind that your costs will include not only the monthly ELB fee but also the data-out charges. Since you applied an uplift to the EC2 spend, these charges should already be accounted for and need not be added in again.

Application Load Balancer

The ALB was introduced a few years ago and is a vast improvement over the classic ELB. An ALB is a Layer 7 network device, so it can understand protocols such as HTTP and can redirect traffic to different server pools based on the URL. This level of integration gives you many capabilities to split your application. Integration is critical when you want to refactor your application in more cloud-native designs. Using an ALB allows you to merge load balancers. Besides being able to look inside a URL, ALBs can also see what host or subdomain you are trying to reach. This vision allows you to use one ALB for up to one hundred different destinations. This function cannot span to different security zones, AWS regions, or accounts. You can't use just one ALB to "rule them all," nor would you want to.

For costing out ALB, you need to plan for how many ALBs you will need plus the number of Load Balancer Capacity Units (LCUs). AWS makes an LCU from four different consumptions: new connections, active connections, processed bytes, and rule evaluations. You are charged for the highest of those consumptions, not for all of them. An LCU contains:

- 25 new connections per second
- 3,000 active connections per minute
- 1 GB per hour for EC2 instances, containers, and IP addresses
- 1,000 rule evaluations per second

Together these create the cost basis of your ALB implementation. Let's look at this scenario to get a better understanding of how you could cost out an ALB.

Scenario 3-2

Anna's company is migrating to AWS, and it has 17 web server farms moving to the cloud. Some of these web farms are under unique domain names, and some are sub-domains of their whizbangcheezeinacan.com. Anna has asked her team to cost out the load balancing functions for these 17 web server farms because she is concerned the cost will be high. Anna had decided that they will run all their websites in two different regions for redundancy. They are the number one cheese-in-a-can manufacturer in the world and have an image to uphold. Besides the 17 production web server farms, Anna's company also has 17 development servers and 17 test servers where they develop and test before the production release.

First let's look at how we have to split up the ALBs for Anna's environment. ALBs cannot go across regions, so her company will need at least two ALBs. They also cannot cross accounts and environments, which means that there needs to be at least four ALBs. That is two for production, one for testing, and one for development. For Anna, the baseline cost of her ALBs will be $65.70 based on the cost in the us-east-1 region at the time of writing.[1]

After figuring the cost of the ALB, you need to start using a bit of fuzzy math. You won't have all the details required to calculate the LCU cost for the ALBs. If I am honest, I am not a fan of the way ALB costs are calculated. The model is convoluted and impossible to predict without running a proof of concept (POC) to gather actual statistics. I recommend multiplying the cost of the ALBs—in this case, $65.70—by four. The multiplication covers the cost of the ALBs and gives you some breathing room for the LCU charges. In this example, the total estimated charges would be $262.80. The data charges that you put in for an uplift will also give you a buffer, because the instances behind the ALB will not go directly out to the internet. Essentially, those charges can be added to the $262.80 as well.

---

1 4 load balancers × $0.0225 per hour × 730 hours in a month = $65.70

Network Load Balancer

The NLB is very similar to the classic ELB. It, too, is a Layer 4 network device, so it cannot see and cooperate with the protocol higher up the stack. The NLB is the replacement for the classic ELB and offers a few new capabilities. The NLB works on not only Transmission Control Protocol (TCP)—which would include HTTP and HTTPS protocols—but also on User Datagram Protocol (UDP), and supports off-loading Transport Layer Security (TLS), which deprecated SSL in 2015. One of the benefits of the NLB is that it supports static IP addresses. A significant change from the classic ELB is that NLBs don't support security groups. With an NLB, you have to allow the source IP addresses of the NLB on the target instances.

Unfortunately, the consumption model for the NLB is like that of the ALB. You pay for the NLB per hour and then for LCUs on top of that. The LCU consumption models are different from the ones for ALB. For the NLB, the consumption is based on new connections, active connections, and processed bytes. I suggest doing the same for NLB as we did for ALB: multiply the NLB base charge by four to create a buffer for the LCU charges.

The NLB service does not support sticky sessions. If you need sticky sessions, use an ALB or classic ELB.

Ancillary AWS Service Charges

When you first migrate your company to AWS, quite a few services will be deployed as part of your landing zone, and their costs need to be accounted for. Like outbound bandwidth, these services are things that you cannot calculate out. The services that need to be included are things like Simple Notification Service (SNS), Config, and CloudWatch. These services are all billed by consumption and are serverless. Since you will not know how many API calls you will make or how many alarms AWS will send, it will be an impractical use of time to cost these out. I recommend a 5% uplift on EC2 spend to accommodate for these charges. Again, if your run rate is $10,000 for EC2, you would spend about $500 a month for these ancillary services.

Assessing Connectivity Requirements

Thus far, we have covered servers, storage, and network. However, it would be a great disservice not to talk about *connectivity*. After all, connectivity could be a large expense, and as we talked about in "Application Connectivity" on page 54, it can be a significant business risk as well. Now that you have completed your discovery, you will have a much better picture of how things connect and interoperate. Choosing your connectivity to AWS is probably best served by following a decision tree. You will want to choose your connectivity based on your business needs and not on the bottom line. I have seen migrations go belly up because the main deciding factor for connectivity was cost. If you want to have a successful migration, you need to give your users and customers the best experience—an experience that doesn't deviate from what they have grown accustomed to while using servers on-premises.

In Figure 3-2, you can see a straightforward decision tree that will help you decide what kind of connectivity you require to best serve your customers and users.

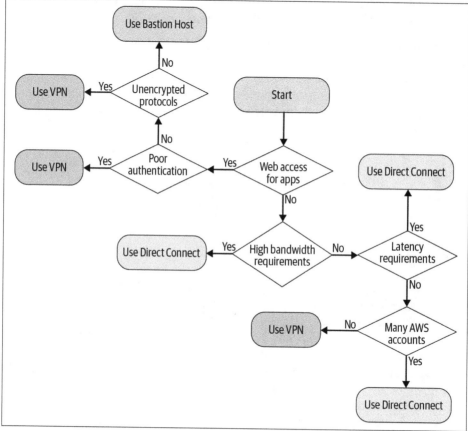

Figure 3-2. Connectivity decision tree

The tree starts with internet access; it is the most cost-effective but has the highest level of restrictions on its use. From there, the tree works down to VPN. VPNs are relatively cost-effective but have limitations with scale. You may arrive at Direct Connect, which offers you the best service and scale. Let's walk through each of the decision points to ensure a clear understanding of why you could choose a yes or no answer:

Do all of your applications have web access?
You cannot have only internet access if your applications do not have a web interface. This limitation makes only internet access a nonstarter.

Do any of your applications require protocols that cannot be encrypted?
Some older applications might use web protocols but cannot be encrypted, such as File Transfer Protocol (FTP) and HTTP. A situation like this would again push you to a VPN solution.

Do any of your applications have poor authentication controls?
Even if an application can support HTTPS and has password protection, that does not mean that it should be on the internet. If your application has an eight-character limit with only alphabetic characters, you would not want it exposed. Another item to include here is if the application does not support account lockout and failed password attempts. It would leave you exposed to brute-force attacks.

Do any of your applications have latency restrictions?
The latency of VPN is not static and depends on the path and amount of traffic on specific legs as your packets head for AWS. If you need low latency, consider Direct Connect.

Do any of your applications have high bandwidth requirements?
VPN is limited in the amount of bandwidth it can push through the tunnel at 1.25 GBps. This limit is based on the AWS VPN device; your internet pipe and the hardware you have on-premises may further reduce VPN capabilities. If you have high bandwidth needs for your application, Direct Connect is your path.

Do you require many AWS accounts or environments?
VPN cannot do transitive routing. If you have many accounts and environments, you will need many VPN connections. The high VPN count will add not only to your cost but also to your complexity and soft management costs. Direct Connect can have 50 virtual interfaces (VIFs) that can connect to 50 accounts.

 Fifty VIFs is the maximum hard limit from AWS. The number of VIFs depends on your provider and the bandwidth purchased. Your limit may be lower.

Do you have a resiliency requirement?
Although AWS offers two VPN tunnels that are deployed to two different AZs in AWS, the limitation of the internet between your office and AWS still exists. Direct Connect typically offers the ability to have more redundancy in the network between you and AWS.

Do all of your applications have a high bandwidth aggregate?
> Even if you do not have an application that has a high bandwidth requirement, you might have a high aggregate bandwidth requirement. You will need to add up all of your bandwidth requirements and make sure the total does not exceed your VPN capability.

At this point, by following the connectivity decision tree, you should have arrived at a decision as to how you will connect AWS to your offices. Most likely, you will have a VPN or Direct Connect connection to AWS. If you wanted to, you could find several ways to work around some limitations and move forward with a lower tier of connectivity. For instance, you could use AWS Workspaces, a virtual desktop service, for a desktop that would allow you to get around needing a VPN. A virtual desktop would ensure that the data that needs to be communicated from a desktop to the server would be protected because that data would never traverse the internet.

The question that you will need to ask yourself is how many workarounds you want to support. For example, if you had an environment where you had 25 web-based applications and one old legacy application used by a handful of people, then maybe using Workspaces as a workaround makes sense. However, if you had five web-based applications and 20 legacy applications with hundreds of users, it makes little sense. At that point, you are trading the maintenance of a VPN for the maintenance of a large virtual desktop estate. When in doubt, say no and move to a higher tier.

Wrapping It Up

In this chapter, we talked about several discovery items that must be done manually. I would love to tell you that the marketplace is ramping up to offer these kinds of capabilities soon, but unfortunately, this is not the case. Advancements are being made, but to have all of these manual items included will take some time for vendors to implement.

I also want to point out that you don't *have* to implement all or any of these items if you don't want to. It is perfectly fine to use what assessment tools suggest and run with that. It will be just as good as on-premises and provide you all the capabilities you currently have. But then what would be the point of migrating to AWS if you are not going to take advantage of the benefits we discussed in Chapter 1?

The important thing to remember is that over time, you want to start moving to AWS services that offer the most automated management. Those services are what will increase employee satisfaction, increase agility, and reduce soft costs. Your timeline might not allow the level of detailed analysis required to review these items. You can always come back and perform these analyses later and make changes to your environment. I cannot stress enough how important it is *not* to treat AWS like a data center.

CHAPTER 4

Building Your Business Case

Migrate, then iterate.

—Nate Gandert, *Chief Technology Officer/Chief Product Officer Getty Images*

Now that you have completed your discovery and made all the manual adjustments, it is time to build your business case. You may be wondering why you need a business case. Very few companies get a mandate down from the board level telling them to move to the cloud. It does happen, but usually there is some significant business objective that they need to address in those scenarios. For the rest of us, we need to show why we should move to the cloud. Unfortunately, the story usually centers on costs, even though agility is the real business value.

When it comes to migration, costs are high. You must operate in two environments for some period, which drives the bulk of your expenses. You will have training, consulting, and potentially software fees as well. Migration also causes a significant disruption to your business units and their timelines. To be blunt, moving forward with migration without having the buy-in of senior leadership is a sure way to get walked out the door. The business case conveys the information that you have gathered about your environment and relays that to management in a digestible format.

The bulk of this chapter will address hard costs, because they are the easiest to get business alignment on and approval to migrate. There are also a few areas to highlight where your costs might go up when you compare them to on-premises. In these situations, it is essential to highlight the additional benefits your company will receive from them. The story really should be more about agility and the capabilities your company will get by moving to AWS. Agility is not always quantifiable. That makes it hard to use in your business case since you cannot directly tie savings or increased revenue to that agility. All is not lost, though; there are some agility benefits you can quantify, and we will cover those in this chapter.

An unseen benefit of the business case process is that senior leadership may ask some questions and require investigation that you hadn't thought of previously. This process guarantees that all the bases are covered and ensures a higher level of long-term success.

Estimating Your Timeline

To craft a proper business case, you need to know how long your migration will run. The length of your migration has a significant effect on the cost of your migration. It will affect your double expenditure, tooling, and any consulting fees. We have not discussed migration planning yet; we will cover it later, in Chapter 7. For now, we will estimate the length based on three factors:

1. The number of servers you have to migrate
2. The number of servers you estimate can be moved per day
3. A buffer for unexpected timeline delays to create the estimated timeline.

Number of Servers

The bulk of the effort in migration comes from the number of servers that you have on-premises. It boils down to the logistics of touching those servers and moving them. You will have to install agents on the box to migrate it to AWS, disable network adapters postmigration on the source server, perform a smoke test, and conduct other operations during your migration. Even with automation, it will still be the largest bucket of time.

Number of Servers Moved per Day

Calculating the number of servers that can be migrated per day can be tricky. It depends on the level of AWS experience of the staff that is performing the migration. It also depends on the types of applications and whether the staff has done migrations in the past. When I was a consultant and computing the level of effort for projects, I would use two servers per day per engineer. These were experienced AWS engineers with multiple migrations under their belt. It would be safe to use this number if you are using consultants or contractors. If you are using your staff, you should target one half to one server per day.

You may ask yourself how your engineers will start the migration and have a server migrated every day. That is a very good question; these numbers are averages. When you migrate servers, you do it in waves and typically have a cutover at night or on the weekend. You might migrate 10 servers with 2 engineers on Saturday, but it would take all week to do the prep work.

Delay Buffer

Delays happen. I do not think I have ever had a project that wasn't delayed. In my management's eyes, I do not miss any targets because I am adamant about including a buffer. Early in my career, I used to keep my timelines tight because I thought it would look good for me to propose a project with a short and optimal timeline. The first time I had to extend a project was not that big of a deal. But the third, fourth, and fifth times, I started to cringe every time I had to tell management I had to extend the timeline. This oversight was a painful lesson to learn.

Since then, I typically like to err on the side of caution, or as I call it, *pulling a Scotty*. If you think back to all those *Star Trek* episodes, they always asked Scotty to do something incredible. The timeline he was given was always too short to accomplish the task, and he would give a longer one. However, somehow Scotty would still pull it off and beat his estimated timeline. For his efforts, they always saw Scotty as the hero. I like to be Scotty when I run forecasts. I would rather estimate a little higher and be praised when the dust settles than shoot low and miss it. It is better to strap on a little extra rocket power to reach exit velocity and not need it than come up short.

For migrations, I would typically add a 10–20% margin of error as a buffer to the migration timeline. If working with an experienced migration team, I would lean toward 10%. Likewise, I would shift toward 20% with a less-experienced team. Besides the team's capabilities, what type of software you have also affects the migration timeline buffer. For instance, if you have a lot of COTS applications, your timeline has less risk than if you have a lot of internally developed software. The reason for this shift in risk is that COTS applications are highly documented and have been moved to AWS by other companies. Blog posts and forum answers are available to help your team resolve any issues. When you have a lot of internally developed applications, the reverse is most likely correct. Typically, documentation is not as strong, and a high degree of tribal knowledge has been lost over time. Since you are the only company that runs the software, there will be no resources on the web to reference either. Because of these factors, I push the buffer toward 20% for companies with large estates of internally developed software.

Before we can move on to see how to incorporate the delay buffer, first we need to touch on employee vacations and holidays. They are a significant component of a migration timeline.

Employee Vacation and Holidays

An often overlooked component of timeline planning is employee vacations and holidays. Employee vacations can have a significant effect on your timeline, and I have seen it forgotten in quite a few estimates. Likewise, holidays can affect the timeline as well, but potentially not how you would expect.

I do not want you to fall into the trap of not thinking about employee vacations. Doing this will delay your migration. The effect gets worse the larger your company is, and the larger your team is, the more vacations you need to consider. The larger the company, the more servers and the longer the timeline, too. The longer the timeline, the more vacation the staff takes. Vacation will have less effect on small companies that do not have many servers, because the timeline will be so much shorter. Let us look at the following scenario to highlight how vacation can affect your timeline.

Scenario 4-1

Beth is preparing her migration timeline and wants to compensate for her staff's vacation times. She has a migration team of six. Her infrastructure is large, and they anticipate that it will take a year to migrate everything. Beth's company also has a decent vacation policy and allows staff four weeks of vacation per year.

The impact on the migration timeline for Beth's situation is sizable. Since she has six staff members on the migration and each have a month of vacation time, she has six months of potential vacation. That is half a year of a full-time person's effort. Since there are roughly 20 workdays in a month multiplied by six months, that's 120 days of effort if her team can migrate 1.25 servers per day, which equals out to 150 servers of missing effort if Beth does not compensate.

Holidays can also wreak havoc on your migration timeline. Most people immediately think about days off and people not being there to work. To be honest, that aspect has little effect on your timeline. What can really hurt is the potential blackout dates that come along with holidays. This is especially true in the retail industry. It is common for a retail chain to have blackout dates from Thanksgiving until after the New Year. That is around one and a half months of inability to migrate. One company that I worked for had blackout dates around every holiday. Valentine's Day, St Patrick's Day, the Fourth of July, and more all came along with one-week blackouts. The impact because of holidays will be very specifically based on your company's individual needs.

I like to compensate for vacation and holidays by decreasing the overall number of engineers that is put into the equation. In "Scenario 4-1" on page 104, Beth would reduce her number of staff from six to five and one-half engineers. This will resolve the discrepancy for the effort that is missing during their vacations. Now that we have all the components, we can move on to putting them into the timeline equation.

Putting the Equation Together

Now that you have the number of servers, the number of servers per day, the employee time off, and the buffer in mind, we can put it all together to come up with the total length of the migration. To do this, I have created an equation to use that will calculate your total migration period. It takes a number of inputs, which are the items that we have just discussed.

Equation 4-1. Timeline equation

$$timeline = \left(\frac{servers}{engineers \times servers\ per\ day} - buffer \right) / work\ days$$

Let us look at another scenario to see how a timeline might look with some actual data points.

Scenario 4-2

Richard is migrating his server estate to AWS; his company has 1,400 servers that will be migrated, and 103 are being left on-premises. Richard's staff is new to AWS, but he has two members of his four-person team that have done migrations to AWS before. The company runs mostly COTS software, only 10% of which is internally developed applications.

Richard will end up with an equation that looks something like:

$$timeline = \left(\frac{1,400}{4 \times 1.25} - 1.13 \right) / 5$$

He has 1,400 servers that will be migrated by four engineers, who can move one and a quarter servers per day. Because half of his staff is trained on AWS, the assumption is that an engineer can move just over one server per day. Last, since Richard's company has nearly all COTS and half of his staff have migrated before, a buffer of 13% makes sense. Richard's staff works a standard workweek, so it all gets divided by five to determine how many weeks of total effort are necessary. Richard's complete migration timeline is 63.28 weeks, or just about 14.5 months long. Based on the number of servers that Richard has, these numbers sound about right based on industry norms.

Now that the timeline is completed, we can start working on the business case. You may be wondering why the migration timeline was completed before the business case and not included as part of it. The fact is that it is inconsequential compared to the rest of the information that will be conveyed to management. You can simply note it and how you arrived at it in the assumptions, which we will discuss later in this chapter.

What Does a Business Case Look Like?

Typically, I have followed the format of starting a business case with a written narrative about the migration and the benefits that migrating to the cloud will bring the company. After the narrative, I follow up with a five-year financial forecast that paints the picture of the savings of moving to the cloud. Finally, I follow up with all the details and outputs of the discovery in an appendix for people to review if they want to. Typically, senior leadership does not concern itself with the nitty-gritty details. However, once a while, the members will want to validate details for an area they are responsible for. In the next few sections, we will dive into detail on each of the components of a business case.

The Narrative

The narrative is the most critical piece of the business case. It is your opportunity to communicate the business benefits that migration to AWS will have. I like narratives because you get to craft a story around the future success of your company. People are more engaged with a story than they are with a PowerPoint flush with a bunch of bullets. Reading a narrative engages people's imagination and has enough detail for them to envision the future. Other forms of communication leave more questions than answers. There is only so much information that you can cram into a slide before it becomes incomprehensible.

Introduction

But where do you start? An excellent and logical place to start is an intro that includes the current state of your infrastructure. I like to focus on some positives and negatives, without any on-premises bashing. It would be best if you appeared impartial, or at least balanced. If you come across as bashing the current state, you run the risk of alienating the leaders that you are trying to get on board with your plan. Your company has been in business for a while, and on-premises has been doing the job. You are trying to convince the same leaders that you or your predecessor did before. These same leaders approved the purchase of the equipment and tooling that is currently running in the data center. Your predecessor might even be the CIO now, and you do not want to call their baby ugly. Doing so will not fare very well for approval, but it will win yourself a major detractor that might have the sway to stall the whole thing. Keep it factual and keep bias to a minimum, and you will gain more support.

FAQ

You have written your introduction covering the current state. Now it is time to start diving into the benefits that will be achieved by migrating to the cloud. The best place to start would be to review the FAQs that you created in Chapter 1. You have already spent significant time developing the questions that you feel will be asked by business units, development teams, and management. At this point, you need to build a compelling story around those specific questions. Let us take a look at this FAQ example and how you might craft a compelling story.

FAQ Question 1

Question
> How is this migration going to affect our staff and operational expenses?

Narrative Story
> Through the past five years, we have seen an increase in operational expenses to maintain our infrastructure. This increase is mostly due to our migration from bare metal servers to virtualization. The ease of deployment and level of consolidation in our infrastructure has allowed us to increase the number of virtual machines (VMs) rapidly. This expansion is not a negative because we have been able to support the business in new ways that were not possible before. Unfortunately, a side effect of VM sprawl is that our operational costs have gone up linearly. By migrating to AWS and using the Systems Management Service (SSM) and CI/CD tooling, we will be able to reduce our operational expenses. Not only will we stave off linear increases in expenses, but we will see an exponential decline in expenses for the infrastructure we have deployed.
>
> SSM will enable us to automate patch remediation as well as apply configuration details to servers without manual intervention. This automation will enable us to apply security changes to meet regulatory guidelines with minimal effort. Currently, we use group policy for security on Windows but do not have a solution for Linux. Using SSM will give us a single point of management for both operating systems.
>
> While performing our infrastructure discovery, we identified that our most significant application is a prime candidate for automated deployment by using a CI/CD pipeline. Automating the deployment will save us 45 staff hours per release and allow us to release more often. By using the pipeline, we can increase our deployments from once a quarter to every week with ease.

As you can see in "FAQ Question 1" on page 107, we did not take a hard-line, negative stance against the on-premises infrastructure. We stated that there would be some benefits from migrating to AWS. The narrative also leads them down a path that hopefully fills in the details they need to form an opinion and limit questions. Let us take a look at how you shouldn't write a narrative.

FAQ Question 2

Question

What is wrong with the way we currently run our infrastructure?

Narrative Story

During our analysis of our on-premises equipment, we found that most of the hardware was archaic and well past its useful lifetime. The aging hardware has led to a horrible user experience. Many people complain that the order processing system "just plain sucks." Many of the operating systems are no longer supported by the vendor and are running on borrowed time. We are just counting the days until we are compromised.

We also discovered that your uninterruptible power supply is at its end of life, and the batteries are leaking. There is no telling whether the system would even keep our servers online in the event of a power failure. Our HVAC system is overpowered for the data center now that we have virtualized everything. Since it is too large, we had to activate the reheater to heat the air before cooling it so that we can correctly remove the humidity. The reheater is adding a considerable expense to our electric bill. Our infrastructure is past its prime and running on borrowed time.

As you can see, this FAQ takes a very different position in the way that it tells a story. The narrative comes off very biased toward the cloud. It also paints a pretty bleak picture for the current state on-premises. The problem that you will run into, using this stance, is that it is your job to ensure that all these discrepancies are addressed. Writing a narrative like this might be signing your own death warrant.

You can continue to progress through the FAQ and pick out the questions where you can build a compelling and exciting story. Some items, like converting to SSD using gp2 EBS volumes, might be a fascinating story to someone technical. However, it probably will not resonate very well with upper levels of management. Using the wrong questions can bore your audience and slow excitement.

Closing

The last part of the narrative should be the closing. It should include a short recap of the essential items that you have discussed. In my closings, I like to envision the future and highlight capabilities that have not yet been used by the company but could be after migration to AWS. The closing is where you can put some out-of-the-box thinking in play and create a vision of some new capability or added customer

---

value. Once your migration is complete and your data is in AWS, there will be a whole host of capabilities that you can tap into. Artificial intelligence and augmented reality are two prevalent technologies that people are thinking of new and creative ways to use across a host of industry verticals.

I tend to stay away from silver bullet technologies for my envisioned future. These would be technologies that, for some reason or another, get massive amounts of traction for solving every problem on the planet. The most recent one is blockchain. Not too long ago, you could not read any tech website without a mention of blockchain to solve a problem. Tennis elbow? Not a problem; rub on some blockchain twice a day. There is no such thing as a silver bullet. In my experience, any technology that is touted as a significant change rarely becomes one. It either dies or becomes a niche player. Blockchain, grid computing, next-gen firewalls, and others have all been on the solve-the-world's-problems train, and they have all derailed. Technologies that change the world take a long time to do so. Look at virtualization, artificial intelligence, virtual reality, and even AWS. These technologies took at least a decade or more to reach a level of maturity to change the world, and some are just starting to gain traction. You want your picture of the future to be obtainable and not fanciful.

The Forecast

You have now written your narrative and painted a wonderful picture of all the benefits and issues that will be resolved by moving to the cloud. Now it is time to get to the brass tacks. You will have to show how much the migration to AWS will cost. Nothing is free, especially when it comes to migration. The double-spend during migration is a major hindrance. However, the spend will not come out to be exactly twice. You should see a cost differential between on-premises and the cloud. In addition, you should see some burn-down on the costs of your on-premises equipment as you migrate. When it comes to burn-down, there is some complexity, and we will cover that in greater detail later, in "Cost Burn-Up/Burn-Down" on page 137.

The important thing to capture in the forecast is when you will start to save money by migrating to AWS. Any good senior leader or board of directors will recognize that the savings will not be instantaneous. It is safe to say that a typical board will look at a three-to-five year return on a major investment like migrating to AWS. Typically, I have seen a return on investment in as little as 18 months, depending on the company's situation. However, I would say that two to three years is probably more common. There is a possibility that companies do not save money by migrating to AWS. Let us look at a scenario that details how this might occur.

Scenario 4-3

Stefan's company has decided to move to AWS from its current data center located in the main corporate office. Stefan's company runs a few SQL servers, a few file servers, the accounting server, and the corporate website. On-premises, Stefan's company runs everything virtualized off a single VMware host with local storage attached. Stefan's predecessor had the server replaced four years ago. The company does not have any other data centers. *Data center* is probably not the word Stefan would use to describe his computer closet.

Hopefully, you can see some significant issues with the way Stefan's firm has deployed the infrastructure. The biggest problem is that there is no redundancy in anything it is doing on-premises. The company probably does not have fire suppression, generators, or physical security. From a technical standpoint, there is no redundancy for the server or its storage. Stefan's predecessor ran the environment as thin as they possibly could. When you compare this type of on-premises deployment to AWS, it could easily cost twice as much to run in AWS. AWS has all these capabilities built in, and it would be impossible to get the costs to align. In this scenario, it is vitally important to focus on the availability benefits that AWS brings to the table over the on-premises environment rather than costs.

The forecast should include several items over a period of at least five years. A good forecast will include:

- Estimated run rate
- Costs for migration, like tooling and consultant fees
- Run rate modifiers, like reserved instances
- Agility savings

Some of these items, like run rate, will come from your discovery, and some, like agility savings, will need to be calculated by hand based on your company's situation. You will want to paint a picture using very high-level costs so that it is easy to digest and understand. The forecast should fit on a single page and should have no more than 10 to 15 rows of data. Add any more, and you risk confusing your audience. Providing spreadsheet after spreadsheet of server lists will not help anyone understand the bigger picture. That information can be saved for the detail section at the end. In addition, some items, which I call run rate modifiers, will adjust your overall numbers to approximate costs, like reserved instances.

Figure 4-1 shows an example of a typical forecast that I would create. It includes all the essential details but makes them as digestible as possible. You can also see that I include a list of assumptions at the bottom that detail where those assumptions were made. You can make the format anything you would like, but simplicity is key. You do not want to overburden the consumer with unnecessary details.

Inputs

EC2	$	1,247,954.00
Storage	$	465,733.00
S3 Storage	$	3,457.00
Tooling	$	6,574.00
Agility Savings	$	157,467.00

Uplift Modfiers

Network	10%
Misc Services	10%

Run Rate Modifiers

Reserved Instances	90%
RI Savings (Avg)	40%

	Year 1	Year 2	Year 3	Year 4	Year 5	Total
Migration %	25.00%	50.00%	75.00%	100.00%	100.00%	
EC2	$ 31,198.85	$ 62,397.70	$ 93,596.55	$ 124,795.40	$ 124,795.40	$ 436,783.90
Storage	$ 116,433.25	$ 232,866.50	$ 349,299.75	$ 465,733.00	$ 465,733.00	$ 1,630,065.50
S3 Storage	$ 864.25	$ 1,728.50	$ 2,592.75	$ 3,457.00	$ 3,457.00	$ 12,099.50
Tooling	$ 1,643.50	$ 3,287.00	$ 4,930.50	$ 6,574.00	$ 6,574.00	$ 23,009.00
Consulting Fees	$ 245,000.00	$ 130,000.00				$ 375,000.00
Agility Savings	$ (39,366.75)	$ (78,733.50)	$ (118,100.25)	$ (157,467.00)	$ (157,467.00)	$ (551,134.50)
Bandwidth	$ 3,119.89	$ 6,239.77	$ 9,359.66	$ 12,479.54	$ 12,479.54	$ 43,678.39
Misc. Services	$ 3,119.89	$ 6,239.77	$ 9,359.66	$ 12,479.54	$ 12,479.54	$ 43,678.39
EC2 Reserved	$ 168,473.79	$ 336,947.58	$ 505,421.37	$ 673,895.16	$ 673,895.16	$ 2,358,633.06
Total						$ 4,371,813.24

ASSUMPTIONS

Outbound bandwidth costs are assumed at 10% of EC2 run rate
Miscellaneous AWS services are assumed as 12% of EC2 run rate
Employee overhead for the cloud engineering team is $100 per hour

Figure 4-1. Forecast example

The last piece that we have to cover is removing the applications that you are not going to migrate to the cloud or, rather, *trim the fat*. Just like your rib eye at a classy steak joint, you want to remove the stuff from the edges that makes your migration less appealing.

Trimming the Fat

Before we can accurately perform run rate modeling, we have to trim some fat. The fat that I am talking about is the applications that you are not going to move to AWS. Amazon has created a methodology called the seven R factors (Refactor, Redeploy, Rehost, Repurchase, Retire, Re-platform, Retain). There were originally six, but Redeploy became a new R factor with more companies having containers or deployment pipelines on-premises. The factors exist to help you categorize your applications to determine whether and how you should migrate your applications to the cloud.

Your discovery tool found everything that you have on-premises and can provide you the right-sized instances. What the discovery tooling cannot do is tell you whether you should move an application. This classification will be a manual process that needs to be completed before we can do accurate run rate modeling. You, of course, do not want to account for costs in AWS that will not move or will be retired. That would inflate your numbers and make your business case less appealing and inaccurate. We are now going to touch on the seven R factors, what they mean, the estimated percentage of your migration for each R, and how you should apply them.

Refactor

Refactoring is the most complex way to migrate to AWS and should be the lowest percentage of your overall migration. Refactoring means converting an existing monolith and dated application into a new, highly decoupled, and cloud-native architecture. The problem with refactoring apps is that often it takes an extended period to complete the work. This extended timeline means that you are spending more on your overall migration running the application in two places or extending your data center footprint for longer periods. The biggest benefit of refactoring, though, is that you will run your applications more smoothly, have a higher degree of availability, have reduced management overhead, and save costs. Refactoring will probably be 5% or less of your migration at this point. In Chapter 8, we will discuss some low-hanging fruits that you can harvest in the initial migration.

Redeploy

The primary use of Redeploy is when you already have a deployment pipeline or containers on-premises. If you already have a deployment pipeline and are migrating, you are essentially changing the endpoint of that deployment. Most tooling already has plugins for AWS. Instead of doing any migration work, you will point the pipeline to AWS instead of to VMware or Hyper-V on-premises.

The same is true if you use containers. Since containers are self-contained workloads, you shift that container over to AWS rather than to on-premises hardware. Of course, there is some more work around migrating these types of workloads, such as DNS changes and whatnot, but the overall effort is lower than, say, a lift and shift or rehost. It is hard to say how much of your migration will be redeployed, because it is highly dependent on your applications.

Rehost

Rehosting will be the bulk of your migration, primarily for speed. When you rehost, you lift and shift the workload into the cloud. The faster it gets to the cloud, the faster you can start turning off resources on-premises. Speed is increased using the block-level CloudEndure replication tool. Rehost is the least sexy migration method but most often the most effective. You get a block-for-block copy of your server into AWS. Your migration will probably consist of 80% rehost workloads.

Repurchase

Sometimes software ages out in your IT infrastructure. These applications are often small, neglected ones that serve an important purpose but do not gain a lot of attention. This lack of attention lets them get old and decrepit, but they still work, so they never get replaced. When you migrate to AWS, it is a great time to age out these applications permanently and replace them with something newer. I have run into quite a few old Visual Basic programs in this category. If possible, I would look at replacing any applications with a SaaS tool, so you do not have to worry about maintaining it going forward. Based on my experience, repurchase will probably account for around 5% of your migration.

Retire

Sometimes you do not need software anymore once you move to AWS. Typically, this software boils down to infrastructure management tools that existed to maintain on-premises workloads. Things like log aggregation, Simple Network Management Protocol (SNMP) monitoring, and other monitoring tools are no longer required once you move to AWS and use native functionality. This reduction saves you both hard costs and soft management costs. The retire R factor is not used very much and will probably account for less than 5% of your migration.

Re-platform

When you re-platform something, you change a small aspect of the application, doing no major architecture changes. This change would be like converting from a database server to RDS. Another potential change would be to upgrade an older Windows OS to a newer, supported version. The key thing to remember here is that you are not making any major changes, like moving from Microsoft SQL to MySQL. Re-platforming is typically more prevalent than many other R factors in the migrations I have been involved with. There are quite a few older operating systems out there that it might surprise you to see you are still running. In addition, if you want to use RDS for peace of mind and to save on some management, you could easily see 20% of your migration be classified as re-platform.

Retain

The last R factor is retain. When you retain a workload, you leave it as is on-premises. Several items will show up in the retain column, but most of it will be applications that need to remain on-premises to keep your offices running. Active Directory would be a good choice to retain on-premises, because you want users to authenticate locally. Other systems might include security systems, Dynamic Host Configuration Protocol (DHCP) servers, and other network management facilities.

Legacy systems might be another item in this category. You will not be migrating your mainframe to AWS because it does not support the hardware. However, since these types of workloads were not detected through your discovery tooling, it will not affect your run rate and probably will not even be listed.

You will probably retain less than 5% of your infrastructure.

Now that you know how to classify all your applications, it is time to review and apply your R factors. When you are done, you will need to capture the run rate for the rehost, re-platform, redeploy, and refactor decisions. These are the run rates that will be put into your forecast. You will not enter them individually. Instead, you should sum those numbers up for a combined total.

Now that you have a high-level understanding of what goes into a forecast, let us dive into detail for the individual items. We will cover what the item is, why it is important to include, how to calculate it, and what assumptions to list. Microsoft Excel, Google Sheets, or a similar spreadsheet software will be required to create the forecast and perform the necessary calculations. A sample file is available as add-on content for this book. You can access the file at AWS Forecast (*https://oreil.ly/4fq4l*).

Run Rate Modeling

The run rate that came out of your discovery process is one of the most important items that need to be included in your forecast. What we want to use here is your modified number that was output by your discovery tooling, which you then adjusted based on the manual discovery items your team reviewed and trimmed by using the R factors. When you start this process, you want to put the full run rate that you have come up with in the input cells for EC2 (C3), Storage (C4), and S3 Storage (C5). Later, you will apply formulas to adjust the numbers based on your inputs, but for now, start with the full run rate. As of now, your forecast should look something like Figure 4-2.

Inputs				Uplift Modfiers			Run Rate Modifiers	
EC2	$	1,247,954.00		Network	0%	Reserved Instances		0%
Storage	$	465,733.00		Misc Services	0%	RI Savings (Avg)		40%
S3 Storage	$	3,457.00						
Tooling	$	-						
Agility Savings	$	-						

	Year 1		Year 2		Year 3		Year 4		Year 5		Total
Migration %	100.00%		100.00%		100.00%		100.00%		100.00%		
EC2	$ 1,247,954.00	$	1,247,954.00	$	1,247,954.00	$	1,247,954.00	$	1,247,954.00	$	6,239,770.00
Storage	$ 465,733.00	$	465,733.00	$	465,733.00	$	465,733.00	$	465,733.00	$	2,328,665.00
S3 Storage	$ 3,457.00	$	3,457.00	$	3,457.00	$	3,457.00	$	3,457.00	$	17,285.00
Tooling	$ -	$	-	$	-	$	-	$	-	$	-
Consulting Fees										$	-
Agility Savings	$ -	$	-	$	-	$	-	$	-	$	-
Bandwidth	$ -	$	-	$	-	$	-	$	-	$	-
Misc. Services	$ -	$	-	$	-	$	-	$	-	$	-
EC2 Reserved	$ -	$	-	$	-	$	-	$	-	$	-
Total										$	8,585,720.00

ASSUMPTIONS

Figure 4-2. Forecast step 1

Breaking up storage and compute costs as shown in Figure 4-2 will make it easier to compute additional costs. In "Overall Outbound Bandwidth" on page 93 and "Ancillary AWS Service Charges" on page 97, you may recall, I recommend adding an uplift to the EC2 spend for these items. Breaking out the compute and storage costs allows easier viewing and adjustment of those percentages.

Once you have entered your run rates in the forecast, you can enter your uplift percentages in cells F3 and F4 for bandwidth and ancillary services, respectively. These are customizable, so you can manually adjust your settings if the output numbers do not align with your expectations. Sometimes you may need to adjust your settings up or down a few percentage points to arrive at a number that reflects your estimated usage. When adjusting, remember to be like Scotty from *Star Trek* and add a buffer. Once you enter this data, your forecast should look like Figure 4-3.

	Inputs	
EC2	$	1,247,954.00
Storage	$	465,733.00
S3 Storage	$	3,457.00
Tooling	$	-
Agility Savings	$	-

Uplift Modfiers		Run Rate Modifiers	
Network	10%	Reserved Instances	0%
Misc Services	12%	RI Savings (Avg)	40%

	Year 1	Year 2	Year 3	Year 4	Year 5	Total
Migration %	100.00%	100.00%	100.00%	100.00%	100.00%	
EC2	$ 1,247,954.00	$ 1,247,954.00	$ 1,247,954.00	$ 1,247,954.00	$ 1,247,954.00	$ 6,239,770.00
Storage	$ 465,733.00	$ 465,733.00	$ 465,733.00	$ 465,733.00	$ 465,733.00	$ 2,328,665.00
S3 Storage	$ 3,457.00	$ 3,457.00	$ 3,457.00	$ 3,457.00	$ 3,457.00	$ 17,285.00
Tooling	$ -	$ -	$ -	$ -	$ -	$ -
Consulting Fees						$ -
Agility Savings	$ -	$ -	$ -	$ -	$ -	$ -
Bandwidth	$ 124,795.40	$ 124,795.40	$ 124,795.40	$ 124,795.40	$ 124,795.40	$ 623,977.00
Misc. Services	$ 149,754.48	$ 149,754.48	$ 149,754.48	$ 149,754.48	$ 149,754.48	$ 748,772.40
EC2 Reserved	$ -	$ -	$ -	$ -	$ -	$ -
Total						$ 9,958,469.40

ASSUMPTIONS

Figure 4-3. Forecast step 2

Migration Costs

Migration cost is not just about the double run rate between on-premises and cloud expenses. Cost is associated with staff time, tooling, consulting, and data transfer costs. When you combine all these expenses, you get an accurate picture of how much the migration will cost. Failure to include any of them can skew the migration cost significantly in favor of the cloud. If you do not include them, it gives any opposition the ability to discredit your business case and can potentially derail your initiative. I firmly believe in painting the most accurate picture I can. Most times, it is completely evident how the cloud will benefit the company and has a large potential to drive down costs.

Although I aim to provide an accurate picture, I do not focus on providing mundane and monotonous details. I also do not waste too much time trying to get "landing on the moon" numbers when "launching into space" numbers for many of these categories will do. In the next few sections, we will dive into these additional expense categories and how to account for them. We will also cover the potential pitfalls of calculating them and how to avoid wasting time.

Tooling costs

AWS has a whole host of tools to help you migrate to the cloud; some of them are free, and some charge fees. Although the tooling from AWS is great, it does not always have the features that your company requires to get the job done. When you run into this circumstance, you have to select an additional tool that will cost more.

Let's run through the tooling AWS offers. These tools assist in migration, and you need to know how to account for those fees. Table 4-1 shows a list of the current tools available from AWS and their use cases.

Table 4-1. AWS migration tooling

Tool	Purpose
CloudEndure	Block-level server replication tool
Snowball	Physical storage device for "through the mail transfer"
Server Migration Service (SMS)	Importation of VMs from on-premises
DataSync	Transfer of files to AWS
Command-line tools	Transfer files to S3
Schema Conversion Tool	Converts DB schemas from one engine to another
Database Migration Service (DMS)	Migrates data between database servers

As you can see, AWS has a healthy portfolio for migrating your systems and data to the cloud. These purpose-built tools fill their roles very well, but unfortunately, all have different consumption and costing models. These different consumption models can seem daunting when you first try to calculate them out. It is not that hard because we are going to estimate for many of them:

CloudEndure
> the AWS tool for migrating servers is now free after Amazon purchased it in 2019. Although the tool is free to use, there is a charge for the instances required to manage the replication. CloudEndure deploys a replication instance for every 15 source disks that you replicate. To estimate the cost of using CloudEndure, you need to find the maximum number of servers that you will be replicating during any of your migration waves. You will want to take the number of servers weekly that you calculated after reading "Estimating Your Timeline" on page 102. In "Scenario 4-1" on page 104, the weekly estimate was five servers. Since 5 is well under the 15 allowed, Richard would only need one replication instance. At the time of writing, a t3.medium instance in us-east-1 is $0.0416 per hour. Multiplying this price by 730 hours will result in a cost of $30.368 per month. Richard's total cost of CloudEndure for his 14.5-month migration is $440.336.

Snowball

AWS Snowball is a physical device that is shipped to your office. You then load this device with data and send it back to AWS. AWS will load all the data on it into S3. In all the migrations that I have done, I have never used Snowball. This is because the data you need to move needs to be relatively static. It takes days to load the data, ship the device, and have it loaded later. Ultimately, the companies that I worked with decided to send everything over the network rather than use Snowball. Using the network allowed them to bypass the synchronization that would be required after AWS loaded the data. If you do have data that would work well with Snowball, such as old backup data, Snowball costs $200 for a 50 TB device or $250 for 80 TB of storage at the time of writing. With that fee, you get 10 days of on-site time included. If you need the device for more than 10 days, you pay $15 per day. If you are going to use Snowball, I suggest that you prep your data and have everything ready to go before requesting the device through the AWS console.

Server Migration Service

Typically, I do not advise using SMS. It only works with virtual machines and is not compatible with physical devices. For most companies, this means that you would need to use two tools instead of one. Since CloudEndure is free and does both physical and virtual machines, I suggest using that tool instead. SMS works by uploading snapshots of VMs to S3 and then creating EBS snapshots. Finally, SMS creates an Amazon Machine Image (AMI) for final consumption and deployment in AWS. An AMI is like a template in VMware terminology. The SMS service itself is free. However, because of the design, there are small numbers of EBS snapshots and S3 storage fees. Overall, these fees are modest and you should consider them part of the uplift for miscellaneous AWS charges we discussed in "Run Rate Modeling" on page 114.

DataSync

DataSync is a newer service from AWS that facilitates moving data from on-premises to S3 or EFS on the file level instead of the server level. This service allows you to transfer data from a SAN or Network Attached Storage (NAS) device with Windows or NFS file shares to AWS. DataSync is a welcome addition as a tool. Before DataSync, most of this type of migration work was done with scripting and the AWS CLI, which was not the most robust solution. DataSync itself has a fee of $0.04 per GB in the us-east-1 region at the time of writing. This service is straightforward to forecast, based on the amount of data you need to transfer. For instance, if you had a NAS device with 1 TB on an NFS share, you would multiply 1,024 GB by $0.04 for a total of $40.96. The $40.96 does not cover the cost of the storage itself, so that will need to be accounted for as well. If it is a small amount of data, the uplift numbers you put in will probably cover it, but if you have dozens or hundreds of terabytes, you will probably want to include those costs as a separate line item.

Command-line tools

If you have a small number of files to move to S3, then using the command-line tools from AWS would be the most comfortable option. None of these tools has a cost, but you will pay for the resources they consume. Since using the command-line tools is not advised for transferring large amounts of data, the uplift should cover the data consumption costs in the forecast.

Schema Conversion Tool

The Schema Conversion Tool allows you to change the database engine for your database. This tool will enable you to switch from one database engine to another, for instance, Oracle to MySQL. The tool is only one piece of the puzzle, though. To change your database engine successfully, you will need to update your software to address the changes necessary in SQL nuances, triggers, and stored procedures. Fortunately, the SCT is free and doesn't have to be accounted for in any forecasts.

Database Migration Service

DMS allows you to transfer data from on-premises to the cloud using asynchronous mirroring. This service enables you to transfer data from a standalone server to AWS RDS. The benefit of using DMS is that it dramatically reduces your outage window for cutover when moving databases, because the service keeps the source and destination in lockstep. If you were to use a backup-and-restore method to transfer your database to RDS, you would experience a much larger outage window. The DMS service uses an AWS instance to do the heavy lifting of your database. It sits between your source and destination. This instance manages the communications and synchronization of the databases and is where the cost of DMS originates. For DMS, I would recommend an instance size of r4.large or larger. Some smaller instances are allowed, like T2/3, but I would not use those to transfer production workloads. At the time of writing, an r4.large instance in us-east-1 costs $0.21 per hour. Running this instance for a month works out to be $153.30. Each replication instance is limited to 20 sources and destinations. This limit means that you can only have 10 pairs of servers in replication per instance. If you need more than that, you will need to account for another DMS replication instance.

If you are *not* changing database engines or moving to RDS, I would use CloudEndure to transfer the server instead of the database.

In Figure 4-4, you can see that I've included tooling in cell C6 on the forecast spreadsheet. The total of tooling should be inserted here. The spreadsheet will automatically populate the tooling in row 14 based on the migration percentages in row 10. We will discuss the "Migration percentages" on page 127 and their use later. If you are planning to use any non-AWS tooling for your migration, you will need to get the pricing from the vendor and add it to the cost of any AWS tooling.

Inputs				Uplift Modfiers			Run Rate Modifiers	
EC2	$	1,247,954.00		Network		10%	Reserved Instances	0%
Storage	$	465,733.00		Misc Services		12%	RI Savings (Avg)	40%
S3 Storage	$	3,457.00						
Tooling	$	6,574.00						
Agility Savings	$	-						

	Year 1		Year 2		Year 3		Year 4		Year 5		Total	
Migration %	100.00%		100.00%		100.00%		100.00%		100.00%			
EC2	$ 1,247,954.00	$	1,247,954.00	$	1,247,954.00	$	1,247,954.00	$	1,247,954.00	$	6,239,770.00	
Storage	$ 465,733.00	$	465,733.00	$	465,733.00	$	465,733.00	$	465,733.00	$	2,328,665.00	
S3 Storage	$ 3,457.00	$	3,457.00	$	3,457.00	$	3,457.00	$	3,457.00	$	17,285.00	
Tooling	$ 6,574.00	$	6,574.00	$	6,574.00	$	6,574.00	$	6,574.00	$	32,870.00	
Consulting Fees										$		
Agility Savings	$ -	$	-	$	-	$	-	$	-	$	-	
Bandwidth	$ 124,795.40	$	124,795.40	$	124,795.40	$	124,795.40	$	124,795.40	$	623,977.00	
Misc. Services	$ 149,754.48	$	149,754.48	$	149,754.48	$	149,754.48	$	149,754.48	$	748,772.40	
EC2 Reserved	$ -	$	-	$	-	$	-	$	-	$	-	
Total										$	9,991,339.40	

ASSUMPTIONS

Figure 4-4. Forecast step 3

Consulting fees

In Chapter 2, we discussed "Contractors and consulting" on page 60 and how they can reduce your business risks through their experience. Many times, consultants and contractors are looked at as expenses during a migration. However, it is important to demonstrate that their experience and capabilities will most likely decrease your timeline. They will also reduce overall risk during the migration. Using consultants is not something to be avoided but rather a tactical decision to help the company along and reduce its migration length. Overall, the dollar amount for consultants will not be small. People are usually the company's greatest expense. Unless you have an existing budget that can cover consulting fees, it is important to put them into the migration forecast.

Consulting fees should be rather easy to obtain. When using consultants, you are offloading the management of your migration to a third party, along with the effort to move your resources. This abstraction allows the consulting firm to price out the entirety of the project for you. The consulting firm will provide you a statement of work (SOW) based on the items that you wish it to complete. The SOW will give you the total amount along with a set of success criteria and work expected to be done. This information can then be recorded in the forecast on row 8. Unfortunately, there is no standard way to split the consulting fees over the entirety of the migration, so you will have to split these fees over the migration years as you see fit. There are no modifiers on the sheet to assist.

When it comes to contractors' fees, they are not as easy to obtain, because you need to calculate them manually. Since you retain management with contractors, you need to determine the level of effort for your migration. Right now, in Chicago, I know that contractors can get typically around $100–$150 per hour. Many contractors work through a placement firm as well, so you will need to add 35% on top of those fees if you use a placement firm. If you do not source your contractor, you are looking at $135–$195 an hour with the added overhead. High-end contractors who work with large enterprises can see rates as high as $300 an hour. Experience plays a big part in pricing for contractors. I would make sure to get certification validation numbers for any claimed certifications and validate that they indeed hold them at the AWS certification site (*http://aws.amazon.com/verification*). The more certifications a contractor holds, the more they will charge. You will want to make sure you are getting your money's worth.

Another option for contractors to be released soon is AWS IQ, a service that allows AWS-certified individuals to register and offer their services available to companies using the platform. The service automatically validates their certifications when they register their account, saving you that step. The service also facilitates payment through the existing AWS marketplace system. The system allows your contractors' fees to show up as part of your AWS bill, reducing the burden on your finance department. AWS IQ charges a minimal 3% fee on top of the contractors' fee for the use of the service.

If you are using a search firm, AWS IQ, or a contractor directly, you will still have to estimate the number of hours you will need such services. Unfortunately, the amount of time you will need a contractor's services is particular to your company's needs, migration timeline, and current staff capabilities. You will need to assess all these items to determine how long and how many contractors you will require. Once you arrive at that length, you can compute how much it will cost to employ them for that period. Let us look at the following scenario to see what a contractor calculation might look like.

Scenario 4-4

At Becca's company, her team is preparing to migrate to AWS. She has calculated that her migration will take around 15 months, based on her current staff. She needs to cut her migration timeline down to nine months and has decided to bring on contractors. She has looked in her area of Charlotte, NC, and found that AWS contractors cost about $145–$188 per hour. When Becca calculated her timeline using her internal staff, she found that her staff could migrate approximately 1.5 servers per day each, and the company has 1,365 servers in total. Becca has three internal staff, so her calculation is *1,365 servers / 1.5 servers per day / 3 engineers / 20 working days per month = 15.16 months*. Becca needs to figure out how many contractors she needs to meet her revised timeline of nine months.

Working backward, Becca's team can migrate approximately 90 servers per month. Currently, her timeline is six months too long. If you multiply 90 by 5, you end up with 450 servers that would not be migrated by month nine. If we divide the overage back into nine months, her intended target, we end up with 50. Becca will need enough contract staff to cover an additional 50 servers per month to meet her revised deadline. If Becca were to target contractors that have AWS experience and have done migrations before, she could get a migration rate of two servers per day from them. With 20 working days in a month, one highly experienced contractor could move 40 servers. Becca needs two to cover her overage and will decrease her overall migration risk, because a second contractor raises the monthly capability to 80 additional servers per month. That is 30 servers more than she needs, further reducing risk.

Based on Becca's need, she will need to account for 2,880 hours of contractor expenses. I would suggest estimating at a higher rate of $188 per hour to ensure greater flexibility. Becca would enter $541,440 into the cell C15 for year one, as shown in Figure 4-5. We know that it is year one because her optimal migration timeline is nine months.

Inputs		
EC2	$	1,247,954.00
Storage	$	465,733.00
S3 Storage	$	3,457.00
Tooling	$	6,574.00
Agility Savings	$	-

Uplift Modfiers		Run Rate Modifiers	
Network	10%	Reserved Instances	0%
Misc Services	12%	RI Savings (Avg)	40%

	Year 1	Year 2	Year 3	Year 4	Year 5	Total
Migration %	100.00%	100.00%	100.00%	100.00%	100.00%	
EC2	$ 1,247,954.00	$ 1,247,954.00	$ 1,247,954.00	$ 1,247,954.00	$ 1,247,954.00	$ 6,239,770.00
Storage	$ 465,733.00	$ 465,733.00	$ 465,733.00	$ 465,733.00	$ 465,733.00	$ 2,328,665.00
S3 Storage	$ 3,457.00	$ 3,457.00	$ 3,457.00	$ 3,457.00	$ 3,457.00	$ 17,285.00
Tooling	$ 6,574.00	$ 6,574.00	$ 6,574.00	$ 6,574.00	$ 6,574.00	$ 32,870.00
Consulting Fees	$ 541,440.00					$ 541,440.00
Agility Savings	$ -	$ -	$ -	$ -	$ -	$ -
Bandwidth	$ 124,795.40	$ 124,795.40	$ 124,795.40	$ 124,795.40	$ 124,795.40	$ 623,977.00
Misc. Services	$ 149,754.48	$ 149,754.48	$ 149,754.48	$ 149,754.48	$ 149,754.48	$ 748,772.40
EC2 Reserved	$ -	$ -	$ -	$ -	$ -	$ -
Total						$ 10,532,779.40

ASSUMPTIONS

Figure 4-5. Becca's forecast

After computing your consulting and contractor fees, you will have an accurate picture of how much it will cost to perform your migration. The forecast sheet will also show you how much your ongoing costs will be postmigration, which you will be able to compare to your current infrastructure operating costs. I hesitate to say the return on investment when compared to on-premises, because often it is comparing apples to oranges. But I would say that for most companies, you will see a reduction in costs when you compare the AWS run rate to on-premises costs. After entering your consulting and contractor fees, your forecast should look like Figure 4-6.

Inputs				Uplift Modfiers			Run Rate Modifiers	
EC2	$	1,247,954.00		Network		10%	Reserved Instances	0%
Storage	$	465,733.00		Misc Services		12%	RI Savings (Avg)	40%
S3 Storage	$	3,457.00						
Tooling	$	6,574.00						
Agility Savings	$	-						

	Year 1	Year 2	Year 3	Year 4	Year 5	Total
Migration %	100.00%	100.00%	100.00%	100.00%	100.00%	
EC2	$ 1,247,954.00	$ 1,247,954.00	$ 1,247,954.00	$ 1,247,954.00	$ 1,247,954.00	$ 6,239,770.00
Storage	$ 465,733.00	$ 465,733.00	$ 465,733.00	$ 465,733.00	$ 465,733.00	$ 2,328,665.00
S3 Storage	$ 3,457.00	$ 3,457.00	$ 3,457.00	$ 3,457.00	$ 3,457.00	$ 17,285.00
Tooling	$ 6,574.00	$ 6,574.00	$ 6,574.00	$ 6,574.00	$ 6,574.00	$ 32,870.00
Consulting Fees	$ 245,000.00	$ 130,000.00				$ 375,000.00
Agility Savings	$ -	$ -	$ -	$ -	$ -	$ -
Bandwidth	$ 124,795.40	$ 124,795.40	$ 124,795.40	$ 124,795.40	$ 124,795.40	$ 623,977.00
Misc. Services	$ 149,754.48	$ 149,754.48	$ 149,754.48	$ 149,754.48	$ 149,754.48	$ 748,772.40
EC2 Reserved	$ -	$ -	$ -	$ -	$ -	$ -
Total						$ 10,366,339.40

ASSUMPTIONS

Figure 4-6. Forecast step 4

Run Rate Modifiers

Now that you know how much everything will cost, it is time to apply run rate modifiers so you can adjust spend based on variables that are highly dependent on a company's circumstances. A multitude of options can affect your run rate; that is one of the beautiful things about AWS. However, I will focus on the largest and most commonly applicable levers available. These levers are reserved instances, savings plans, migration percentages, agility savings, and management savings.

Reserved instances

Reserved instances (RIs) are probably the easiest way to save a significant amount of money running in AWS. A reserved instance is when you agree to use an instance of a specific type and operating system for a period of one or three years. By agreeing to use the instance for a longer period, you are offered a discount on the total run rate for that instance. The discount you receive is based on how long you purchase your RI for and how much you prepay. There are options to prepay all the instance cost, called an all up-front RI, down to no up-front prepayment. Of course, the highest discount is offered on the three-year all up-front RI purchase. RI purchases can save you an average of 40% for one year and 60% for three years. However, I am not a fan of three-year RIs for these four reasons:

Contrary to agility

The number one benefit of AWS is business agility, so why would you lock yourself into a three-year instance? In three years, a new service might come out that is serverless or on-demand that might save you thousands.

Instances improve

AWS continually releases new instance types; some of these are significantly faster than their predecessors. You have locked yourself into a Ford when you could have a Tesla.

Cash outlay

You have to pay for your servers up front for the biggest benefit, so you have a large cash outlay like you do for on-premises operations (although you use amortization instead of deprecation).

Decreased pricing

AWS drops the pricing on instances from time to time. With a three-year reservation, you've already bought it and can't take advantage of the decrease.

You can resell reserved instances on a marketplace and purchase convertible reserved instances. These two capabilities allow you either to change your RI, as with convertible reserved instances, or to sell off, using the marketplace, but you have to ask yourself whether you really want your staff to be wasting time with these levels of mundane management. Or do you want them to add business value?

There are many reasons and methodologies to purchase reserved instances, and I could easily write half a book on the subject. I will instead focus on an easy way to adjust your forecast to compensate for purchasing RI. Including instance information in the forecast would reduce its life span and increase its complexity. Ultimately, we don't need that level of precision. Instead, we will work with generic discounts based on RI type and length.

To adjust the RI footprint on the forecast, you change the percentage in cell H3. The percentage represents the amount of the estate that is *not* reserved. Typically, I recommend 10–20% to be left as on-demand. This on-demand buffer ensures that your RIs are always used. Since RI is based on OS and instance size, if you are not running an instance with that configuration, the RI will go unused. Therefore, leaving a percentage as on-demand ensures that all your RIs are used. The on-demand percentage also allows you to change your environment. For instance, after you migrate, you might update an application so that it can support auto scaling. By changing the application to use auto scaling, the reserved instances that were purchased for the application will be left available when the application scales back during low periods.

If your infrastructure has much auto scaling, then you may want to adjust the percentage up, and if you use a lot of COTS applications without auto scaling, and do not change often, you will want to adjust the percentage of on-demand lower. If your company is small and you do not have many servers, you will probably have an excellent idea about your estate and its growth. When this is the case, you will want to have a very low on-demand rate.

Savings Plans

In 2019, AWS released a new capability to buy compute resources called Savings Plans. Savings Plans offer a discount when you guarantee to use resources, just like reserved instances. The primary difference between Savings Plans and reserved instances is that Savings Plans offer a significant amount of flexibility. Savings Plans are purchased based on the amount of compute you intended to run per instance family. See Table 3-1 for a refresher. In addition, Savings Plans are not tied to any region as RIs are. This means that you can significantly reduce your risk and management overhead by using Savings Plans.

Of course, there is a potential downside to using Savings Plans. The level of savings in a Savings Plan is about 10% less than purchasing RIs. If you have a medium-sized business, then I suggest using Savings Plans. If you are a very large enterprise, the 10% decrease in savings might justify your increased employee overhead for managing RI purchases. For a small business, I would stick with RIs, because you probably know your compute infrastructure usage intimately. There are no specific cells to accommodate Savings Plans in the forecast template. If you plan to use Savings Plans instead of RIs, you should change the percentage in cell H4 from 40%, which is the average RI savings, to 27%. You make this change because the average cost reduction of a one-year savings plan is 27%. At this stage in the process, Figure 4-7 should be a similar representation of your inputs.

Inputs		
EC2	$	1,247,954.00
Storage	$	465,733.00
S3 Storage	$	3,457.00
Tooling	$	6,574.00
Agility Savings	$	-

Uplift Modfiers			Run Rate Modifiers	
Network		10%	Reserved Instances	90%
Misc Services		12%	RI Savings (Avg)	40%

	Year 1	Year 2	Year 3	Year 4	Year 5	Total
Migration %	100.00%	100.00%	100.00%	100.00%	100.00%	
EC2	$ 124,795.40	$ 124,795.40	$ 124,795.40	$ 124,795.40	$ 124,795.40	$ 623,977.00
Storage	$ 465,733.00	$ 465,733.00	$ 465,733.00	$ 465,733.00	$ 465,733.00	$ 2,328,665.00
S3 Storage	$ 3,457.00	$ 3,457.00	$ 3,457.00	$ 3,457.00	$ 3,457.00	$ 17,285.00
Tooling	$ 6,574.00	$ 6,574.00	$ 6,574.00	$ 6,574.00	$ 6,574.00	$ 32,870.00
Consulting Fees	$ 245,000.00	$ 130,000.00				$ 375,000.00
Agility Savings	$ -	$ -	$ -	$ -	$ -	$ -
Bandwidth	$ 12,479.54	$ 12,479.54	$ 12,479.54	$ 12,479.54	$ 12,479.54	$ 62,397.70
Misc. Services	$ 14,975.45	$ 14,975.45	$ 14,975.45	$ 14,975.45	$ 14,975.45	$ 74,877.24
EC2 Reserved	$ 673,895.16	$ 673,895.16	$ 673,895.16	$ 673,895.16	$ 673,895.16	$ 3,369,475.80
Total						$ 6,884,547.74

ASSUMPTIONS

Figure 4-7. Forecast step 5

You can use a combination of a Savings Plan and RIs. However, I would advise against doing this unless you really comprehend the ramifications of using both.

Migration percentages

Migrating to AWS is not an instantaneous process. No form of migration is an instantaneous process. If you think back to recent history, you will see the same timelines migrating from physical servers to virtual machines, even by VMware from one data center to another. In this regard, migrating to AWS is not anything new. It is only the capabilities that have changed.

You've already gone through discovery. You know how many servers you have. You have calculated how much work your team can perform, and you have accounted for contractors and consultants. You have entered all these values into the Microsoft Excel forecast. As it sits right now, you have five years of spend and each year is the same, the full migrated run rate.

Since we are talking about run rate modifiers, we will adjust the migration percentages that are on row 10. The sheet starts with the value of 100% across all five years. It is as if a magical fairy migrated all your servers for you. Now you want to go back and adjust them based on your timeline. For instance, if you have a two-year time-frame, you have approximately 50% in year one, and years two through five will remain at 100%. If you have a three-year migration, it would be 33% for year one, followed by 66% for year two, and 100% for years three through five.

A large enterprise should anticipate a three-year migration timeline. A small business should be estimated at less than a year for its migration, and medium-sized businesses would be about two years. Once you enter all the information, it will automatically calculate the run rate based on those percentages.

You might have noticed that we are just working with percentages here, and this goes back to my analogy of blasting into space. We haven't done migration planning and, therefore, don't have the minute details. Like many processes before, we don't want to get stuck in the tar of more information right now and have it slow down your migration process. We will cover migration planning later, in Chapter 7, and cover the timeline in more detail. At this stage in the process, Figure 4-8 should resemble your inputs.

Inputs			Uplift Modfiers		Run Rate Modifiers	
EC2	$	1,247,954.00	Network	10%	Reserved Instances	90%
Storage	$	465,733.00	Misc Services	12%	RI Savings (Avg)	40%
S3 Storage	$	3,457.00				
Tooling	$	6,574.00				
Agility Savings	$	-				

	Year 1		Year 2		Year 3		Year 4		Year 5		Total
Migration %	33.00%		66.00%		100.00%		100.00%		100.00%		
EC2	$ 41,182.48	$	82,364.96	$	124,795.40	$	124,795.40	$	124,795.40	$	497,933.65
Storage	$ 153,691.89	$	307,383.78	$	465,733.00	$	465,733.00	$	465,733.00	$	1,858,274.67
S3 Storage	$ 1,140.81	$	2,281.62	$	3,457.00	$	3,457.00	$	3,457.00	$	13,793.43
Tooling	$ 2,169.42	$	4,338.84	$	6,574.00	$	6,574.00	$	6,574.00	$	26,230.26
Consulting Fees	$ 245,000.00	$	130,000.00							$	375,000.00
Agility Savings	$ -	$	-	$	-	$	-	$	-	$	-
Bandwidth	$ 4,118.25	$	8,236.50	$	12,479.54	$	12,479.54	$	12,479.54	$	49,793.36
Misc. Services	$ 4,941.90	$	9,883.80	$	14,975.45	$	14,975.45	$	14,975.45	$	59,752.04
EC2 Reserved	$ 222,385.40	$	444,770.81	$	673,895.16	$	673,895.16	$	673,895.16	$	2,688,841.69
Total										$	5,569,619.10

ASSUMPTIONS

Figure 4-8. Forecast step 6

Agility Savings

When assisting companies with migrating to AWS, I always emphasize the importance of doing as much lift and shift as possible: copying servers block for block to AWS, not focusing on refactoring or making significant changes to the application or infrastructure. I make this suggestion because while you are migrating, you are spending twice as much. I focus as much as possible on decreasing the timeline and decreasing those costs. There are a couple of areas that I do recommend capturing the low-hanging fruit for agility and management savings. I would not classify these changes as refactoring but rather as augmentation. These are changes that I recommend companies take advantage of and are easy to obtain.

After all, agility and reduced workload are the main reasons people want to migrate to AWS. It makes sense to take advantage of some of those capabilities from the get-go. I will talk primarily about deployment pipelines and the AWS Service Catalog. These services are the most effortless capabilities to consume. They can even work with COTS applications, making them applicable to nearly any workload and company.

Automated deployment

Deployment pipelines are what many associate with internally built applications, but that is not always the case. Pipelines could be used for the deployment of COTS applications as well. Typically, I see deployment pipelines for COTS applications in highly secured environments. In a high-security environment, you would want to rehydrate your servers every week. Rehydration is the process of destroying the old machines and creating new machines with the latest patches and applications installed. You would do this in a high-security environment because it ensures that any potential malware, virus, or trojan is removed. Rehydration helps reduce the attack footprint of the COTS servers and can be a vital tool for managers in regulated environments such as financial services. However, for most people, you want a deployment pipeline for your internal applications.

Deployment pipelines help significantly reduce the manual overhead associated with deployment and testing. On-premises, you most likely have an individual on the engineering team or operations team who would receive the application once it was built and deploy the application. Not only does this cost your company hard dollars with manual effort, but it is a tedious and mundane task that can demoralize employees. Manual deployment is also prone to human error, which leads to security concerns and customer outages. By employing a deployment pipeline, you reduce all these risks and their associated costs.

The service that Amazon has for pipelines is called CodePipeline. It can be triggered manually by a person or automatically triggered based on several triggers, such as when a new file is deployed to S3 or when a new check-in is made in your code repository, or you can schedule it with a CloudWatch event. Out of these options, I have seen most companies deploy automatically after a code check-in. You could also create a pipeline that has to be triggered manually, although I have not seen it in practice. However, I do see manual checks implemented in an automatic pipeline, such as approvals before the production release.

CodePipeline has many capabilities. However, we will look at a few key capabilities, such as automated unit testing, load testing, and other functions that help reduce employee overhead further. CodePipeline does charge for its use. However, the cost is very low unless you have some very specific use cases. These might be when you are using a lot of unit testing or load testing that would increase the cost. I would say that the uplift for miscellaneous AWS services that you already have in your forecast is enough to cover CodePipeline.

Right now, we are talking about forecasts and want to recognize potential savings by using CodePipeline in your environment. To do this, we will need to find out some information to calculate those savings. The first piece of data will be the average cost per hour for personnel who do your deployments. It is essential to calculate the actual employee load, not just the base salary. You will want to make sure that your hourly rate also includes vacation, benefits, and payroll overhead to get real representation. For the sake of this exercise, we will use $100 per hour as our employee rate. The next piece of information we need is how much time it takes to perform a deployment of your software. This number would be the amount of time that it takes an engineer to get the software, log on to the server, perform any backups, install the updates, and perform smoke testing and any other functional test. Let us use four hours per environment for our exercise. The last piece of information we need is how often updates are applied. Typically, updates are most frequent in development environments, less frequent in test environments, and significantly less frequent in the production environments. You want to find out how often you deploy for each of those environments to calculate accurately how much an automated deployment will save you. For this exercise, we will use one implementation for development per week, one deployment per month in test, and one deployment every three months for production. These numbers are a typical average that I see at most companies.

Let's start doing some math. We will take the 4 times of 4 hours, for a total of 16 hours per month spent deploying the development environment. That is 2 days of effort per month in a year that is equal to 24 days, or more than an entire working month. The 24 days is just for the development environments. Next, we want to calculate just how much that costs. We said we'll use $100 an hour, so let's multiply 100 by 8 hours, bringing the daily total to $800. Now we multiply that $800 by the 24 days of effort for the year. That brings the total to $19,200. As you can see, this is a major expense for your company. Now that we have the development cost, we want to repeat the process for the test and production environments.

For the test environment, it will be one-fourth the cost of development, because it is deployed only once a month. Test will take four hours per month or one day every two months, which works out to be six days for the year. We multiply six days by $800 to get the total cost of the test at $4,800 per year.

Production is only being deployed once every quarter. Production will be two days per year or $1,600 in employee effort. You can see that this company is spending tens of thousands of dollars ($25,600) to deploy the application, so automating the deployment of applications can save your company a significant number of dollars. This cost represents just one application. Most companies deploy multiple applications or several pieces to a large application. This application sprawl leads to a significant number of wasted company resources and potentially multiple headcounts.

You want to repeat this operation for any application that you can deploy automatically and update your total savings in cell C7. You do not wish to do this for an application that currently requires a significant number of manual changes and configurations. These would need to be automated. That will take longer to set up, and it will extend your migration timeline, reducing any savings that you would have achieved.

The wonderful part of deploying CodePipeline automated deployment is that you can significantly increase your company's agility. Your company probably is not rolling out as many updates to your product as you would like. It is not because the developers are not making changes. It is because the cost of deployment is substantial, and the risks that are involved with it counteract the benefits. Once you create your pipeline, you can significantly increase the number of production updates that you are doing and deliver value to your customers faster. It is not uncommon to hear companies that have adopted an agile and automated deployment process to push as many as 10 production updates per day. This velocity is a vast improvement for time to market over most companies that roll out updates only every quarter or longer. Development deployments could be done daily or multiple times per day. Testing and production could follow suit to reach multiple production updates per day. To obtain this level of agility, your company will have to invest in more than a simple deployment pipeline and increase the automated testing to ensure a quality release.

Service Catalog

AWS Service Catalog is a service that allows you to create products with CloudFormation templates, which deploy AWS infrastructure as code (IaC). CloudFormation enables you to automate the majority of your AWS infrastructure deployment. For example, look at the following code snippet:

```
InstanceSecurityGroup:
  Type: AWS::EC2::SecurityGroup
  Properties:
      GroupDescription: Allow http from the internet
```

```
VpcId:
    Ref: myVPC
SecurityGroupIngress:
- IpProtocol: tcp
  FromPort: 80
  ToPort: 80
  CidrIp: 0.0.0.0/0
SecurityGroupEgress:
- IpProtocol: tcp
  FromPort: 80
  ToPort: 80
  CidrIp: 0.0.0.0/0
```

Your operations team can then allow access to these products by semitechnical staff to deploy the infrastructure required for their workloads. Service Catalog is an excellent way to save money postmigration to AWS. I have seen many companies significantly reduce the strain on their operations department by implementing Service Catalog.

In many companies, the operations team or cloud management team is a choke point and single point of failure in the deployment of infrastructure. By implementing Service Catalog, you allow your business units to deploy their infrastructure, thereby reducing the dependency on your operations team. This enablement removes the choke point, reduces delays, and overall increases the quality of service.

When you are planning to migrate to AWS, I recommend approaching Service Catalog by looking for repeating patterns in your current applications. The identification of these repeating patterns allows you to maximize the impact of Service Catalog. Your team can then translate those repeating patterns into infrastructure as code and a Service Catalog product. Once the products are complete and added to the catalog, access rights can be assigned to allow employees to deploy them.

Finding out how much you have saved by Service Catalog is different for every company. To help with assessing your savings, we will look at two scenarios. The following scenario focuses on the automated deployment of EC2 instances, and "Scenario 4-6" on page 134 addresses S3 buckets with corporate hardening applied.

Scenario 4-5

Bridget's company migrated to AWS about four months ago; at the time, it didn't consider rolling out Service Catalog. Before Bridget commits the resources to deploy catalog products, she wants to find out how much it will cost for the effort. She will then compare this to how much she will save by enabling company staff to self-serve.

Bridget's organization has 14,026 servers and has identified 403 applications during the discovery phase of migration. It is a mixture of COTS and internally developed software. Many design patterns and software were purchased over a period of 25 years. One of the problems that Bridget's company is faced with is being in a regulated industry. Its regulations require many systems to be validated after deployment. This requirement imposes a significant load on Bridget's team. Not only do they have to create the system and deploy the software, but a second member of her crew must come back and validate that all configurations are correct.

For the past few months, Bridget's team has been manually creating, hardening, and validating new system images. They create these images for deployment every time AWS puts out an updated OS image. Bridget would like to automate this process and enable staff to deploy their own systems. Currently, Bridgette's team deploys, on average, 80 systems per month, and it takes three and a half hours to apply the hardening and validation.

When reviewing your infrastructure for patterns, you will often ingest a lot of noise. If your company is like Bridget's, it probably has many servers, applications, and design patterns. However, sometimes the answer is staring you right in the face, and you must clear the fodder to see it. I purposely added much extraneous information into this scenario to demonstrate this fact. We are looking for repeating patterns to optimize the impact of Service Catalog. It does not matter how many servers or apps Bridget has. You might have started going down the mental path of thinking about the infrastructure side: how servers, load balancers, auto scaling groups, and similar items were laid out. For your infrastructure, these might be viable options. In Bridget's case, the fact that her company is regulated and it has to put three and a half hours of effort into deploying each system is a massive amount of energy.

If we use $100 an hour for her operations team for easy calculations, we see that it is costing the company $28,000 a month to deploy these servers,[1] or $336,000 a year. Now I don't know about you, but I don't want that number in my budget, and I'm sure my staff would much rather do something more interesting.

To calculate how much Bridget will ultimately save, we also need to calculate the amount of time it will take for her team to create the Service Catalog product. Based on the description of her environment, I think it would be overly safe to say three weeks of effort to perform the work. This timeline would include creating the required CloudFormation and automation scripts and testing of the product once it was completed. Based on the cost per hour, it will cost Bridget's company $12,000 to create the product.[2] Next, we need to know how much it will cost to deploy the product. Let us say that it takes 10 minutes to log on to the AWS console, select the product, configure its options, and deploy. That means it would cost Bridget's company

---

1 $100 × 3.5 × 80 = $28,000.

2 $100 × 15 × 8 = $12,000.

$16,000 of employee effort to deploy the same servers over a one year period.[3] Bridget's company will save a total of $308,000 in year one by implementing this product.[4] That is a significant return on investment and would be very worthwhile for the company to implement.

Scenario 4-6

Kurt's cloud engineering manager has come to him with the proposal to create a Service Catalog product for deploying S3 buckets for the company. Currently, the cloud team does this deployment. The process is not entirely manual; they have created CloudFormation templates that deploy the infrastructure. The cost is not in the implementation of the S3 bucket but instead in the management of the overall process. The cloud engineering team supports the entire global company with several hundred thousand employees and dozens of business units. The engineering team is deploying thousands of them a year. Even though it only takes about five minutes to deploy the S3 bucket, about an hour of total effort is necessary due to the documentation and ticketing process. The engineering manager would like to create the Service Catalog product and have it deployed directly from the ServiceNow ticketing and workflow system, which would eliminate all of the workload on the team.

In total, the cloud engineering team deployed 3,546 buckets last year for a total of 1.7 person-years of effort (3,546 / 2,080 = 1.7), bringing the total cost to the company to $354,600 per year, based on an average engineer hourly cost of $100.

I would love to say that it is an absurd scenario that would never happen. However, this is one of those *life is stranger than fiction* situations. It is by no means odd to see a mundane technical task overloaded with administrative burden. Kurt wants to save the $354,600 that his company is currently spending on a mundane and low-value task. ServiceNow has a connector that Kurt's company can leverage that would enable employees to deploy AWS infrastructure directly without logging on to AWS. Using the connector enables his company to leverage the existing workflow and approval capabilities of ServiceNow without the manual intervention of the cloud engineering team. Even if Kurt has to pay for consulting services to set up the connector to interface with the AWS Service Catalog, he still achieves a significant return on investment (ROI) in the first year.

Service Catalog can offer significant savings for your company, depending on your organization's size. Obviously, if your company has only a few dozen people, the return on investment would probably not justify the cost of implementation. The

---

3 $(100/6) \times 80 \times 12 = $16,000.

4 $336,000 - 12,000 - 16,000 = $308,000

service catalog also allows you to help maintain financial expenditures by only approving infrastructure sizes appropriate for your organization. Users will often also have an improved user experience. Service Catalog will enable them to see the products easily that they have already deployed, and when an update is published, they will be automatically notified.

Now that you see a couple of ways Service Catalog and pipelines can save significant amounts of money for your organization, it's time to enter it in the forecast worksheet. These savings are designed to be entered in cell C7, Agility Savings. At this point in the process, your forecast should resemble Figure 4-9.

Inputs			Uplift Modfiers		Run Rate Modifiers	
EC2	$	1,247,954.00	Network	10%	Reserved Instances	90%
Storage	$	465,733.00	Misc Services	12%	RI Savings (Avg)	40%
S3 Storage	$	3,457.00				
Tooling	$	6,574.00				
Agility Savings	$	143,500.00				

	Year 1	Year 2	Year 3	Year 4	Year 5	Total
Migration %	33.00%	66.00%	100.00%	100.00%	100.00%	
EC2	$ 41,182.48	$ 82,364.96	$ 124,795.40	$ 124,795.40	$ 124,795.40	$ 497,933.65
Storage	$ 153,691.89	$ 307,383.78	$ 465,733.00	$ 465,733.00	$ 465,733.00	$ 1,858,274.67
S3 Storage	$ 1,140.81	$ 2,281.62	$ 3,457.00	$ 3,457.00	$ 3,457.00	$ 13,793.43
Tooling	$ 2,169.42	$ 4,338.84	$ 6,574.00	$ 6,574.00	$ 6,574.00	$ 26,230.26
Consulting Fees	$ 245,000.00	$ 130,000.00				$ 375,000.00
Agility Savings	$ (47,355.00)	$ (94,710.00)	$ (143,500.00)	$ (143,500.00)	$ (143,500.00)	$ (572,565.00)
Bandwidth	$ 4,118.25	$ 8,236.50	$ 12,479.54	$ 12,479.54	$ 12,479.54	$ 49,793.36
Misc. Services	$ 4,941.90	$ 9,883.80	$ 14,975.45	$ 14,975.45	$ 14,975.45	$ 59,752.04
EC2 Reserved	$ 222,385.40	$ 444,770.81	$ 673,895.16	$ 673,895.16	$ 673,895.16	$ 2,688,841.69
Total						$ 4,997,054.10

ASSUMPTIONS

Figure 4-9. Forecast step 7

Assumptions

Now that we have covered everything in the forecast, it is important to discuss assumptions around technology, capabilities, and costs. Throughout this book, we have made numerous assumptions. We have talked about migration percentages and agility savings and approximation of the bandwidth charges, to name a few. In total, you probably made dozens of assumptions throughout the process. Unfortunately, human nature dictates that when you write something down, you set it in stone. Inevitably, someone will read that and expect it to be 100% accurate. That is why documenting your assumptions is critically important.

You might be wondering what assumptions you should document. It is not uncommon for me to record 30 assumptions, although I cull those items from a significantly more extensive list. Typically, I do not document obvious assumptions. For instance, I would not list that the migration timeline is an estimate; this is an undeniable truth because you do not have a crystal ball. What I would recommend documenting are things like the employee overhead per hour for the cloud engineering team that you used in an agility savings assessment. To assist you in generating your assumptions and getting the creative juices flowing, I have included a list of potential assumptions in Table 4-2. These assumptions cannot be used verbatim, but they should be usable with some minor tweaking and adjustment. It may also give you other ideas that are relevant to your environment.

Table 4-2. Assumption examples

Assumption	Assumption
Outbound bandwidth costs are assumed at 10% of EC2 run rate	Miscellaneous AWS services are assumed as 10% of EC2 run rate
Employee overhead for the cloud engineering team is $100 per hour	Engineers can migrate two servers per day on average
Application WidgetWidow takes four hours to deploy	Holidays have been included in the migration timeline
Vacation time of three weeks per engineer is included in the timeline	Auto scaling groups have a minimum of three baseline instances
Microsoft SQL servers will be migrated to RDS	Oracle databases will be migrated to MySQL on Aurora
Development instances will only run during office hours	Values used in the migration timeline calculation
RDS deployments will run in multiple-AZ mode for redundancy	80% of the infrastructure will use one-year reserved instances

The Excel workbook has a section named "Assumptions" for the documentation of your assumptions. This allows them to remain with the forecast and eliminates a significant number of questions. In my experience, it is best to document them with the forecast directly instead of as an addendum or additional document. This proximity allows easy flipping of back-and-forth between the assumptions and the forecast for easier analysis and ensures their visibility. With your assumptions documented, your forecast should now look like Figure 4-10.

Inputs	
EC2	$ 1,247,954.00
Storage	$ 465,733.00
S3 Storage	$ 3,457.00
Tooling	$ 6,574.00
Agility Savings	$ 143,500.00

Uplift Modfiers	
Network	10%
Misc Services	12%

Run Rate Modifiers	
Reserved Instances	90%
RI Savings (Avg)	40%

	Year 1	Year 2	Year 3	Year 4	Year 5	Total
Migration %	33.00%	66.00%	100.00%	100.00%	100.00%	
EC2	$ 41,182.48	$ 82,364.96	$ 124,795.40	$ 124,795.40	$ 124,795.40	$ 497,933.65
Storage	$ 153,691.89	$ 307,383.78	$ 465,733.00	$ 465,733.00	$ 465,733.00	$ 1,858,274.67
S3 Storage	$ 1,140.81	$ 2,281.62	$ 3,457.00	$ 3,457.00	$ 3,457.00	$ 13,793.43
Tooling	$ 2,169.42	$ 4,338.84	$ 6,574.00	$ 6,574.00	$ 6,574.00	$ 26,230.26
Consulting Fees	$ 245,000.00	$ 130,000.00				$ 375,000.00
Agility Savings	$ (47,355.00)	$ (94,710.00)	$ (143,500.00)	$ (143,500.00)	$ (143,500.00)	$ (572,565.00)
Bandwidth	$ 4,118.25	$ 8,236.50	$ 12,479.54	$ 12,479.54	$ 12,479.54	$ 49,793.36
Misc. Services	$ 4,941.90	$ 9,883.80	$ 14,975.45	$ 14,975.45	$ 14,975.45	$ 59,752.04
EC2 Reserved	$ 222,385.40	$ 444,770.81	$ 673,895.16	$ 673,895.16	$ 673,895.16	$ 2,688,841.69
Total						$ 4,997,054.10

ASSUMPTIONS
Outbound bandwidth costs are assumed at 10% of EC2 run rate
Miscellaneous AWS services are assumed as 12% of EC2 run rate
Employee overhead for the cloud engineering team is $100 per hour

Figure 4-10. Forecast step 8

Cost Burn-Up/Burn-Down

The burn-down rate and burn-up rate refer to the incremental decrease and increase of spending as you migrate your infrastructure. When you migrate servers to AWS, you burn up, as in adding more cost to your run rate in Amazon. The other half of the equation is the burn-down: as you migrate off, you recoup some costs on the on-premises equipment. However, these two rates are not equal. The burn-up rate is typically a linear path with a small amount of stepping as you migrate applications. An example of a burn-up can be seen in Figure 4-11.

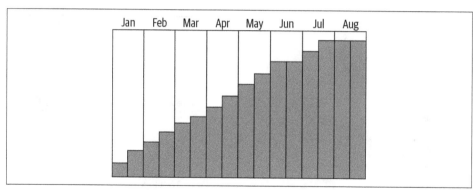

Figure 4-11. Burn-up example

Figure 4-11 shows a company migrating from on-premises to AWS. As you can see, the overall trend is quite linear but has steps as each of the significant migration waves are completed. Some of the waves had applications with more server counts, which is why some of the steps are larger than others. In Figure 4-12, you can see a burn-down graph, which is significantly different from the burn-up.

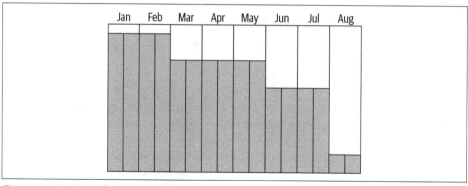

Figure 4-12. Burn-down example

When you are migrating from on-premises, the removal of a server does not necessarily indicate the removal of all the underlying infrastructure. This latent removal is not true for physical servers such as a large database server where the equipment is removed immediately. However, most companies have a highly virtualized infrastructure. In such an infrastructure, most components are shared among dozens to potentially hundreds of thousands of servers. In the typical case, you will have to remove many servers on-premises to see cost reduction. Therefore, the steps in Figure 4-12 are significantly longer in duration and shorter in decreased spend when compared to burn-up. Most of the cost reduction in the burn-down does not occur until the very end of the migration. This reduction is when the most significant components of the on-premises infrastructure can be shut down, such as SANs and the facilities themselves.

Typically, I do not include a burn-down analysis in the migrations that I have worked on, mostly because of the amount of effort that would be required to compute it. To calculate the burn-down, you need to know which servers are physical and virtual, and if the latter, what host and SAN they are attached to. It would be best if you then allocated the appropriate costs for those assets to those servers and where they are in the migration to create a burn-down. Burn-down calculations add several weeks to an overall migration timeline and yield a very low value to the business. Burn-down analysis also cannot occur until after the migration planning phase and is not included in the forecast. The reason I have included it in this chapter is that for many people, it makes sense to include burn-down as part of the financial forecast. At first glance, this does make sense, but once you understand what is required to complete a burn-down properly, you will see how it is impractical to include it in the forecast.

Wrapping It Up

In the grand scheme of things, building your business case is probably one of the smaller efforts in the migration process. Most of the information is already available from the previous processes, and it is more about adjusting and properly conveying the material that is important for the business case. Building the narrative is probably the lengthiest process. However, thankfully, you should have a good source of information from the FAQs that were built as part of Chapter 1.

The business case is a pivotal point in your migration to AWS; it's the final piece that conveys your intent, costs, and business value. At this point, you will be at a crossroads; one path takes you forward to your migration, and the other leaves you on-premises. I cannot express enough how important the business case is in taking your company forward in its competitive capabilities by migrating. It deserves attention and should not be viewed as onerous. Hopefully, your business case shows the value you have uncovered, and your migration efforts are approved. To prepare you better to start migration, Chapter 5 will cover addressing your company's operations in preparation for migration, and how to build a successful story that you can carry forward to other departments to gain adoption.

Addressing Your Operational Readiness for AWS

We have covered much ground in your migration journey so far. At this point in the process, you have just received approval for your migration, based on your business case. Many people at this phase of the process think it is time to move resources. I would not recommend that approach. There is still a hefty amount of planning you need to do if you want your migration to go forward without significant disruptions. One of the critical areas that needs planning is your operations once you move into AWS. In this chapter, we will cover how to address your operational readiness to ensure that you reduce your risk of operating in the cloud.

Many consulting firms and even AWS have a phase in migration around assessing your operational readiness. I see nothing fundamentally wrong with this approach. Still, it has been my experience that many companies find little value in *evaluating* their readiness. Let me explain. Most companies looking to migrate into the cloud do not have any applications there currently. Maybe they have some, but they are limited to disaster recovery or development. They have yet to use the cloud in a meaningful way. They know they are not ready to operate production workloads. Therefore, there is no reason to assess their readiness. Performing analysis for a company at this stage usually ends up with a spreadsheet filled with red boxes denoting inefficiencies that they need to resolve. Ultimately, you end up calling their baby ugly and pointing out many things they already know.

Instead of this approach, we will come at it from another direction. We will assume that you are not ready and do not have any of the vital operational items in place. We will show you proactively what you need to address and why. This way, you save the time that would be spent evaluating your current state. If your operations were ready for the cloud, you probably wouldn't be reading this book in the first place because you have migrated. Hopefully, this approach will move your project forward faster by eliminating the analysis piece and going directly into solving the problem.

This chapter will not cover every possible aspect of operating in the cloud. Instead, it will focus on the key areas that every customer should address. These items are what should be considered a minimum point of entry in cloud consumption. By focusing on these items now, you will prevent issues for your company long-term. We will focus on the business operational changes, because they differ significantly from contemporary on-premises thought. Before jumping into details, we will first discuss in more depth why these changes are necessary.

Why Your Operations Change After Migration

We have previously covered some areas where your operations will change after you migrate. I covered many of these items in Chapter 1, such as "Change to Operational Expenditures" on page 35 and "Disaster Recovery/Business Continuity" on page 31. Operating in AWS gives you a very different tool set to operate with when compared to on-premises operations. The services AWS provides have been engineered toward reducing your operational burden by taking over mundane management tasks. Even though your staff will no longer have to perform a lot of these mundane actions, it does not mean that no work will be involved. As you transition to increasingly managed services, you need to realign your operations to address those shifts. The net of the situation is that your staff will indeed have less work. However, the work that remains becomes significantly more important than the remedial actions that were replaced.

Sometimes when I mention to companies that the work they will do will become more critical and more valuable, they become nervous. Many people associate a higher-value task as more complicated. For example, if you work in a regulated environment on-premises, you must perform a lot of remedial actions. These actions are usually around securing the physical environment, a perspective that is managed by AWS once you migrate. AWS has removed the work of managing access logs and videotapes. Left in its place is a simple yet significantly more valuable action of collecting the documents having to do with regulations and compliance from the AWS Artifact service and delivering them to your auditors.

 AWS Artifact is a service that allows you access to download audit and compliance documents. You can find the AWS ISO certifications, Service Organization Control (SOC) reports, Payment Card Industry (PCI), and other regulatory documents there.

Operational changes are not something new. The difference is that the changes are more significant when you are operating in the cloud, in comparison to previous changes throughout technological history. The last significant technological change that made a substantial impact on operations was the transition from mainframe to workstation/server-based computing. The workstation/server model differs significantly from that of the mainframe, which had one central compute node and dozens of terminals that received screens from the mainframe. The terminals performed no processing themselves. Therefore, when companies transitioned to the workstation/server model, a significant number of operational changes needed to take place. Items such as updating and patching the workstations were completely foreign. The more recent transition from physical servers to virtualized servers also entailed operational changes, although they were not as significant as the transition from the mainframe. Virtual machines offered consolidation but operated fundamentally the same as their bare metal predecessors. Migrating to the cloud introduces a significant amount of operational process change, just like the transition from mainframes did. You can use this parallelism between mainframe and the cloud to help frame your thought process.

It is essential to keep an open mind and understand that operating in the cloud is not the same as operating on-premises. You could continue to work in the cloud as you did on-premises. However, in the timeless words of the movie *Mr. Mom*, Miriam Flynn as Annette said, "You're doing it wrong." By continuing to operate as you did on-premises, you are not taking full advantage of the capabilities and benefits for your business.

Business Operations

Since the primary driver for migration is business-related, it makes sense that the greatest number of changes required to your operations exist on the business side of things. You might ask, "Are there not changes to technology that require changes in my operations?" The answer is absolutely. However, take a second to think back on the past couple of years of your business. Think about all the changes that took place, both technologically and business process–related. You will quickly discover that you have implemented dozens of technology changes and maybe different web frameworks, languages, and applications. Now think about all the operational business changes you made. The list is a lot shorter and might bring images of the Hindenburg to mind.

The fact of the matter is that technology changes all the time; we are used to it and used to adapting to it operationally within IT. Business operational changes involve people across significant swaths of your organization. Many of these often-siloed segments of your business are not used to that rate of change. Let me be very direct: your company's ability to shift business processes directly relates to how well your organization adopts the cloud.

Now that we have covered why your operations need to change, we can discuss how you can go about making these changes an integrated part of your business. In the next sections, we will cover my process for adopting and transferring operational changes throughout your organization. I call my process *building a pyramid.*

Building a Pyramid

I call my method building a pyramid for two reasons. First, for all things to succeed, you need a strong foundation, like the rock under the base of a pyramid. When migrating to AWS, the strong foundation is represented by your executive sponsor. It is that leadership that gives strength, validity, and purpose to your message. Without this foundation, you are building your pyramid on sand. Second, to transform your organization, you will not need a handful of people. You will need everyone's help, just as though you are building a pyramid.

In Figure 5-1, you can see that my process has four major components. The foundation, or executive sponsorship, is the stone foundation. The base of the pyramid is where you create and refine the new processes inside of the IT organization. These changes include items such as change management and security and compliance, to name a few. Once you have established your base—the correct operations internally in IT—you can then add the next layer to the pyramid, the department expansion layer. It is in this phase that you reach out to a key department to envelop it into the new processes. This department helps you prove out your processes and build an ally external to IT. Once you have created an ally and additional sponsor for the changes, you can finally assemble the apex, in which you deploy the changes to the rest of your organization.

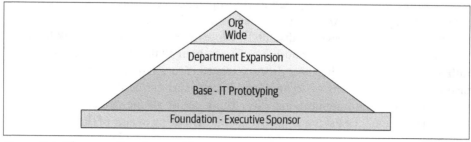

Figure 5-1. The operational pyramid

The Foundation: Executive Sponsor

Before we delve into addressing the processes that need to be changed to be ready to operate properly in AWS, we need to cover the foundation of a vital component to the success of the implementation. To drive the changes in the business, you will need an executive sponsor (see Figure 5-2). A high-level C-suite executive is preferable because that person has the clout and leadership strength required to drive the business units to a common goal. Having lower management from the IT organization as your executive sponsor will more than likely impede progress. You will have a more difficult time getting the rest of the organization on board with the transformation. This alignment is required to be effective. A great candidate would be the chief operating officer. For obvious reasons, the officer in charge of operations would be the ideal candidate for operational change.

Foundation - Executive Sponsor

Figure 5-2. The operational pyramid foundation

I cannot stress enough how important it is for your cloud journey to have a C-suite executive as your executive sponsor. I have seen migrations fail when the appointed individual is not a member of the C-suite. In the company I am recalling, the executive sponsor was the director of the cloud department. Unfortunately, this sponsor did not have the authority or leadership panache to get the job done. In this circumstance, the only part of the IT organization that he could get on board was a single development team and the team that created hardened virtual machine templates for use by other departments. Without the security and business units on board, he could not drive the business results and agility the company was looking to achieve. Having an actual executive-level sponsor is vital to your company's long-term success.

The other important factor to consider is whether your executive sponsor wants to *see* it work or *make* it work. There are two types of people that will work on a task. The first is in the *see it work* crowd, tasked with completing objectives that they do not believe in deeply. They work at the issue until they see or do not see it work. At this point, they will stop. The second group is the *make it work* crowd, who are deeply passionate and inspired by the situation and will do everything in their power to make it work. They will not give up at the first sign of trouble and will power through the issues until the task is complete. I hope it is obvious what type of person you want to be your executive sponsor. They will need to navigate some tough situations with parts of the company that are resistant to change, and they will need the drive to see it through.

The Base: IT Prototyping

When it is time to build the base of our pyramid, starting in IT is probably the best choice because this is where you have the largest sphere of influence. The staff probably understands the impact of migrating to AWS more than other departments, and it gives you the ability to crack a few eggs without affecting many people or revenue streams. You can test out methods and processes within the comfort of your own home, if you will. Once you have established that base, you can take the lessons and processes that you learned and move forward with other departments. The key concepts you need to address in the base are security and compliance, change management, and agility. We will cover these in the next few sections and discuss why they are important to your base and some potential processes to target. At this stage, your pyramid should look like Figure 5-3.

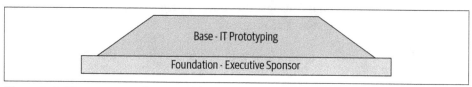

Figure 5-3. The operational pyramid base

Security and compliance

When you were operating on-premises, the IT security department probably handled your security operations in their entirety. The security department made and reviewed any changes to firewalls and other security equipment. The security department would create a single choke point in the cloud if this design were to continue. Also, this single-threaded concept does not work very well with automated deployment in the cloud. When you migrate to AWS, your security and compliance operations need to change from being the doers to being the reviewers. To reach the highest level of velocity, you will want to deploy as many automated systems and automate as many processes as possible. You will also want to push the deployment of infrastructure out from the IT department and into the hands of developers as IaC. To meet these automation requirements, you need to retool as many components of your security and compliance as possible with a new operational process.

Since your development teams throughout the company can deploy by IaC, they become the individuals that create the necessary security rules for the application. They are the ones that have the most intimate knowledge of how the application interoperates between its pieces and what communications need to be allowed to maintain least privilege. The question to answer is how the security team reviews it. Since you are operating your infrastructure as IaC, you should be checking it into a source code repository to keep it safe and track changes. This code repository then becomes the vehicle used to facilitate security review by the security team. Your deployment pipeline can orchestrate this review process. You can include a security review checkpoint in the process, which will prevent the code from being deployed until security reviews it and approves it. Once approved, the pipeline will continue to deploy the code into the environment.

Security can review the security of the deployed application though the source code repository. On the first commit or saving of the code to the repository, the security team will need to review all the IaC to determine whether it includes all the security and compliance controls that your company requires. Once they complete this review, they can approve it in the pipeline, and the deployment process continues.

This process gives you a true two-party review of your security controls. The person who implemented the control is not the same person from the security team who reviewed and approved it. This duality works well with certain compliance control frameworks such as those found in banking.

When the next commit happens, the pipeline will then again ask for a security review of the code. However, the security team does not have to review the entire application again. Since you are using a code repository, the security team can perform a difference evaluation between the last code the security team reviewed and the new code. This difference comparison will highlight all the changes that have occurred, and the security team only reviews those. It streamlines the process compared to on-premises.

One of the critical components of creating your base is being able to demonstrate the essential concepts and their new processes to other departments within your company. Security and compliance are no exception. Security becomes increasingly important as time goes on. Criminals have found that finding victims through technology is lucrative, and this is why I have positioned security and compliance as the first and most important cornerstone in your pyramid. Strong security will ensure that your company makes an unappealing target for criminals. You want your company to be as unenticing to potential hackers as possible. By developing this pattern within the IT department, you can demonstrate to other departments how the new cloud methodology streamlines the process. You can demonstrate how it ensures a proper security review and enables your staff to implement security directly without having to wait for the security team to do it for them.

Change management

Change management is another area where significant changes take place regarding the operational process. Your existing change management process probably is not a good fit when implementing automated pipelines. Many change management processes require a review by a change board that meets on a specified cadence. This method does not fit well with the continuous nature of automated deployment. Contemporary change management processes are quite honestly an agility inhibitor. Let us review this scenario to see how damaging a legacy change management process can be.

Scenario 5-1

Tim is consulting for a financial services company thinking about moving to the cloud. The company is very large and has many siloed divisions and departments across the globe. The change management process is very slow to navigate and implement changes. Last month, Tim needed to get some firewall changes put in place to

---

> allow a new server to communicate with an existing server. He was told that it would take 45 days for the firewall changes to be implemented.

I have a confession to make; in this scenario, I am Tim, and this happened. You may think this story is total garbage, but I assure you it is true. You probably would not believe me if I told you they made a mistake on the work order on the first attempt and made me wait another 45 days to fix their error. Sadly, this is also true. This scenario is a prime example of how business processes can impede business progress.

Ultimately, this kind of situation cannot last if you want your company to remain viable in the long term. Acting like this is like buying a Ferrari and leaving it with an empty tank in your garage while your competition is lapping the track. Now, this scenario is an extreme instance that I thank the electron gods I have never seen again. However, it does an excellent job of illustrating the business process traps lurking around the corner and dropping your company's agility into a tar pit.

The whole point of change management is to decrease corporate risk. Risk management ensures that situations such as the following occur:

- Two major changes are not implemented at the same time
- Production changes are not made outside of maintenance windows
- Rollback plans exist
- Proper testing was done

Ultimately, you want to make sure that any changes done don't affect your customers or your company's operations. You are probably putting together a good story in your head about why a conventional process might not be advantageous in the cloud, and you would be right. We want to change the process, but we also want to ensure that it still addresses the critical items we listed. We just do not want to throw caution to the wind and scrap the process altogether.

Let's walk through these four significant items and address how they are de-risked in the cloud and how a revised change management process might look. These four items are not the end all be all, but they are solid items that would apply to every business. You may have some others specific to your business, such as compliance reviews, documentation updates, and other things you want to de-risk:

Simultaneous changes

When you work on-premises, many of your systems, equipment, and databases are very intertwined and heavily connected. This interconnection creates an inherent amount of risk to other applications. When you update more than one application, database engine, SAN controller, and so on, you can disrupt operations of a tertiary system. It then becomes difficult to trace the cause of the issue.

Was it the changes you made in application A or was it the firmware update you applied to the firewall? When you migrate to AWS, the posture of your systems changes drastically. In AWS, you can create very decoupled applications that do not intersect as they do on-premises.

Moreover, you are not responsible for the networking, firewall, NAT gateways, and all the other AWS managed services. Together these inherently de-risk performing changes at the same time. An additional de-risking factor is that you will be doing many more updates with a much smaller change volume. Instead of performing a major update once every six months, you will perform a couple of small changes per day in the development environment.

Maintenance windows

When you move to an automated deployment model as we discussed in "Automated deployment" on page 129, you can control the pipeline and when it performs actions. You could set constraints so that development timelines can operate at any given point in time, but production only happens after midnight. You might also want to limit production changes to the weekends or some other time of low usage. Having a programmatic control significantly decreases the risk of production changes being implemented outside of the maintenance window.

Rollback plans

When you migrate to AWS, the need for rollback plans does not disappear. Just like most of the other items that we talked about previously, it is something that becomes more automated in the cloud. With the advanced technologies available to you in AWS, you can use more advanced deployment methods such as blue-green and canary. These deployment methods allow you to build rollback into the process itself with automation. This automation allows you to de-risk changes made to your application in AWS, ensuring that a rollback plan exists by default.

Proper testing

Testing is another item required for change management that can be automated in the cloud to reduce change risk. With an automated deployment model, testing can be included as part of your pipeline and automated like rollbacks and maintenance windows. You can perform different types of testing, such as unit tests, performance testing, code quality tests, and code security testing, to name a few. Thresholds for all these tests can be set, and deployments can fail if they do not meet your criteria. By implementing these tests, you mitigate the testing risk that would require review by a contemporary on-premises change review meeting.

Since you can automate and mitigate most of the risks involved with deployment in AWS, we can now cover what a new change management process might look like. We just covered how the implementation of deployment pipelines significantly reduces your risk when changing your environment. As you can probably see, your change management process after migration will be a meld of technology and process. Therefore, many companies struggle after they migrate. They have not modified their change management process to consume the agility fully that the cloud has to offer.

My recommendation is to implement your change management processes within your deployment pipelines and other automated processes. By combining the two processes, you eliminate the possibility of steps being missed or change management not occurring and being bypassed by staff. You can implement security reviews, rollback, testing, and maintenance windows all as part of the process, as we have just discussed. It may also make sense to include manual approval for production deployment as the final step to ensure that everything is correct and there are no extenuating circumstances that should prevent the change from going through. A good example of this might be a change blackout window during Thanksgiving week. Although the change is safe, you might not want to roll it out until the next week, when potential exposure is lower.

 Change management can also be automated if you implement it as part of your service management system. ServiceNow is a tool that has adapters that interface with AWS, and I have seen many companies succeed at implementing their change management as a ServiceNow workflow (*https://www.servicenow.com*).

Build pipelines are just one example of how the process can be integrated directly into technology. Change management can also be integrated into items such as golden template creation, EC2 instance patching, and VPC deployment, to name a few. The level of automation and risk mitigation is only limited by your imagination. AWS provides the hooks and tooling to automate nearly everything on the platform.

It is vitally important to experiment with the different processes in your organization, because they are unique to you. This experimentation continues to build the base of your operational pyramid. Just like security and compliance, you want to demonstrate that the processes work before taking them to other parts of the organization. It is always more effective to show someone a proven path than to talk about hypotheticals.

Agility

Agility is a difficult topic to discuss or define, because it is not just one item, such as automated deployment, or using an agile method of software development. The root of agility goes much deeper into the organization itself. Business agility is the ability of a company to respond to changing market conditions rapidly. It isn't something you can just buy and say you're agile, and unfortunately, slapping a label of "agile" on something does not make it so. Agility is a collection of processes, technology, and company spirit. Unfortunately, nailing down what creates agility in an organization isn't something we can cover within the scope of this book. Instead, we will focus on the few items that have been known to stifle agility. It may take you many years to reeducate your entire company on being more agile. Still, it will only take you a few days to stop doing these items to help your agility along. The three main items that we will address are:

- Teams that are too large: loss of traction
- Too many cooks in the kitchen: decision atrophy
- Process for process's sake: wasted cycles

These three items are probably the biggest offenders in slowing down your operations and your overall agility.

Large teams. I find team size and efficacy quite an interesting conundrum. You would think that if you want to get something done faster, adding more people to the mix would accomplish that goal. However, this is hardly the case in most instances. You need to find the sweet spot where efficiency and efficacy are maximized, when adding just one more person will reduce the efficacy. When you keep increasing team size, you become increasingly efficient at doing the wrong things. As you add people, they spend too much time on questions like who should do what. Smaller teams are much easier to manage.

Just as it makes sense to break up your monolithic applications in AWS, an excellent way to achieve agility is to break up your monolithic teams as well. By breaking up your teams to work on smaller segments of work, you create efficiency within the overall team. It will reduce those extra cycles that were wasted and make your company more deliberate in its execution. Amazon is a firm believer in small teams, and it is one of the major reasons that it continues to be agile, given its massive size. Amazon adheres to the concept of a two-pizza team. This rule is employed throughout Amazon, and it states that no team can be bigger than you can feed with two pizzas. Small teams = agility.

To see how breaking up teams makes an improvement, you will need to take some measurements, so you have something to evaluate. Items that make useful yardsticks are things like:

- How long does it take to complete a new software release?
- How long does it take to see a shift in competition and react?
- How long does it take to hire a new employee?
- How long does it take to approve features to add to applications?

There are many kinds of project management techniques and software. It would be difficult to make any direct recommendations on how to measure them. You will have to assess your situation and determine the best metrics to use for your evaluation. In addition, there might be a ticketing system, HR systems, or another tooling that exists outside of project management that will be able to provide insight. One potential risk in breaking apart your teams is that you are disrupting employees' reporting structure. Whenever you make an organizational change, it has the potential to make employees uncomfortable. As we discussed in Chapter 2 in the section "Staffing and Expertise Loss" on page 65, you should be aware of employees' potential fears and address them appropriately.

Too many cooks.   I did not want to use the cliché *too many cooks in the kitchen*, but it sums up the issue so perfectly. In this case, we are not talking about too many people on a team but, instead, too many people involved in the decision-making process. I cannot count how many times I have been in a meeting where everyone had a say in a decision. We would just go around and around and around the table, and nothing would ever get accomplished. I have seen this increasingly as of late as business has changed. In the United States, we created companies in a hierarchical structure based on the military chain of command. The upper tiers develop the plan. As you trickle down the ranks, the lower tiers figure out how to execute and make it a reality. More recently, I have observed a trend in which the company tries to make the process more inclusive among the ranks, allowing lower tiers of management and staff to be more in control of their destiny. However, in being more democratic and inclusive, they have sacrificed decisiveness.

I am not bashing the new process at all; on the contrary, I believe it helps with employee morale and can extract great ideas from a larger audience. The issue is that no one in those meetings is empowered to decide. This lack of a decision maker causes the merry-go-round of decision making to carry on indefinitely.

I experienced this firsthand when I was working as a consultant. The company I was working for deployed eight people to work on a customer. Five of these eight people thought they were in charge. Every meeting had infighting, and we never made decisions, because there were too many cooks. What was worse was that those five people started doing what they thought was best and were sending very mixed signals to the client. The project was on the brink of failure.

The client was upset, and we were told we had a week to get everything in order, or they would cancel the contract. To be honest, I did not do much other than lay down the proverbial law and make decisions. I was not supposed to be in charge of the project, but no one else had done it up to this point and corralled the others. I heard everyone's opinions and made a decision. This strategy aligned everyone to a common goal, squashed the infighting and vying for position, and increased our customer's confidence.

Your situation might not be as dire as this one. However, this sort of situation happens to some extent in every company I have worked for or with. The way to address this issue is to ensure that a decision maker is involved in every meeting. Ultimately, there should probably be a process for how meetings work and what is expected. This level of administration for meetings might sound odd, but articles are circulating around the internet about how Amazon doesn't allow presentations in their meetings. Google actually had, or possibly still has, a rule that a decision maker needs to be appointed for every meeting. Having controls for meetings works, and appointing a decision maker is more common than one would think and will drive your agility.

Process for process's sake. One thing that can slow down agility is process for the sake of process. I have worked for quite a few startups and small companies and some very large companies. One item that allows smaller companies to be agile and move quickly is the lack of processes that are not completely necessary for the operation of the business. When a company is small and lean, you only have time to do what is necessary. Many processes are not added until much later. If you need to take a day of vacation, you ask your boss, and all is well. Later, as the company grows, a process is added because the number of employees goes up, and you need some process to keep things running smoothly.

Where things start to derail is when process starts getting invented for no necessary reason. I am reminded of a company that was particularly bad in this area. Its mentality was that to be a big business, it had to act like a big business. This company, which was of a decent size, started to implement every possible process you could imagine. Everything had to be done as if we were General Electric with thousands upon thousands of employees. In the end, not much work ever got done because you were too busy filling out paperwork.

For every process you consider implementing, you need to ask yourself whether this process would make things more efficient or detract from accomplishment. Not all processes need to be scrapped; some need to be adjusted to remove the bloat that is slowing you down. Just remember the mantra: process is good, filling out forms in triplicate is bad.

Calling out these three items will help you gain some agility in your organization. They won't guarantee that your company will become like Amazon or a startup, but they will help. These changes are just the tip of the proverbial iceberg, because there are many other things to implement to gain maximum agility. However, as part of building the base to your pyramid, you should have some good discussion points for other teams, specifically on how you optimized your processes and removed the dead weight by following these suggestions.

Building Onto Your Base: Department Expansion

Now that you have spent the time within the IT department building your solid base, addressing your agility, security, compliance, and change management, it's time to add the department expansion layer (see Figure 5-4). At this phase, you will look for a team you have worked with in the past that you know is open to change and willing to work closely with IT. You have built a functioning base and can demonstrate that it worked for IT. You can show the improvements it made and how you could optimize it and get more work done. Unfortunately, managers in other departments will take it with a grain of salt. They will say, "Well, that's IT; your teams are used to this kind of change." That is why it is so important to take your next step with an ally of IT.

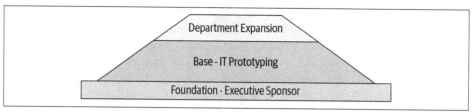

Figure 5-4. The operational pyramid expansion layer

By working with a friendly team, you are building your credibility with a business unit outside of IT. By working with this team, repeating the processes and enhancements you made within IT allows you to create that next great story. That story will buy credibility with other units within the company because they will be more willing to accept that it is something they can accomplish, and not just an IT thing.

There will probably be issues with some changes within this pilot department or business unit. They are not IT and are probably not as accustomed to change as the IT staff. It will be critical for IT to keep the lines of communication open and establish a cadence with the team to ensure that any issues are addressed as soon as possible. The worst possible thing that could happen in this critical stage is that the team becomes disillusioned with the process. If this were to happen, you would not have a great showcase for the rest of your organization. It is important to keep the positive energy and excitement for the process high.

I have had great success with this method of building my pyramid in the past. When I was prototyping virtual desktops when they were first coming out, they were a great play for the company to meet some critical disaster recovery issues that we were having. We prototyped them initially in IT, but this was not a very good indication of how end users would respond. IT staff will just fix the problem and move on without really thinking much about it. The automatic repair will lead to a poor end-user experience when those nontechnical users run into those same issues.

To rectify this issue, I used this method: I built the base in IT and then used the investment department to refine it before mass rollout. I chose a department where the VP was a friend of mine. By forming this alliance, I guaranteed that I would have cooperation on her team. On the opposing side, I was personally motivated to ensure that my team did not screw it up and provided excellent service and attention. Her department was the gold star standard that I wanted to promote. Even if they are a friend to IT, you still need to put your best foot forward.

Finishing the Apex

Once you have completed your work and built a success story with the pilot team, it is time to take your success forward to the rest of the company as shown in Figure 5-5. Having a great story to tell is a fantastic way to sell your ideas to the other areas of the business. Being able to sell is not something that most IT management thinks about, but it is what you are doing. It is just a different type of sales from selling products and services to clients. An IT manager effective at selling has more overall success in their career. We are not talking about used car salespeople, but it is selling nonetheless.

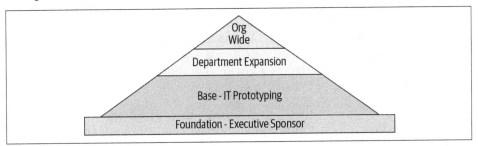

Figure 5-5. The operational pyramid apex

Ultimately, now you are selling your new processes to a team that might not even know they need your product. Your product is agility and a refined process to make that agility a reality. You could draw a similarity between cloud processes and operations when the first iPod was released. There was nothing like it; at first glance, it seemed odd that you would need a device that stored every piece of music you ever had and bring it with you. Apple solved a problem that consumers did not even know they had. This example is very similar to your operational situation. You can use this similarity to help you envision how you will communicate to the teams; you are selling a vision.

At this point, you need to craft your message and your value proposition for those departments. It would make sense to create an overall storyboard to walk your potential clients through what their journey would look like and the added value it brings. You have done this twice before with your pilot and the base built in IT. You have the data; now, it is just about crafting a compelling story. Feel free to refer to your whys from Chapter 1 to help draw inspiration from your narrative to inspire people to adopt your improved processes.

You might think this is overkill, and to be honest, when I first started in IT I would have said the same thing. In the earlier parts of my career, this was a mistake in my judgment. Things that seemed so simple and obvious to me are not so simple and obvious to people who do not understand the technology or concepts. I did not see success until I abandoned that mentality. Remember your overall goals for cloud migration and the benefits that it brings to your company. If the message about operations doesn't transform your company, you won't be able to maximize the potential of the cloud and will revert to an on-premises state.

Finance Capabilities

With building a pyramid, we walked through the process of driving operational changes through the entire organization. The items that we discussed are universal across all of your business departments. However, one department needs special attention when you migrate to AWS. One of the biggest operational changes will occur in your finance and accounting departments. The change to operating expense from capital expense and the ability to consume an endless supply of resources requires some retooling in how you account for and allocate those expenses. Without the proper controls, it is easy to see your costs spiral out of control. Shadow IT or systems that are created and forgotten about and not shut down can become a significant problem if not contained. These are critical items to keep costs under control and why we will cover these financial operations controls separately.

One story that can exemplify this problem comes from a client I was consulting on a discovery and migration planning project. They had not yet migrated to AWS, but this example shows how the lack of these types of controls can lead to issues in the cloud. The customer wanted my firm to evaluate their 9,600 servers on-premises and determine what should be moved to the cloud and what they should leave behind. This client was a highly agile company that made a lot of changes and innovations. However, they did not have any good controls in place from a financial perspective to ensure that they kept expenditures in check.

While evaluating, we found that around 6,000 of the 9,600 servers they were running were unnecessary. I was shocked, and I had a hard time wrapping my head around how they even got to this point. After having many conversations with staff during the application interview process, the problem became evident. Time after time, we heard the same thing: "I thought those servers were shut down two years ago"; "That was a pilot we did for some new service a few years back"; "Those servers were spun up to test and update in a nonproduction environment." The reasons were different but all very similar. They needed a system temporarily and, for some reason or another, forgot to shut it back down again. Nearly two-thirds of their entire infrastructure was unnecessary. Because of the company's growth, the expansion of their on-premises infrastructure was masked and thought to be part of that growth.

This example is, hopefully, one in a million. Still, with the nearly unlimited capacity of AWS you can experience this type of runaway infrastructure without the proper operations. Some ways that this occurs in AWS are:

- Unconstrained resources
- Misconfigured pipelines
- Poor tagging
- Lack of chargeback/showback

We will discuss further how these items can contribute to financial risk while operating in the cloud and how you can address your finance operations to mitigate said risk.

Unconstrained Resources

Unconstrained resources refer to resources that are provisioned in AWS that should be constrained by process. You need to have some control over who can deploy and how they deploy. You should have some process to approve resources and sizes to be deployed and ensure that they are properly shut down when no longer necessary. This process can be implemented in several ways. For instance, you can use Service Catalog as discussed in "Service Catalog" on page 131, or you could use a service management tool like ServiceNow. Honestly, you could use a spreadsheet and email if you had to. The point is that it is essential to have control to prevent the sprawl of servers.

Besides the control of resources being deployed into the environment, it is also important to implement a sandbox account for developers. By creating a sandbox account and the necessary processes, you can ensure that developers do not leave test and prototype infrastructure running long-term. You want your developers to play with new technology. You in no way want to inhibit their innovation. That innovation will enable your company to surpass your competition, but you also do not want to give them your Amex card for a shopping spree. Typically, I implement a sandbox account and allow developers a free-for-all area in which to play with any of the AWS technologies, but buyer beware. Anything that lives in that account will be purged on a daily or weekly basis. This action does two things. First, it makes sure your bill stays lean by deleting all the resources. Second, it ensures that your developers get comfortable with IaC. If they want to pilot something for a few days or weeks, they will deploy it repeatedly. They will quickly learn that the best way to do that is to follow company policy and use IaC.

You can source AWS account cleanup scripts from GitHub (*https://github.com*). There are several available, depending on your company's needs. A popular one is AWS-Nuke (*https://oreil.ly/YSpA3*).

Misconfigured Pipelines

Pipelines are a blessing to companies. The capabilities they bring and the sheer volume of monotonous work they remove are astronomical. However, if they are improperly configured, they are also a way to drive up your bill quickly. There is a multitude of reasons for how this can happen, but here we'll cover the largest.

Most deployments want some form of rollback so that if something goes wrong, you can revert your environment to the last known good state as fast as possible. This process is to reduce the impact on your customers. The deployment can be done with blue-green deployments. In such a deployment, you deploy a completely new set of infrastructures to support your application, install the application, and then cut over to this new set of servers. But what would happen if there was something wrong with the cleanup part of this process? At some point, you are running on the new version and no longer need the older one; you have no intention of rolling back. If this process does not work out properly, you can end up with servers always being created and never removed. You can imagine the damage that this could do to your AWS bill. Imagine if you were super agile and did 10 production updates a day! Yikes!

Thankfully, it is easy to address your process to compensate for this malfunction. You could do something as simple as using a notification to alert you when the cleanup portion of the pipeline is complete. It is not the best solution, though; although simple, it is best to avoid true positive email notifications. They turn into just noise, but eventually, someone will notice that they didn't get the email and investigate what was going on with the process.

The better way to address this would be through tagging of the infrastructure attached to the pipeline, monitoring the spend, and looking for anomalies. This analysis can be accomplished by using the AWS Cost Explorer tool to monitor spend by using cost allocation tags.

Cost Management

Tagging is the most important component of the cost process in AWS. It is how you can allocate the costs to departments, applications, teams, even specific developers or purchase orders if you wish. It has also been known for large companies to use tagging based on marketing events so they could directly tie the cost of supporting a marketing campaign to the revenue it generated. Without tagging, everything ends up in big buckets by service on your AWS bill.

We covered tagging in "Resource tagging" on page 69, which you can refer to for a refresher on risk mitigation and tagging suggestions. Besides those concepts, I also want to include some information here about the AWS Cost Explorer. The Cost Explorer is a service that allows you to create and generate reports about your AWS usage and graphically display them. You can think of it as a business intelligence tool for your AWS costs. It allows you to break down your costs by service or region, account, and tagging. This tool allows you to see the costs associated with any tags you configure.

To enable the use of tags for cost exploration, you need to enable them first in the billing console. The configuration can be a hangup for some because the setting is not in the AWS Cost Explorer console. You need to access your billing dashboard and select Cost Allocation Tags from the menu on the left, as shown in Figure 5-6.

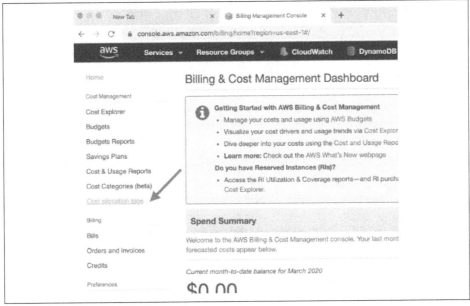

Figure 5-6. Cost allocation tags

From there, you can use the User-Defined Cost Allocation Tags section to add any tags you wish to show up in the various billing tooling AWS offers. You select the tags that you wish to use by clicking the checkboxes and then clicking the Activate button, as shown in Figure 5-7. It would also be beneficial to enable the aws:cloudformation:stack-name tag. Being able to see the cost of a CloudFormation stack can be very fruitful, especially if tagging was not properly implemented on the resources contained in the stack.

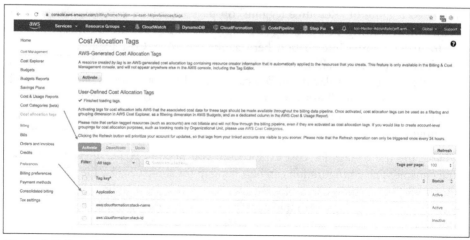

Figure 5-7. Cost allocation tag activation

The Cost Explorer service also allows you to export the data in a comma-separated values (CSV) format. This reporting allows your finance team to import to Microsoft Excel and do more advanced analysis. You can put many automations in place with Cost Explorer to perform the collection and downloading of the reports for you. It is possible to automate the process completely if you have a large company with many departments. If you are a smaller organization, it might be enough to create a role that has access to the Cost Explorer service and allow finance to interface directly.

I cannot emphasize it enough to have your tagging schema designed and implemented before migrating to AWS. Without the proper implementation, it can take much effort to go back and rework which resources belong to which department. Without proper tagging, it will be significantly more difficult to track down cost overruns and where they are coming from.

Lack of Chargeback/Showback

We briefly touched on this topic in "Chargeback and showback" on page 70. When you migrate, your financial operational processes must change. You will take on a more agile and fluid infrastructure than you had in the past, and your financial processes must adjust to compensate. Think back for a second on how you did budgeting on-premises. You probably created your budget once a year and checked it every so often when you were making purchases to make sure you were not going over. In the cloud, this could be a risky process, given the dynamic nature of the consumption.

Chargeback and showback are the best ways to give teeth to controlling your department's spending in AWS. Most large enterprises already have this practice in place and it probably is not a significant change. However, small and medium businesses probably do not practice it as much. It is also possible that your organization might practice this partially. One company I worked for, where I was in charge of the IT budget, was good at charging back to the business when it was launching a new product or service. It would have to include the capital for the IT infrastructure as part of its business case, and then it would be allocated against the business unit. This process was great in the short term because it did not affect my budget immediately. The unfortunate part was that after year one, the responsibility for the funding to keep the application running fell under the IT budget, and an increase in spending was my responsibility to justify.

If you were to follow the nonchargeback model or partial chargeback model in the cloud, you would put the burden of monitoring all the resources and the appropriate level of spend on the IT team. Unfortunately, the result is that IT would not have the resources or the time to track the expenditures appropriately. It would default to having more funding approved. The result would be that your cloud costs would continue to increase over time with no checks and balances to ensure that they were appropriate.

By changing your financial operational processes, you can spread this workload to all the departments to crowdsource the work. By having chargebacks, you ensure that the department will address any cost overruns because of the impact on its profit and loss (P&L) statement.

Wrapping It Up

By addressing the concerns we discussed in this chapter, you should be on the way to a much smoother and successful long-term journey. By following the building of your pyramid, you will craft a successful change in your company's operational process. You built your foundation by getting a strong executive sponsor to spearhead adoption of cloud operations. You built your base of operational readiness in the IT department and refined the processes. Once you completed your base, you worked with a single department to gain adoption outside of IT. Finally, you put the apex on the pyramid by rolling out the operational processes to the rest of the organization. The concepts discussed in this chapter are probably the most difficult to implement and will take a significant amount of time, much longer than the migration itself.

The processes covered in this chapter are not an end state, because technologies and staff capabilities will require refinement of your company's operations. Your processes need to be just as agile as the technologies and development methodologies that you employ. The key to long-term survival in today's business economy is the ability to adapt continually.

These are the last vital items to be addressed before you can start rolling out your environment in AWS and begin your migration. In the next chapters, we will get into the meat of migration, starting with Chapter 6.

Defining Your Landing Zone and Cloud Governance

Now that you have addressed your operational readiness for AWS, it is time to address the design of your landing zone and cloud governance. The concept of a landing zone was introduced in Chapter 2. As previously discussed, the landing zone provides baseline security controls and guardrails, account structure to segment environments, and security notifications. Now we will cover specific design concepts and best practices to build on and round out your understanding. We will follow the landing zone discussion with cloud governance, which comprises the controls developed for your operations in the cloud to maintain stability and security. By addressing these items now, your team can start the deployment of the landing zone and governance controls while you are performing your migration plan, which we will discuss in the next chapter. This parallel workflow will save a month or two on your migration timeline. You might want to postpone the deployment of your landing zone if there will be a lapse in time between your migration plan and your actual migration. By deploying the landing zone, you will start to incur AWS costs because resources such as NAT gateways and VPNs will be online at this time. If you expect a delay between planning and the start of migration, it might make sense to hold off on the landing zone until you are closer to your start date.

Frequently, the landing zone and cloud governance don't get the attention they deserve because companies view them as necessary components and matter of course and gloss over them. This chapter will highlight just how important these concepts are for your business—they are the foundation of everything you do in the cloud. In Chapter 5, we talked about building the foundation of your pyramid with the support of your executive leader to ensure successful adoption of cloud operations. Similarly, you need to build a foundation here for your actual cloud deployment. If you were to build a house, a great amount of time and effort would go into the design, validation, and inspection to ensure that the foundation would support your home. Although it's a necessity and uninteresting, your foundation isn't something you, the city officials, or your general contractor would just gloss over. You wouldn't want a crooked and crumbling cloud deployment any more than you would want a crooked and crumbling house. Let's start building that foundation with the landing zone.

Landing Zone

Think of a landing zone as like an airport. In your landing zone, you can think of your accounts as airport runways where your workloads land, depending on the criteria, such as whether you need an account for PCI compliance. You can consider the logging controls to be like the airport taxiways in which your vital access logs are guided to your protected logging account. Similarly, your security and compliance controls are like the airport control tower. If any of these items were missing from an airport, it would be utter chaos. The same rules hold true for your AWS environment. The first concept we will cover regarding your landing zone is account structure and how that relates to your company's size and structure.

Account Structure

When it comes to landing zone deployment, the one thing that you really need to get right from the start is your account structure. It doesn't get much attention on the internet, and quite a few companies struggle with how to structure their accounts. Your account structure is very specific to your organization's business unit structure and how you account for costs in the finance department. I break down the account structure into three classes:

1. Business unit–based
2. Environment-based
3. A hybrid model that incorporates both concepts

We will cover these in detail in the next sections.

All structures should have a base design that is consistent between all three for the baseline security controls. There is no set way to accomplish this, but there should be a master billing account, shared services, and an audit or logging account at a minimum. AWS Landing Zone also deploys a security account for security operations for a service such as the AI-powered threat-detection service, AWS GuardDuty. However, it is not uncommon to see these services used for the master account instead.

Business unit–based

A business unit–based account structure gives each business unit an account to hold its resources. One of the main reasons for this is cost control and chargeback. Tagging is not guaranteed to be correct or added to all resources. In companies with many business units, these potential missteps can be seen as potential risks that should be avoided. To prevent this situation, a designated business unit account automatically bills all resources for that account to that account. That way, costs are allocated and don't get lost.

Large companies often have merger and acquisition and divestiture activities. Having a business unit–based account structure facilitates this type of workload shifting. A business unit account can be added and removed from your organization with ease. The account would just need to be either added or severed from your logging, master, and shared accounts. In the case of divestiture, the account could then be transferred to a new master billing account when you give the root account credentials to the purchasing company. There is, of course, much work to be done around access management when you take over an AWS account, but that is out of the scope for this book.

The business unit account structure also helps companies with regulatory compliance requirements that vary between accounts. Having the unit separated by account allows you to control the access and security controls by account. You can then restrict the accounts with compliance requirements without affecting any other business units. If you were to have an environment-based account structure, you would have to restrict all the business units to accomplish this same regulatory control.

Most often, I recommend the use of an environment or hybrid model. I don't use the business unit model very often because I have a deep security and compliance background, and I don't feel that the business unit model will provide the required level of segmentation between the environments. That said, in an unregulated company or a company with many COTS applications in play, where development and testing environments aren't as extensive, the business unit model makes sense.

Environment-based

In an environment-based account structure, you distribute your workloads to accounts based on the environment that they belong in, that is, development, testing, or production. This account structure works well for smaller organizations without an expensive estate. This design is simple and easy to maintain but requires proper tagging to ensure that your finance department can appropriate costs correctly.

Unlike the business unit design, the environment structure is not conducive to divestitures. In a divestiture, part of the organization is being sold off or segmented, and any workloads that are contained in an environmental account will have to be migrated out of the source company's account because it contains other workloads that are not part of the divestiture. Those workloads will have to be placed into a new account under the purchaser's control. In the reverse circumstance, when you merge or purchase a company, you must migrate the new workloads into your existing environmental accounts even if they already use AWS. This limitation is another reason the environmental design is not the best choice for larger organizations.

The major benefit of the environment-based account structure is the ability to segment the controls and data that are used in your different environments. This structure is especially beneficial to regulated industries such as health care and financial services. These industries require customer personally identifiable information (PII) to be protected. By grouping accounts by environment, you ensure that no data leaks to environments lower than production without some form of obfuscation. The environment design also allows you to control the access controls by environment. This level of control enables you to give more rights in the development environment to engineers and developers but more restrictive controls in production.

Hybrid model

The hybrid account model is a combination of the business-unit and environment-based design models. In this design, each business unit gets separate accounts for development, testing, and production. Although this design is the most complex and contains the largest number of accounts, it gives the greatest level of flexibility. Not only does it work well with mergers and acquisition activities, but it also is conducive to segmenting the environments.

I would say that if you have over 300 servers, the hybrid model would be the best choice for you. With anything lower than that, the overhead of operating the extra accounts probably does not make sense. For each new account, you will also have more federation groups in your directory services to manage access, further increasing management overhead. You can automate most of the deployment, using IaC and compliance tooling. The real level of effort with the many accounts created by using the hybrid model comes into play with access and authorization hygiene, which must include auditing access to ensure that the correct people in your company have access and others do not.

You may be beginning to think that having all these new accounts adds a burden to the finance department. The number of environments and the number of business units should be consistent across all three design methods. The difference is in the financial firewalling that occurs in the business and hybrid models; they ensure that all costs are properly associated.

Recommended Accounts

Although the account structure covers the bulk of your environment, several required accounts are outside that structure. Accounts such as logging and shared services create a fundamental layer to the infrastructure upon which you build your account structure. You will connect these too, either logically or by a network connection, to the other accounts that you deploy in your selected account structure. The other accounts we will discuss are the sandbox account and the PCI account. If necessary for your business, you will use these accounts to offer segmentation in your environment to increase security and compliance.

Shared services

The shared services account hosts the services that all the other accounts access. This account would hold software deployments like Active Directory, Chef, Ansible, Salt, Splunk, Elastic, and security tooling like Nessus. The shared services account creates a hub-and-spoke design by which all other accounts communicate, as shown in Figure 6-1. By using this design methodology, you eliminate the need to deploy these types of resources repeatedly in each account.

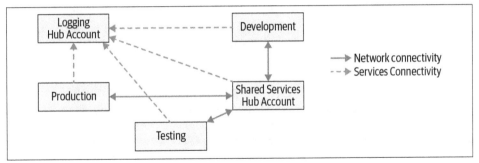

Figure 6-1. Hub-and-spoke access

The shared services account also can host your bastion hosts. A bastion host is a hardened instance that can withstand attacks and allows IT staff access to backend servers by using the Secure Shell (SSH) protocol for Linux servers and Remote Desktop Protocol (RDP) for Windows servers. Although you can access your servers directly through VPN or Direct Connect connections, I would instead recommend the use of bastion hosts to access your servers. It provides an additional layer of security for your servers that a hacker would need to penetrate to gain access to your environment. It also allows you to eliminate routing your on-premises workstation segment to your critical database segment. In this design, the only way to access your critical data layer would be to use a bastion host or the server that directly needs the data on the database server.

For larger organizations that need many administrators to access the bastion hosts, I recommend the use of Amazon Workspaces, a virtual desktop interface (VDI) environment that grants each user their own virtual workstation to operate from. This design allows for an additional layer of protection from malware by segmenting the users individually versus using a service such as Remote Desktop Services. With Remote Desktop Services, the server allows many users to access it at the same time by presenting each user with their own desktop session. By using workspaces instead, you also lessen your blast radius from an outage. Depending on your Remote Desktop Services deployment, an outage could offline all your administrators at once.

The shared services account is also a good account to locate certain AWS services, such as Amazon Chime (enterprise video conferencing), Amazon QuickSight (business intelligence tooling), and Amazon Route 53 (DNS). You can also share these services between environments and accounts. The master account should be reserved for command and control functions. It would be best not even to have a VPC in your master account. Eliminating the VPC will ensure that no servers are deployed there. One service that should be deployed to the master account rather than to the shared account is Route 53 and domain restrictions. Route 53 doesn't need any ancillary services to operate, and every account uses it, making this the only recommended candidate for the master account.

 A good practice for deploying DNS in AWS is to host the domain name registration in the master account (mydomain.com). Once that is set up, you can create subdomains for each account (dev.mydomain.com, test.mydomain.com). You can delegate authority for the subdomains in the master domain. The Route 53 subdomains will then become an authority for all hosts in their subdomains. Using this configuration allows you to implement DNS configuration easily for server deployments through Cloud-Formation, which cannot span accounts to enter DNS records.

Hopefully, you now see that the shared services account plays a critical role in your environment and makes maintaining security through consolidation easier. Next, we will cover another critical account, the logging account.

Logging account

The logging account or audit account, depending on your nomenclature, is the account that stores all the AWS Config and CloudTrail logs in your account structure. This account is one of the most important in your whole landing zone design. The sole purpose of this account is to protect the logs in a read-only fashion. This segmentation prevents anyone from manipulating them. The best way for an attacker to get away with their attack would be to cover their tracks. They would also want to cover up ongoing theft. The best way to do this is to erase the evidence of their access by manipulating these two services' log files. By creating the logging account, you create a safe haven for these logs where they cannot be manipulated.

In AWS, you can allow access to resources through several avenues. You can grant access to users, groups, and roles and trust specific AWS services. Trusting specific AWS services is a critical security component. For instance, this trust allows you to create S3 buckets that can *only* be accessed by AWS services. If you want to create a location that can only be read, you can create an AWS role that allows write access to the AWS Config and CloudTrail services (individually, not together). This control will allow only those services to write to the buckets. You can then create policies and roles for your users that only allow read access to those buckets. You can further protect those buckets by setting explicit "deny write" access rules that trump all allow actions for more security. If that is not enough, you can activate S3 versioning. This control will keep modified versions of files so you can always go back in time and see what the file looked like originally. This setting also prevents someone from permanently deleting files, and the previous versions will still be stored. Your logging account can become your impenetrable fortress of security. Well, at least an impenetrable hall of records to see when an attack happened, how the access was gained, and what was done during the attack. Adding a logging account is critical for your business and should be included in your landing zone deployment. Next, we will cover the sandbox account; although optional, it is a critical component.

Sandbox account

We have touched on the sandbox account twice before in this book, in Chapters 1 and 5, but it bears repeating here because the sandbox account is one of the most critical accounts for your company's innovation. One office I worked in had a sign on the wall that said, "Create something today, even if it sucks." This is my mantra, and I try to practice it every day. I end up trying many things; often they break and suck, but when they do not, it feels like magic, and something new and awesome is created. That is what the sandbox account is for. This is where the magic happens.

You cannot innovate if your staff is afraid to get in there and experiment and break things. However, it is perilous to test things in your other accounts, which is where the sandbox comes into play. This special account is segmented from the rest of your environment; it isn't part of the hub-and-spoke model with shared services. This isolation prevents any experiments from disrupting your daily operations or raising concerns about data leakage. The sandbox account is quite honestly the best way to move your company forward. Hopefully, you now see how important this often overlooked account is, and you incorporate it into your design.

We now have one last optional account to cover: the Payment Card Industry (PCI) account, which should be deployed if you are processing credit cards and need to store card data.

Payment card industry data security standard

For companies that need to meet the Payment Card Industry Data Security Standard (PCI-DSS or PCI), a special account configuration would be most advantageous. In PCI, the term *infectious data* refers to cardholder data (CHD), which contains critical credit card information such as card numbers, zip codes, and so on. PCI classifies this data as Category 1. Any system that stores, transmits, or processes cardholder data is a Category 1 system and is within the scope of a PCI audit. Category 1 systems can become infectious when other systems have unrestricted network access to those systems.

If you were to put your PCI Category 1 systems in with your production environment, it would increase the scope of your PCI audit and therefore increase your audit costs. If you are paying attention to what has been said about least privilege, you might wonder why putting a PCI Category 1 system in the production environment would increase the scope. Least privilege would ensure that those servers would be segmented through security groups and would not have access to PCI systems. Unfortunately, auditors will want you to prove that they do not have access to the servers. Proving a negative is not a pleasant experience. You must show that every production server that is not in the PCI scope has the proper security group rules to prevent access to CHD systems. If you have dozens or hundreds of servers in this account, it will become very costly and time-consuming.

The better solution is to create a separate PCI account to store Category 1 CHD systems. By creating another account to store these systems, you create a barrier between servers that is easier to prove and keeps your PCI scope contained. Congratulations, you have just decreased the cost of your audit significantly. I suggest taking this a step further to reduce expenses by deploying a new managed directory to run the environment. AWS offers managed Active Directory services that reduce the burden of management. AWS takes care of the updates and security patching; your company only needs to worry about the group policy and user controls. By creating a managed directory explicit for your PCI environment, you significantly reduce your audit scope. A separate directory accomplishes this by removing all the users, groups, and policies that are in your main corporate directory from the scope. This segmentation allows auditors to audit the controls and users explicitly for PCI account and server management. AWS account segmentation and managed directory services make it significantly cheaper to manage your PCI environment than you could ever do on-premises.

We have covered the additional required accounts, logging, and shared services, as well as the optional PCI and sandbox accounts and what they mean for your environment. Before we can move forward with deployment, we need to touch on how you can deploy your landing zone.

Landing Zone Deployment Methods

Many design concepts should be considered for a landing zone, but we will only cover the account structure here. There are a couple of ways to deploy a landing zone in AWS, depending on your needs and company size. Unless you are a small company, it makes sense to use the AWS Control Tower service to deploy your landing zone. Control Tower is a service that automates the deployment of AWS Landing Zone, which really isn't a service but a product, like software you would buy. For small companies, the AWS Landing Zone product might be too expensive to operate. You get little control over the base deployment to turn off some features that a smaller company might want. For instance, the AWS landing zone deployed by Control Tower uses highly available NAT gateways to all accounts. For a smaller company, it might not make sense to spend an additional $75 a month for two other gateways in the second and third availability zones.

Since most companies will probably be using Control Tower, we will not dive into the technical specifics of a landing zone deployment. If you wish to deploy a landing zone, there are several deployment packages on GitHub (*https://github.com*) that you can use or use as reference points. I would not recommend building your landing zone by hand without IaC. It will be very hard to maintain compliance or add new accounts if necessary. You should start with a base configuration found online in IaC and modify it based on your specific business needs.

Now that we have covered the landing zone, account structure, and deployment in depth, we can move on to the second critical component of your landing zone deployment, cloud governance.

Cloud Governance

Mentioning cloud governance is enough to send chills down the spine of an IT manager's back. It is the technology, people, and processes associated with your cloud operations. Typically, cloud governance means risk mitigations put in place that make doing your job in IT more difficult. Thankfully, the items that we will discuss here will not have a marked impact on your ability to complete work. They will, however, ensure that your environment stays secure. Since the infrastructure in AWS is so vast, and the ways to access it are plentiful, some controls need to be in place to ensure that your engineers and admins stay in their lanes.

We will not be diving too deeply into the realm of technical controls and service controls. Instead, we will focus on several higher-level items that need to be configured and selected that are of interest to the IT manager. Items such as AWS Support Plans, business continuity, and access and authorization can significantly affect the operations of your business. I recommend defining these cloud governance items before deployment of your landing zone and migration to create policies on how and when changes should be made. As with most items in the cloud, they need to be able to change and shift based on your company's current needs. These are not, nor should they be, set in stone. We will first look at AWS support, which is a vital service to have when something goes wrong. Often, it isn't addressed at the beginning of migration and ends up an afterthought. By addressing it first, you ensure that if something goes sideways, you will have the support you need.

AWS Support

AWS support falls into the process category of cloud governance. When something breaks, you follow a process or workflow to resolve the issue. When operating in the cloud, many of the items that would have been addressed internally, such as managing the hypervisor, are managed by AWS. This shift in responsibility means that you might need to involve AWS to resolve an issue. Without the proper level of support, your company may be left floundering, unable to resolve the issue on your own. Amazon offers different levels of support, based on the requirements of your business. The support runs from free (no support, only limit increases) to over $15,000 per month for Enterprise Support.[1] Support is not a flat fee, either. A base fee is charged (based on the level selected), and then an additional fee is charged (based on the amount of spend in each account). For Enterprise Support, the additional fee is based on an aggregate of all your account charges.

The question at this point in your migration is what kind of support your business needs. If you are a large enterprise, the question is very easy to answer. If you chose the hybrid account structure, you would have many accounts for your business units and environments. Since AWS charges for support by account for service levels lower than Enterprise, these charges could rack up quickly if you choose the Business tier. For instance, if you have 100 accounts and choose business-level support at $100 a month, you would spend nearly the same amount as Enterprise Support without the added benefits.

If you are a medium-sized organization, the question is a little harder to answer. You need to choose your support based on the workloads you are running and how vital their operations are to your business. Based on the criticality of the environment for a

---

1 For more information about support plans, visit the AWS website (*https://aws.amazon.com/premiumsupport/plans*).

medium-sized business, Enterprise Support probably makes sense. In the grand scheme of things, the cost of Enterprise Support for a medium-sized business will not be a significant expense compared to your resource consumption.

For smaller organizations, support gets even trickier. A small company will most likely not be consuming massive amounts of resources, and support will be a major part of the spend. Even if a small organization uses the environment-based account structure, it would still end up with six accounts that need support. For a small organization, a minimum of $600 a month could be a sizable amount of the overall spend. If you are a smaller organization, you may want to investigate using the Developer Support level for lower-level environments such as development and testing. However, the small amount of money that you would save is likely not worth the delays in support. The support SLAs for the Business level of support is significantly better, with less than one hour response time for a production system outage versus up to 12 hours for Developer Support.

The important part is to decide on your support level before you move resources into AWS. You do not want to run into an issue without this critical piece of cloud governance. You want your support in place when the accounts are rolled out, especially if you will move forward with Enterprise Support, which comes with a Technical Account Manager (TAM). The TAM is a technical point of contact that can assist with guidance and best practices for deployment into the cloud. Both can be a great resource to ensure that your environment is as healthy as it can be.

As part of the support exercise, create a policy stating when you will shift your support levels. It's unlikely that you would downgrade your level of support, but sometimes you will want to raise it. The big question is *when* you should upgrade to Enterprise Support. After all, $15,000 a month is a large nut to crack if you have a smaller infrastructure. As with most critical things in a business such as security, the question you should probably ask is how much it will cost not to have it. The adage "an ounce of prevention is worth a pound of cure" is a good yardstick to follow with leveling up to Enterprise Support. If your workloads are critical to your business and having those offline for any amount of time will cost you significantly more than $15,000, then go for Enterprise Support.

Region Management

The AWS regions all around the globe are a benefit and potentially a risk to your company if not properly managed. All regions launched prior to 2019 are enabled by default. This default means that engineers can spin up resources in any region around the globe, even if you do not want them to. You want to avoid a governance risk if you have data sovereignty and regulatory concerns. Having all regions available can also pose a risk for data leakage. Without control of the regions that are being used, it is possible for a bad actor that has access to AWS to deploy resources that may not be discovered if stored in an obscure region.

Region management should be a cloud governance item that is put in place with the deployment of your landing zone. It should be limited to only the regions required for the operation of your business. The newest regions are disabled by default, and you do not need to take any action to account for these. Unfortunately, the controls that are in place for new regions are not available for the older regions that were deployed by AWS before 2019. Those regions require you to implement controls in IAM to prevent access to them.[2]

Another cloud governance item that should be created before migration is the controls and criteria governing how new regions are enabled to meet changing business objectives. At some point in time, your business may very well require the use of additional regions that were not activated as part of your initial migration. Establishing the criteria and controls necessary to expand regions safely at the outset is a vital governance action. You do not want your business to have region sprawl any more than you want server sprawl. By establishing new regions, you start to duplicate expenses for items such as NAT gateways and security controls. Your business controls for region expansion should consider the costs and increased risk of region sprawl.

 Having a strong landing zone deployment in place will help lessen region-sprawl risk. However, your blast radius continues to increase with each region.

Some items that may be indicators for region expansion are:

- Increased business continuity capabilities
- Business expansion into new regions
- New data sovereignty concerns
- Customer latency issues

These items are just some potential triggers that could be part of your expansion controls. There are potentially others, but these items probably cover the requirements for most companies. I would recommend a policy that details these triggers and what approvals, such as security, should be involved.

---

2 There are other ways and tools to ensure that resources are not created in other regions that are outside the scope of this book.

Account Management

Now that we have covered how to add governance for region controls, we will move on to account management governance. We talked about account structure in "Landing Zone" on page 164. However, this is not the only item regarding accounts that needs to be addressed at this point in your migration. There are a couple of account governance items that need to be discussed: consolidated billing and root account management. Without these governance items in place, you can run into some billing and security issues. The concept of creating an account and having it align to a structure are key components to your landing zone. However, along with those structural actions, you need corresponding governance controls to maintain your security posture and cost controls.

Consolidated billing

Consolidated billing is an AWS capability that allows a company to roll account bills into a central account called a *master payer*. Consolidated billing makes paying your AWS bill significantly easier because it acts as a single point of contact for your finance team. Most companies will want to activate consolidated billing across the entirety of their estate. However, some organizations, primarily very large companies, may want to have more than one consolidated billing account.

One of the primary reasons for more than one billing account is that a company is multinational and set up with multiple legal entities around the globe. Whether you have more than one billing account is ultimately determined by how your company splits apart its finances. If your company has separate profit and loss (P&L) for each entity, then it may make sense to have multiple master payer accounts. The business unit accounts under that legal entity would roll into each of their respective master payer accounts. This structure would simplify the finance controls and contain them within each entity. The alternative would be to have one master payer set up under the main corporate entity. The drawback to this approach is that the main corporate entity would have to charge the legal entities around the globe for the consumption of resources.

As you can see, having one master payer with global entities could be a significantly larger amount of effort. This effect would most likely be more work for the finance team than the multiple master payer model would be. One item that you forgo when using the multiple master account structure is the savings you get from some services based on consumption. AWS prices services such as S3 and data transfer on a graduated scale. If you use more, you pay less per gigabyte as your consumption rises. When you break your spending into multiple master payer accounts, you segment your consumption and your savings. People's salaries are most likely your company's largest expense, and saving effort for your finance teams probably outweighs the savings on these services.

Using multiple master payer accounts can also complicate the use of an Enterprise Discount Program (EDP). The EDP is a program in which companies guarantee a certain amount of AWS spend and will prepay to receive a discount on that consumption. When you have multiple master payer accounts, you would need more than one EDP, which increases the burden on your legal teams around the globe. Each of these legal entities will have to negotiate and sign its EDP contracts.

 The EDP program is only available for AWS customers that spend more than $1 million a year on services.

For small, medium, and even large corporations that do not have these multinational entity concerns, the answer is much less complicated. For the companies that fall into this category, your master payer account is all that is necessary. You may want to sketch a brief policy if it becomes necessary to split your master payers and describe what the triggers for that split may look like. I would say that of all the items listed here, creating new master payer accounts will be highly improbable.

Root account management

You would think that securing and maintaining your root accounts would be an obvious practice. Unfortunately, if you google "AWS root credentials compromised," you will find link after link of people saying their account was compromised. Each AWS account that we discussed will have a root account. Your root AWS accounts have access to everything in the account and have the power to delete the account itself. The root account can also disable other users, groups, and roles. With the right know-how, an attacker could disable your ability to log on to the account to stop them. You could say that your root account is the one ring to rule them all.

There are primarily four ways in which you can become a victim of root account compromise:

1. The exposure of root access keys

2. Password compromise by an internal bad actor

3. brute-forcing the password

4. failure to follow best practice and create access keys for your root user.

All four can be easily avoided if you secure your root account properly. The last thing you want is your company to be listed in any of those Google search results.

The first thing that should be done when setting up your landing zone is the creation of a backup administrator account. Once you create this account, you should no longer require the use of your root account. Your root account should not be used *ever* once the backup administrator is created. The next step in securing your root accounts is to create a hardened password. AWS IAM has a maximum password length of 128 characters. Do you need your root password to be that long? Probably not, but I use 32 to 64 characters and a password manager to store it. You do not want your password to be brute-forced; making it long and complex is the best way to do that. You do not want anyone memorizing it either.

> There are 10 tasks that always require access to the AWS root account, such as changing the AWS support plan or closing the account. You can find a complete list online (*https://oreil.ly/UzeRH*).

The next step is to secure your root account with a physical multi-factor authentication (MFA) device. I am a personal fan of the Yubico YubiKey, which is very easy to use and is highly reliable. I deployed more than 6,000 of them for a banking application, and as part of my testing, I sent them through the washing machine multiple times without issue (not by design but great validation nonetheless). It is very important to have a physical device and not just a software token, because a physical device can be locked up in a safe or vault, adding another layer of protection. By implementing a physical MFA device, you prevent two potential attacks: (1) brute-force attacks, which, even if a hacker were to guess your password would not yield the physical MFA device; and (2) the internal bad actor. By implementing a physical MFA device, even the bad actor would not be able to gain access to your root account.

The final piece for securing your root accounts is never to create access keys for the root account. Just as you do not want people logging on to the console, you also do not want them logging in through the command-line interface or programmatically by using the root access key credentials. You want to implement least privilege in AWS, and allowing the root account to have access keys to the environment programmatically is the opposite of least privilege. To help drive the root security point home, let us look at three scenarios in which people's accounts were compromised.

Scenario 6-1

Tonya got a frantic call from the CIO this morning. Their website was under a distributed denial of service (DDoS) attack, and customers couldn't access the site. Tonya's company provides online storage for customers' documents. When Tonya arrived at work, she logged on to the AWS console to see how hard their servers were being hit and whether there was any way she could scale them to absorb the load. Upon logging on to the console, she saw a message in one of the EC2 instance tags that said they needed to pay a ransom of $200,000 to stop the DDoS attack. Tonya immediately let the CIO know what was going on and changed the root user password to resecure the account. Tonya checked the servers, and everything looked OK; the private keys to log on to the servers were not in AWS, so the attacker had no way to log on to them. The CIO talked to the CEO, and they decided that since they had changed the root user password, the account was safe and they were not going to pay the ransom. Later that day, Tonya and all the engineers lost access to the AWS console again. This time, the site went offline. By the end of the day, Tonya's entire AWS estate was obliterated, and the company was forced to file for bankruptcy and was dissolved.

There are a number of things that Tonya's company didn't do right in this scenario. The obvious one, which started the whole incident, is that the root account was not protected by MFA and could be brute-forced. If MFA had been implemented, the attack wouldn't have been possible, even if the password had been discovered. The root account should always be MFA-activated. The second mistake is that they were obviously using the root account as the password, which was easy to guess so that administrators could easily remember it. Using the root account for daily activities is also against best practice in AWS. The final death blow to Tonya's company wasn't the fact that they didn't pay the ransom but that they didn't do any forensics to see immediately what the attackers had done. If they had done so, they would have seen how the attackers gained access and what changes were made.

If you follow the guidance in this chapter, you won't make the mistakes that Tonya's company made. In addition, if your accounts were somehow compromised, your proper account structure and logging account would give you the ability to perform proper forensics and investigate what was done. You would be able to see whether the attacker created another IAM user as a back door to continue gaining access even after you changed the access keys. Let's look at another scenario about how your account could be compromised.

Scenario 6-2

Betty's company recently started working in AWS. It runs an open source project and has a paid subscription plan for enterprise customers that wish to use its product commercially. To allow access to its AWS environment, it created access keys for the root account so it could get started right away. It has a client that is pushing for it to support AWS, and that client is a major source of revenue for it. For the first phase of support in AWS, the company released an open source package to deploy a few AWS components automatically, based on custom configurations. About two weeks after the release of the new tool, it started getting billing alarms in AWS stating that it had spent over $15,000. They were quite concerned, because they were running only two servers in AWS at the time.

Unfortunately, this scenario happens quite a bit. People will inadvertently check in code with access keys embedded in it without obfuscating them first. Hackers scan sites like GitHub for AWS access keys to exploit. They use these keys to create botnets or ransom your infrastructure. Therefore, it is vital not to create access keys for your root account. If these keys were to escape your environment, it would expose all your infrastructure to attackers. The first step that Betty should have taken was to create a new user with only the permissions required and save the root account for emergency use only.

Scenario 6-3

Maria works as the CIO of a large US firm that performs tax services for the public. The firm runs its call center on AWS Connect. Last week, it had to let an engineer in the cloud department go for poor work performance. When Maria was driving in to work today, she received a frantic call from the manager of her cloud team. It appears that the AWS account that hosted their Connect call center is gone. They cannot log on with the root credentials nor with those of any other users. The whole call center is offline, and no customers can call in for support or to ask questions. The tax deadline is nearing, and it is Maria's company's busiest time. They cannot afford to be offline. They later realized that the engineer they let go had the AWS root credentials and was able to commandeer their account.

One would think that with the number of stories floating around the web about incidents like this one that people would make sure this doesn't occur. Just like the other scenarios, this is completely avoidable. Maria's cloud team should never have been using the root account for any operations, and the engineer should not have had access to the password. They also should have been using MFA, so if someone did have the password, they still would not have gotten access.

Hopefully, these scenarios demonstrate, in a very real way, the risks involved with managing your AWS root accounts. Hopefully, you address them properly and promptly with the deployment of your landing zone. Next, we will cover some additional access and authorization governance items that will further reduce your risk of operating in AWS. These access and authorization controls will ensure that your environment stays secure by reducing the overall complexity of IAM controls.

Access and Authorization

We covered why you need to secure your root accounts, but now it is time to dive into how to protect the rest of your accounts in AWS. There are two key items that I want to cover to achieve that. The first is a single sign-on, and the second is IAM user accounts. These two key cloud governance items will ensure the long-term security of your AWS environment. We will cover when to use them and when not to use them.

We will also detail the reasons for these contexts so you can gain a strong understanding of their importance. In the end, you should have a solid plan forward as well as a policy to ensure that your environment is secured.

Single sign-on by federation

You can probably remember a time when there weren't any single sign-on capabilities in any of your applications. Managing security in this environment was a total nightmare. You had to create users in a bunch of disparate systems, the password criteria settings were never the same, and your users had multiple accounts and passwords to manage. You do not want to repeat this pattern in AWS; implement account federation instead. Your AWS estate will hold all your sensitive infrastructure. The last thing you would want to do is create separate IAM user accounts for your administrators. You would be creating yet another set of accounts for you and your administrators to manage.

By implementing SAML Federation, you have one directory to control the access your administrators have and one account to disable when they leave the company. The most common way to achieve this in AWS is to create an IAM identity provider that uses Security Assertion Markup Language (SAML) authentication against your directory. There are several ways to do this, but the most common pattern I have seen is the implementation of Active Directory federation through Active Directory Federation Services (ADFS), Okta, SailPoint, and more. Alternatively, for organizations that use Google Suite, Google single sign-on (SSO) capabilities are available. Both solutions provide the single sign-on capabilities that your organization should be looking for to secure your environment.

By using federation and single sign-on, you also decrease the learning curve for the staff that provisions access in your environment. They will use the same tooling they have in the past. For example, in a company that is using Active Directory, your team would create user groups that correlate with AWS roles. Let us say that you have a built-in role in AWS that allows the administration of your Amazon Chime configuration, which is a conferencing tool like WebEx. You would then have a group in Active Directory that represents this role. To grant Chime administrative access, all that would be necessary is to add the required administrator to that Chime group in Active Directory. When the user accesses the login portal, they will be represented with the Chime role for the correct AWS account. If you use IAM users and groups, all management actions would need to be performed in AWS and require additional training.

As a cloud governance item, you will want to construct a policy that states that all administrator, operator, and developer access is to be provided by federation. The policy should specifically state that IAM user accounts will not be used for these purposes. The policy should also contain the contexts in which you should include the instances in which you would use IAM user accounts, which we will detail in the next section.

IAM user accounts

Federated account access is the preferred method for administrators to access the AWS console and CLI. Still, there are situations in which you will want to create an IAM user, but they should be used sparingly, primarily for the reasons we just discussed in "Single sign-on by federation" on page 180. The two situations I recommend using an IAM user for are when you need a service account for a third-party tool, and when you create the backup root account, which we discussed in "Root account management" on page 176.

Many third-party tools are available to supplement and augment AWS capabilities. Many of these tools help with cloud governance, deployment, security, and reserved instance recommendations. These services will need access to your environment to perform the actions that you want to supplement. Creating a user in your directory service would not be the best method for these types of services due to the complexity of receiving long-term (90-day) access keys. This situation would be a good use case to create a user account specifically for the tooling and assign the appropriate role to that user. The primary method that third-party services use to connect to your AWS account is by access keys. By creating an IAM user, you give yourself a bit more control over how these accounts can access AWS. When you create an account, adding a password is optional. By not creating a password, you disallow the user from accessing the AWS console, forcing only API access to your account. Even without a password, you can create the required access keys for the user's account. These access keys are then used by the third-party service to perform its work.

Although we have already covered the need for a backup root account to protect your master root account, I do want to make one more point around IAM policy as you are crafting it. Because IAM users are a critical part of cloud governance, you will want to define the reasons for using an IAM user, such as for connecting to a third-party service we just covered. It's also important to define whether they are authorized to log on to the console. You want to make sure that the number of IAM users you have stays low. User sprawl increases risk and management, and a well-defined cloud governance policy will ensure that the number of accounts is kept to a minimum.

Key Management Service

The AWS Key Management Service (KMS) is the service that creates and manages encryption keys for your company. By default, AWS creates a master customer key that can be used in most of the services. You can use this key, but it would be better to create new keys to help with the blast radius in case of key compromise. If you create more KMS keys, you protect yourself on two fronts: key compromise and blast radius due to key access. The greater your key segmentation, the more refined the access you can grant to those keys, lessening exposure. In addition, the more keys you use, the fewer systems will be affected by any one key compromise. As a cloud governance item, establishing the KMS key controls and policy during landing zone construction will save you from needing to change keys later on.

If you use the default key to encrypt everything and that key is somehow compromised, you have potentially exposed all of your data. This exposure would occur even if you created another key and still used it across all your estate. At the time of writing, KMS keys cost $1 in the us-east-1 region. At this price point, it makes sense to break up encryption in your environment to create more segmentation and decrease your blast radius for this type of compromise. How you break up your infrastructure depends on the size of your company and which account structure you have selected to use. For instance, if you are a small company, and you have selected an environment-based account approach, then it would make sense to create at least one KMS key for each account. This deployment type is very cost-effective yet offers a good deal of segmentation. If you have a larger organization, you could use a per-account KMS key for all of the business units, or even down to hybrid account structure.

Using an account-based KMS key structure helps minimize the blast radius for key compromise, but it can cause another problem. When you create keys based on account, all the engineers and developers need access to that account key. Now you have a potential issue with blast radius due to the expanded scope of employees who have access. If you cannot trust your employees, then who can you trust? Unfortunately, there are bad eggs out there who are the exception to the rule and do something malicious. Your engineers' account might also be compromised, and the bad actor would have access to your keys. It is these one-off situations that you need to protect yourself from. It may make sense for larger organizations to break down their KMS keys further to segment and protect the company as much as needed. You may want to make it a policy to segment your encryption by the development team, or potentially by the application. This level of segmentation will allow you to constrain the access to those keys further and reduce your attack footprint.

Regulated companies may also want to add a component to their KMS governance policy to address specific workloads. For instance, if you must meet PCI compliance, you may want to detail how those specific workloads are all encrypted individually with their KMS keys. This policy will allow you to severely limit the blast radius for key exposure and key compromise. It makes sense to use this approach for all the regulatory requirements such as Health Insurance Portability and Accountability Act (HIPAA) and Gramm-Leach-Bliley Act (GLBA). Again, a well-crafted cloud governance policy early in the process will save you from the significant work of trying to rectify it later.

Business Continuity

Business continuity is the last cloud governance item that we will discuss. As we touched on in "Disaster Recovery/Business Continuity" on page 31, the major change that you should address during migration is the mindset change from disaster recovery to business continuity (BC). To achieve the desired state, it becomes critical to create some BC governance controls to control the way applications are deployed in AWS. Your business units and engineers will then use these BC governance controls to determine how each of your applications are deployed to AWS.

Not all applications can be adapted to a higher level of BC. Legacy applications can be very difficult to change into a highly available design. These same applications might not have an adequate return on investment to refactor, either. On the other hand, having a highly available application increases the cost of operation. Not all applications require a higher level of availability; therefore, those costs are unnecessary.

Because of the possible deficiencies that some applications may have, and the lack of business necessity, it becomes prudent to construct BC governance using a tiered approach. This isn't new to AWS and the cloud. The concept has been around for some time on-premises. I recommend the bronze, silver, gold, and platinum approach to BC. Although this approach is not sexy or new (it's been around on-premises for years), highly effective constructs rarely are. These four tiers should cover nearly all of your BC needs. They will, however, have very different designs based on the new capabilities at your disposal in AWS. We will now cover the recommended configurations for each of these tiers, which are primarily geared toward legacy-type applications. Cloud-native applications would look different, but legacy applications are what you will be migrating.

Bronze

In the bronze tier, you won't have any business continuity. This tier is reserved for applications that have no critical business impact and are safe to be brought back online. The critical difference that happens in AWS as opposed to on-premises at the bronze tier is that in the event of an AZ failure, at least one if not more AZs are available to you to restart the system in. To have that level of redundancy in AWS, you will need to take snapshots of the server. You can do this with DLM, custom scripts, or manually if changes do not occur often. EBS snapshots are stored in S3, and just like everything else in S3, they are replicated to the other availability zones. This replication allows your staff to easily restore a snapshot of the server to a volume in another AZ and bring that server online. What would have taken a long time on-premises can be quite short in AWS. This timeline depends on the level of workload for your staff at the time of the event. This tier is the cheapest method of recovery available in AWS.

Legacy applications, such as those written in Visual Basic, will fall into the bronze tier due to their limited capabilities.

Silver

Now that we have covered the basics, let us cover applications that have some sort of business impact and need to be online faster than bronze. It is at the silver tier in AWS where you move from DR to BC. Because of the multi-AZ capabilities of AWS, the silver tier introduces multi-AZ HA capabilities. In this tier, database servers would operate in an active/passive mode across two AZs. The application servers and web servers would exist in at least two AZs fronted by a load balancer in an active/active configuration. This design can withstand the failure of one AZ and automatically failover to a second AZ with no disruption.

Failure without disruption is based on the technology used to replicate and failover the database tier.

Gold

In the gold tier, we are explicitly talking about applications that have a significant impact on your business. These are applications that not only need to survive an AZ failure but also the failure of a complete region. In this tier, you can use AWS native technologies such as region copy and DMS to replicate data from one region to another. In the gold configuration, servers are made HA, using the same methods as the silver tier. Then the servers are replicated using snapshots and cross-region copy to another region. The snapshots allow a cold image of the servers to be available in the event of a complete region failure. These servers would be restored from the snapshots before resuming operations. For the database tier, the databases could be replicated from one region to another by using DMS. The DMS not only can replicate servers for migration, but it can also be used as a long-term replication tool. The benefit of using DMS is that it replicates asynchronously and does not affect the performance of the production environment. DMS allows your database to remain in lockstep with the primary region; this allows the database to be considered hot and readily available for use.

Most applications will fall into the gold tier of business continuity.

Platinum

In AWS, the pinnacle of business continuity is the platinum tier. In this tier, all servers and databases are replicated and operating in more than one region at the same time. This tier is the most expensive and should only be used for the business-critical servers that always need to be available. Unfortunately, many applications cannot support this level of redundancy without some modifications. At the platinum tier, servers would be deployed with multi-AZ configurations in multiple regions and balanced by Route 53 DNS based on geolocation or latency. This configuration is not inherently complicated, because most applications can deal with this type of deployment. However, it gets trickier with the multiregion database implementation. There are many ways to solve this problem, but they are much too technical for this book. The database tier will most likely be the limiting factor for the platinum level.

 Only the most critical applications will require the platinum tier and may be limited due to technical constraints. Most often, an application may require significant code changes to be able to handle this level of availability.

Wrapping It Up

When you address the key cloud governance and landing zone issues we discussed in this chapter, you add strength to your base deployment, and you ensure that your initial migrations are successful. The proper cloud governance ensures that you do not have to rework designs around security and compliance issues. At this point, the prework for your migration is complete, and your team can start deploying the landing zone in preparation for migration. Many more items must be discussed for cloud governance, but those discussed here should give you a decent start on the process.

In Chapter 7, we will cover migration planning, which can be done in tandem with the deployment of your landing zone. We will cover technology blocker analysis, migration planning, and how to categorize your applications by using the seven Rs method. Migration planning accounts for the second-largest component of your migration to AWS.

Planning Your Migration

Well, we have finally made it to planning your migration. We have covered all the required preliminary work and can now get to the meat of the process. Migration planning will consume a lot of the information you have already gathered as part of your discovery process, which we covered in Chapter 3. The discovery information not only forms the rough version of your plan, but also helps you maintain the constraints between dependencies as you refine your plan. However, before we can start, we need to review a few things, such as what kind of methodologies to use for the plan, plus blockers and changes in your business that have occurred since you started the overall process. Once we address these items, we can move forward with developing a comprehensive migration plan. To start the process, let's look at what types of companies need a plan.

Who Needs a Plan

Not every migration needs a plan. Let me rephrase: not every migration needs a *documented* plan. If you are a small business and have only a handful of servers, you can probably create a plan in your head. If you do not fall into the small-business category, you will need a migration plan. The larger your estate, the more complex your plan becomes. Unfortunately, the complexity is not linear, either. With the increase in application sprawl, you will experience exponential growth in complexity. The more applications you have, the greater the level of interconnectivity between them. You will also have more teams to account for in a larger organization, which is another reason having a plan is critical.

It is common for a very large migration to have multiple iterations of a plan. You should not consider your plan as set in stone, either. There needs to be a certain amount of flexibility in your plan, and it should be considered somewhat agile. You never know when something unexpected will happen, such as an application update that needs to take precedence over migrating it. There are other potential disruptions as well. Critical staff leaving a department, funding issues, and the occasional reorganization are just some potential issues you might face. You need to be flexible to adapt to these changes. Since the possibility exists that you can't be completely agile, we need to discuss what types of plans you can use, and we will cover those next.

Agile, Waterfall, or Combination Plan

There is a lot of talk in the migration world about using agile methodologies to migrate your workloads to the cloud. To be clear, we are specifically talking about the migration plan and execution at this point. We will cover development methodologies later in this chapter. Unfortunately, you can only be partially agile with your migration due to dependencies, and ultimately, a lot of waterfall might be included in your migration. A waterfall plan flows in a predetermined and unmovable path, just like a waterfall in a stream. You must progress from A to B to C before you can get to D. Your migration might require a predetermined path for certain applications. For instance, Active Directory, Chef, file servers, and other highly shared components need to be moved over first, because many or all of your applications depend on them. You may also use some form of waterfall methodologies in your migration in application subsets, due to a smaller interdependence within that application cluster. Databases are also often tightly coupled to applications, causing a dependency that cannot be migrated out of order. Ultimately, you will end up with an *agile waterfall* or a combination of both types. Sections of your plan will need to be sequential but have many surrounding pieces that are agile. Be as agile as possible, but do not be obstinate and think you can make the whole migration agile.

You will want to plan your migration in sprints. Although a *sprint* is an agile term meaning a time-boxed level of work effort, nothing says you can't put a waterfall effort in a sprint. Waterfall sprints become fixed and can't be moved, whereas an agile workload sprint can be moved at will.

It doesn't matter whether a sprint will contain an agile or waterfall work effort. It is important to set the sprint length properly for your migration. I have found that a sprint size of two weeks works well for most applications. Some small applications could be completed in a week's time frame, but most will require two. In one project I worked on, the project manager was attempting to create one-week sprints. This length of sprint might make sense with a development team working on small application modifications and feature requests. When migrating to AWS, a one-week sprint does not afford enough time to complete the required amount of work for most applications. Depending on how complex your applications are, you might need three or four weeks, but in this circumstance, you can couple two two-week sprints and achieve the same effect without overcomplicating the migration of smaller apps.

I like to make a sprint equal to the time it takes to move an application in its entirety. You can break an application down further into the individual pieces and have shorter sprints. Still, I find that shorter sprints add a bit of management overhead that people are not ready to absorb. Besides, most teams are not used to running in an agile fashion. They can get overwhelmed with the level of management required for smaller sprints. When it comes to migration, there is no *right* way to split up your work (even though there are probably plenty of people who will tell you otherwise). You need to determine what your team can work with and the level of management overhead you can absorb.

If you are working with a consulting firm, the process will be different. It will be the one running the project with its project managers and engineering staff. It will use its methods, and sprint lengths will be based on its process. Its teams will be much more coordinated and used to the work involved with migrating, because they do it so frequently. Although consulting firms can be more effective at migrating you to AWS, remember the risks I talked about in "Contractors and consulting" on page 60. You must ensure that you create the proper documentation to take the work over after they have walked out of the building.

Preplanning

Several components go into the migration planning phase. The bulk of your time will be spent evaluating the applications and determining which method of migration, or lack of migration, you will use. Amazon uses a specific methodology called the *seven Rs* that we will touch on a bit later in greater detail. The rest of the process will be dedicated to a bit of preplanning that occurs. You will need to address three precursor items before the planning portion. First, it is important to review your infrastructure and company to determine whether there are any technology or business blockers. Second, once that is complete, you move into selecting methodologies for development. Third, the last item before planning is selecting the tooling that you will use to do the workload migrations. When you complete these three items, we finally move into migration planning.

Blocker Analysis

Even though we have put much effort into crafting a great migration story, built a business case, made a thorough discovery on your infrastructure, and addressed operational readiness, a few technical and business blockers will interrupt your migration. We will address a few technical blockers, such as outdated and unsupported operating systems. From there, we will cover a few business blockers that might have come up since you started your migration, such as mergers and acquisitions. There are not that many, and it will not take much effort, but addressing these blockers is important nonetheless. With each step, we refine the process a little more and get closer and closer to landing on the moon. At this point, you have already blasted into space. Let us look at some technology blockers first.

 One thing that I want to make sure to say is that it is OK to leave something behind on-premises. Sometimes it just makes sense if the blocker is too costly to rectify. Having all of your infrastructure in the cloud is great, but it isn't always practical.

Technology Blockers

In Chapter 3 we talked about discovering your workloads and how you locate your systems and applications. If your company has been around for a while, there is a high probability that you have some legacy technology that was not discovered in the initial discovery process. Now is the time to put a final point on the discovery and determine whether any technology blockers can cause an issue during your migration. These blockers will boil down to three categories: unsupported and outdated operating systems, and unsupported hardware. We will cover these in more depth in the next sections.

Unsupported and outdated operating systems

You may run into some operating systems in your environment that are not supported by AWS. These operating systems (OS) are different from ones that are unsupported by the vendor. In this case, the OS is not supported by AWS and cannot run. The primary cases that I have seen are the Solaris operating system or macOS (if you had an old Apple server hiding somewhere). These operating systems are unique in that they run on x86 hardware, which might give you the impression that you could run it on AWS, but the drivers needed to support the virtualized hardware, such as the network and disk controller, are not available and would be a critical blocker to running it on AWS.

Unfortunately, the applications that run on these servers will need to be ported and recompiled, repurchased, or potentially refactored. To be able to recompile, you need to own the source code and have the capabilities to make that kind of change within your team. If you do not own the source code, then you are at the mercy of the vendor. If the vendor still exists, there may be a possibility of converting your license from Solaris to Linux to enable you to move the application to AWS. If the vendor for the software no longer exists, then you have little recourse other than leaving the server as is on-premises or purchasing a compatible replacement tool.

Beyond some unsupported operating systems, migrations often run into problems with outdated operating systems as well. Almost every migration that I have been a part of has had some form of outdated operating system running on-premises. You could have Windows 2003 somewhere in your environment, or maybe an outdated version of Red Hat. It does not matter what vendor it comes from; if it is unsupported, it is a risk to your migration. Without correcting this issue, you do not receive security updates and critical patches for those operating systems. These bugs and security flaws are significant business risks, even if they are only on one server. After all, a chain is only as strong as its weakest link, and you could have a paper clip in your chain depending on the issues with the operating system. Before you migrate to AWS, you will want to address these issues.

Sometimes the software that runs on an outdated operating system cannot run on a newer version of the OS. Although this may seem like a dead end, all hope is not lost. Some tools can package up your application and make it compatible with newer operating systems. One such tool is part of the End of Support Migration Program (EMP) at AWS. The tool is an Application Compatibility Packaging solution. This tooling allows you to package a legacy application into a container to run it on a new operating system. The term *container* in this context is not the same containerization referred to in the Docker technology. It is just another case of technology reusing a naming convention. If you are familiar with Microsoft App-V and VMware ThinApp, the concepts are very similar. An *application emulation bubble* might be a better term. This packaging technology allows you to bridge the gap between the time you migrate and the point in time at which you have to replace the application while still maintaining security and patching of the OS.

 You may be tempted to move outdated operating systems to the cloud since you can bolster your security model in AWS. Avoid falling into this trap. Although you can increase segmentation, you still cannot remove the flaws. You only make them harder to access.

Unsupported hardware

The second major technology blocker that you will run into while migrating to AWS is incompatible hardware. At this point, most of the world is probably running on x86 hardware. However, there are still significant portions that run on mainframes, midframes, and other RISC CPU–based hardware. These types of hardware are not supported in AWS, and alternatives will have to be sought out to replace them or leave them on-premises.

One of the concerns about leaving them on-premises, particularly for mainframes, is that usually the ancillary systems cannot move as well.[1] Many ancillary systems, meaning any applications that are required to talk to mainframes, need low latency to perform their work, and the round-trip time to and from AWS is too long to be

---

1 Mainframe migration has a very different process than migrating typical IT workloads and is outside the scope of this book.

practical for your business. Your company then sees a large and most likely business-critical chunk of your infrastructure left behind. The ultimate impact can be quite negative, because these critical systems then become less agile than the rest of your applications. The mainframe, in effect, becomes a massive anchor holding your business back. The decision to leave your mainframe alone and not refactor it to a more cloud-friendly environment can have a major impact on your overall business long-term. This decision should be given the proper amount of thought and should not be taken lightly.

Business Blockers

When you started your migration process, you were operating under a set of business assumptions. These assumptions did not preclude you from moving to the cloud and are why you began the process in the first place. Since you began the migration process, several months may have passed, and business objectives and the assumptions around its operations might have shifted. At this point in the process, you will want to reevaluate these assumptions and determine whether any potential business blockers need to be addressed. You will want to address them now or build them into your migration plan.

Only a few blockers will pop up now. Some of these items might be very sensitive, such as mergers, acquisitions, and divestitures. In contrast, others are just a shift in priorities and objectives caused by major bugs or competitive needs. In addition to mergers and acquisitions (M&A) activities, we will cover changes in management and priority shifts. These major categories involve several subcomponents such as divestitures for M&A or vertical management changes that can affect your migration plan. We will cover these individually in detail and demonstrate how they may affect your schedule and how to compensate for them.

M&A activities

Mergers and acquisitions can affect your migration plans significantly. Unfortunately, depending on your position in the company, you may not always be privy to M&A activities until the later stages in the process (or potentially after the deal has closed). Consuming an entire IT staff and infrastructure can have an enormous impact on your migration timeline and costs, depending on the source state of the acquired company. If the company you have just purchased is in AWS, you are in luck, because the impact is not as significant. If the company's estate is on-premises, your entire migration plan might shift in favor of moving the acquired resources first, with your existing estate taking a back seat in the process. If you do have to consume on-premises estate, you would have to start a discovery process on the infrastructure to determine what is there and what your run rate would look like. You will not have to build a new business case, but as you learned in Chapter 3, you cannot properly create a plan without the details contained in the discovery.

Let us look at the items that you would need to address if you acquired a company that was already in AWS. When you consume an existing AWS account, the primary changes will be the master payer, alignment to your governance controls, and any modifications to the federated access to the AWS accounts. If you have been following along and following best practices, then the consumption of AWS accounts and alignment to your controls should not be an overwhelming amount of work. If your teams have been following best practices, the items that need to be implemented to align the accounts are already programmed in IaC and can be readily deployed. Since the landing zone controls and governance that we discussed in Chapter 6 are the bulk of the items needed, you should be in the process of deploying them now or have already completed them. The two things that your team will have to do manually is switch the master payer account to your master payer and configure tagging on existing resources in the consumed accounts. These two items ensure that the resources are properly paid for, there is no interruption in service, and the resources are properly charged back to the relevant business units.

 If the company being purchased is a divestiture, additional work will need to be done for access controls and your directory service. Since the users that operated and consumed the resources in the AWS accounts were in the selling entity's directory, you will have to migrate those users and transform the permissions of the access controls to new users in your directory. This work can significantly add to the migration timeline. It doesn't matter whether the infrastructure is on-premises or in AWS; the level of effort is the same.

On the other hand, if you are the company being purchased, the news could be awesome or a total disaster for your existing planning. If the acquiring company is not in AWS, the probability of your migration going forward is probably low. You most likely will have new management, and it might want to start over at the business case and make its own decision about the process. If it is already in AWS, the news is probably good, and it will be much more receptive to your plan and existing documentation because of its own experience. Ultimately, either way, there will be a high level of disruption to your existing thoughts on migration, governance, landing zone, federation, and a whole host of other items if your company is being purchased. Outside of the discovery and business case, much of the work will need to be reviewed and adjusted to compensate for the corporate changes.

Divestitures

In a divestiture, or when your company sells off a business unit, the impact on your migration will not be very large. It will probably make migrating easier than before because there will be fewer workloads to move. The complication that divestitures create is in the retention of on-premises resources. When a part of your company is sold off, part of the contract details how long the purchasing company has to move the relevant resources to its ecosystem. These contractual obligations can affect your burn-down, as we discussed in Figure 4-12. Depending on how your migration timeline aligns with the divestiture timeline, you could end up having to leave services and equipment on-premises longer than you expected.

The other issue that can arise from divestiture is that some of your staff might be moving to the new company. It would not be unheard of for IT staff to be divided up with the sale of a portion of the company. A purchasing company will want to minimize the impact that tribal IT knowledge would have on the acquisition. This impact can be greater with a larger number of internally developed applications. If your company has mostly COTS applications, this risk is minimized for the purchasing company. If staff will be changing companies, you will need to keep this in mind when adjusting your timeline for migration. As we discussed in Chapter 4 in "Estimating Your Timeline" on page 102, you should recompute the amount of work that your new and reduced team can perform based on its skill set. After you can recalculate the capabilities of your reduced team, you can adjust your timeline.

Changes in management

Finally, we arrive at changes in management. When there are shifts in management at a company, there is always disruption. The old managers are out, and the new managers are in, and they want to make a name for themselves. Unfortunately, when they come in, the first thing that they want to do is make a bunch of changes. These changes are not necessarily bad. Often companies can become stale, and a fresh outside look can inject new life into a company. Other times, changes can just be for the sake of not doing it like the last guy, and these changes are often a waste of everyone's effort. In the following sections, we will cover vertical management changes (such as in your management) and horizontal changes (such as in your peers). Both management changes can have negative effects on your migration. However, their effects will be felt differently.

Vertical changes.   The change in your management chain can have a significant impact on your migration. I would say the risk is the same if you are an IT manager or a CIO. The higher up the change, the greater the potential risk to your migration. For instance, if you are an IT manager and have a director, VP, and CIO above you, a change to your direct manager will probably have little effect on your efforts. But as you climb the ladder closer to the CEO, the risk goes up. A new CIO might come in and say no to the cloud completely, or they might come in and say that everything is going to the Google Cloud Platform (GCP). Of course, the reverse might come into play as well, and they mandate that the company will move to the cloud. The fact of the matter is that you just cannot know until it happens. Hopefully, if you did have a change in your management during this process up to now, you know where they stand. If not, you can follow the processes that we discussed in Chapter 4, such as in your why narrative and FAQ, for gaining traction and acceptance. It can be unfortunate to have to restate your business case; it can feel like you are starting over, but your company needs to move forward. You have shown the value to the business before, and you can do it again.

The level of impact by a vertical management change can also be affected by the size of your company. A larger organization is a lot harder to get moving in a direction. Thus, once it is headed in that direction, it becomes a lot harder to shift and take into a new direction. If you work for one of these larger organizations, you will have less potential risk of your migration being derailed. I have personally experienced this in a couple of migrations that I worked on. The companies were all in the Fortune 1000 and had made changes to IT management during the migration assessment and business case. In each of these instances, the company had committed to migrating already. It had committed to AWS and consulting firms, and potentially even made public statements to the shareholders. In these cases, even though no workloads had yet been moved, it would have been career suicide for new management to derail the effort.

The risk of migration derailment increases as you move down to smaller organizations. For a small company, there can be a significant risk, because it does not have the momentum that larger organizations have. You will be at the mercy of the new manager's bias, good or bad.

Horizontal changes. In a horizontal management change, a peer manager changes during the migration process. Unlike in a vertical manager change, there is less impact on your migration with this type of change (unless it was your chosen department for expanding upon the base of your pyramid that we discussed in Chapter 7). This is not to say that this won't have any impact at all and you will be sipping martinis on the beach at sunset tonight. Rather, it does not have the potential to derail the entire migration. The new manager could still throw up roadblocks for moving a particular business unit to AWS. Just as with a change in vertical managers, you may want to go through the FAQ process with them to answer any questions they have and reassure them about any potential concerns.

Ultimately, the only thing that a horizontal management change will affect is the migration timeline. Since they are coming in late to the game, they might not feel at ease with the migration, given their overall understanding of the company. They must learn the people, processes, and applications for the business, and the migration will just add more fuel to the fire. If you were to purposely move the migration of that business unit's applications toward the end and give them more time to onboard before that kind of disruption, you could probably earn quite a few brownie points with them. This positive action is something to keep in mind as you complete the migration planning process.

Priority shifts

Another thing that might have changed since you began the migration process is a shift in priorities. Let's face it, the world does not stand still, waiting for us IT managers to get everything we need all lined up and ready. Business priorities shift, based on current trends in the marketplace, economy, and political situation. As with most of the topics we have talked about previously, there is a never-ending litany of items that we could cover, and we need to hone our focus. Instead, we will cover major application bugs and competitive requirements, which can affect many of your business units and are quite common to many companies.

Major bugs.   Nobody likes bugs, and it goes without saying that no one likes major ones. It does not matter whether you are running mostly COTS or you develop your own software; bugs can still affect your migration. In my experience, major bugs only affect a particular business unit and not the entire enterprise. Most enterprise-wide applications have become quite refined, and most big bugs have been worked out. When was the last time there was a major bug in your email or SQL server? You might not even remember. This is not the case with internally developed software and why major bugs typically affect only one business unit. When it comes to your migration, the question you must answer is how your timeline will be affected. The answer lies in whether the application in question is COTS or internally developed.

With an internally developed program, you have more control over the release of updated software. When you encounter major bugs in your application that need to be addressed by internal engineering teams, the impact is reflected in your migration plan. You should be able to move a couple of other applications around to compensate for the repair of the bug. This adjustment will ensure that the engineering team will have its full focus on migration when necessary. Its undivided attention is necessary for a successful migration. Typically, the impact to your plan should be relatively small if the development team is using an agile development model. If the team uses waterfall and intends to put the fix out in a new release rather than with a hotfix, you may need to adjust your plan and your timeline. The timeline might need to be extended to address any delays due to the long release cycle.

If you have a major bug in your COTS application, the potential for your migration timeline to extend is significantly higher. You are at the mercy of your vendor's release timeline, and unless you are a major customer for the vendor, you probably do not have enough sway to make the vendor change it. Depending on how long it will take to get the new release, you might have to extend your timeline. I would not suggest moving the application to AWS before the bug fix, because you are potentially changing a causality variable from a known state to an unknown. This might cause the application to work properly without a fix, and you will never know whether it will happen again. For instance, the bug might be caused by a race condition that is now changed based on the amount of RAM and CPU that is available. This condition then might reoccur in the future when load increases, and RAM and CPU become constrained again.

The only time that I would recommend moving an application to AWS prior to receiving a bug fix is when the timeline is too far out of bounds. For instance, if your software vendor is telling you that the fix won't be available until the next major release is out in six months, it might make sense to move that application ahead of that time. You obviously can't put your migration on hold, supporting your environments for one trailing application.

Competitive requirements. The business world is a highly competitive one. There is constant vying for position between companies, each of them striving to be a market leader. Sometimes a competitor puts out a product or feature that your company must address. Without it, your company will continue to lose customers, and you need to address it sooner rather than later. In this situation, you have two options regarding how it will affect your migration plan: delaying the migration or accelerating it. Depending on the capabilities that your company needs to enhance to remain competitive, you might want to accelerate the migration to AWS.

AWS offers an amount of agility that you cannot replicate on-premises. Not only can you accelerate the deployment of new versions by using automated tooling, but you can also try a new technology without any sunk equipment costs. By migrating the application to AWS sooner, you open the door to better data analytics, artificial intelligence/machine learning (AI/ML), specific database options such as a cryptographic ledger, and the internet of things (IoT). These services would be available instantly to developers once the application was moved.

 You might be tempted start creating new resources in the cloud and leave the application on-premises, but this will introduce potential latency and data transfer concerns.

On the reverse side, it might make sense to leave the application on-premises longer and move it to a position later in your plan. If the application does not need any of the new features available on AWS, it might make sense for your company to just leave it for the time being and focus on adding the new features rather than concerning the engineering team with moving it. The priority is addressing the business need, not your migration.

With any priority shift, the important part is to keep your eye on the ball, and the ball is your business. I have seen many managers get hung up on the migration and lose sight of the main purpose. Moving your company forward is the main purpose; sometimes that does not prioritize the migration, and sometimes it does. Migration is a bit like the water moving down a river. It can't be rigid, or it will get hung up on the rocks and not go anywhere. You need to be fluid and adaptive.

Now that we have addressed how priority shifts might affect your migration, it is time to look at development methodologies that need to be selected prior to building your plan.

Development Methodologies

You might be asking why we are looking at selecting development methodologies at this point during the migration planning phase rather than later in the process. At first glance, it might make sense to talk to the development teams about what method they prefer when you are migrating their applications. However, this is one time when you need to drive business agility forward. Your company probably doesn't have a consistent method of development, and it might not be agile. Some prerequisites are required in the cloud to truly gain the agility that you are looking for in your business. Having an outdated development methodology will not give you that agility. Like we talked about in "Building a Pyramid" on page 144 in Chapter 5, you can leverage the IT department to set a new standard on how your company operates. Because we want to drive agility in the business, this is a good point in the migration at which to discuss development methodology. In addition, by choosing your methodology now, you will also lay the framework for the AWS tooling that you will need to support your agile deployments to meet those needs, such as CodePipeline and CodeGuru. This preparedness ensures that the first migrated applications follow best practices and will not need to be reworked postmigration.

Throughout this book, I have probably mentioned agility a thousand times. You cannot be agile if you do not develop your application in an agile way. A couple of business units in your organization might still follow the waterfall development methodology. These business units will have to be coached to change those methods to maximize the benefits of AWS. You might think that you could save this change for a later time, but I have worked with enough companies to know that you will never come back around to it. The best day to inject agility in the business is today. Enveloping it into the migration process forces the issue and increases the return on investment of your migration immediately.

Before we get into these individually, let's go over some core principles of agile development. There are 12 principles from the Agile Manifesto that are instrumental in all agile methods and can serve you as a guiding north star as you communicate the necessity of agile development to your business units.[2] We will touch on a couple that are particularly relevant to agility in the cloud:

---

2 For more information on these principles, you can read the full manifesto online (*https://agilemanifesto.org*).

Customer satisfaction

This principle is my favorite, and it aligns well with the Amazon leadership principle of being customer-obsessed. The problem with the waterfall methodology is that you do not know how the customer feels about your software until the whole release is out the door (or potentially during beta testing), which is much too late. By this stage in the release cycle, you cannot afford to go back and change much to address the issue because you are too far along in the process. If you miss the mark with the customer, why even bother shipping the release? By using an agile methodology, you can receive customer feedback sooner and adjust to meet those needs faster with less rework.

Working software measures progress

When working in an agile methodology, you can directly measure progress by how much of the software is working. Each time you release a new feature, it is rolled out to your customers and becomes usable immediately. This acceleration means that you continually add to customer satisfaction as you go. There is no "big bang" release to talk about, but customers would prefer an incremental improvement that will help them today rather than waiting for months for all the features to arrive. Many features that are released in a waterfall method might not apply to every customer. You essentially make your customers wait for features they might not use. This is not the case with an agile methodology.

As you can probably see, these two principles play well with the cloud story. You want to provide a high level of customer satisfaction quickly, hopefully making your competition play catch-up all the time, putting it on the defensive. Now let us look at the types of agile methodologies and their key components.

There are several agile methodologies in the wild. We will not cover them all in-depth, but we will go over the most popular to give you an overview. This baseline knowledge will enable you to assist your teams in selecting the proper methodology for their product and team:

Extreme programming

Extreme programming (XP) focuses on iterative small releases that allow you to adjust requirements based on customer feedback. Where XP differs the most from other methodologies is that it focuses on code quality by using programming methods like test-driven development (TDD). In TDD, you write the unit test before you write the actual code. By working backward, you make sure that your code does what it is supposed to, from the get-go. If you automate the unit testing using a deployment pipeline, you get instant feedback on your code quality, and the defective code is never deployed. The pipeline will fail out of the unit tests and send an error message. This error handling allows your programmers to address the issue quickly.

Scrum

Scrum is probably the most common agile methodology. In Scrum, work is completed in units of work called sprints. Sprints usually last from two weeks to two months, whereas XP work is split into a maximum of one- to two-week sprints. Scrum does not prescribe any engineering methods like TDD and instead focuses solely on project management. Scrum is also more rigid than XP and does not allow for the changing of priorities once a sprint starts. Because Scrum is closer to waterfall than XP, it would probably be the methodology of choice when converting to agile. This framework allows your team to keep its familiar engineering methods and keeps priorities locked in for the sprint.

Feature-driven development

Feature-driven development (FDD) is a bit different from other methodologies in that it starts from the required feature and works backward from there. I particularly like the FDD methodology because it starts with the customer and the features that they desire. In today's competitive economy, time to market (TTM) is critical, and FDD focuses on delivering usable software in a short period.

These are the three most popular methodologies that I see deployed. There are more, such as Crystal, Kanban, and Lean. I would begin with one of the three most popular methodologies to get started. Once your teams become more comfortable working in an agile mode, they can experiment and use methodologies that might fit their particular needs better, or even blend methods to create their own. I view agile frameworks as a great starting point and adapt them to my own needs as necessary. Once you have selected your development methodology, you can move on to selecting your tooling for migration.

Migration Tooling Selection

Migrating to AWS requires tooling. You do not want to have to re-create all your servers in AWS. You want to be able to capture the work that was done on-premises and move that into AWS. AWS offers two main tools that you will want to use and, potentially, some third-party tooling. Of course, the tooling from AWS is essentially free, save for some instance costs. However, sometimes you require some additional functionality, which is where third-party tools come into play. The primary AWS tools that we will cover are CloudEndure, Database Migration Service, and DataSync. The selection of tooling is not just about which tools to use but also when to use them, which we will discuss in the next sections.

CloudEndure

CloudEndure is a block-level replication tool that can copy the disk drives of your servers to AWS asynchronously, so that the data only needs to be committed to the source server for operations to continue. Thus, it does not affect the performance of your applications, which is a very important fact to remember, because business own-ers might become concerned that CloudEndure will slow the performance of their application on-premises. It will be your number one tool for migration. CloudEndure does an excellent job, has a very simple user interface, and is integrated with AWS Migration Hub, a service that essentially creates a single pane of glass or a unified console or dashboard for management of your migration activities.

CloudEndure is used when you want to replicate a server in its entirety from on-premises to the cloud. It isn't really designed for partial migrations in which not all the drives and data are replicated. Typically, you would do this to replicate application servers and, possibly, web and database servers. Most of the time you only want to replicate one web server in a web farm. A typical use case for this feature is when there are many servers in a load-balanced cluster. Since all the servers are the same (or should be), you only need to replicate one. You then create an image of that repli-cated server to add to an auto scaling group. The auto scaling group would then han-dle the spin-up and termination of servers for you. This scaling saves you from replicating all the servers.

In my opinion, CloudEndure is the only service you should use to migrate your servers to AWS. There are other options, but they are not seamless or as easy to use. They ultimately create more work for your staff and will drive up the cost of your migration. CloudEndure can work from both physical and virtual servers, so there is only one tool to learn. Other tools, like the AWS Server Migration Service, only sup-port virtual servers from VMware and Hyper-V. The other tools also work using snapshot technology, making the migration timeline longer than CloudEndure, with its continual replication the only logical choice.

You won't use CloudEndure for moving database servers if you will use AWS Rela-tional Database Service. To perform that kind of migration, you would use DMS, which we will cover in the next section.

Database Migration Service

Database Migration Service will probably be your second most used AWS tool to migrate to AWS. To recap, DMS runs on an AWS instance and connects to the source database and the destination database. It then replicates the database asynchronously to the destination. Like CloudEndure, the asynchronous replication does not affect the performance of the production on-premises database and application. As part of the operational cost savings, you will want to move as many database servers as you can to RDS. As discussed before, RDS will save your teams a lot of effort with patch-ing, backups, and high availability that you will want to take advantage of.

DMS can also help you move data from one database engine to another. For instance, you might want to migrate from an Oracle database engine to MySQL. DMS can help you move the data between them. Unfortunately, this is only part of the equation. You will most likely have to perform a significant number of code changes in your application as well. These manual code changes are what usually derail database engine conversion.

Unlike CloudEndure, which competes against AWS Server Migration Service, AWS does not have any competing products for DMS. It will be your only option while using AWS native tooling. There are other options in the market that can perform the same type of asynchronous replication, such as GoldenGate. Unless you need some enhanced capabilities such as partial or multiregion replication, DMS will most likely fit your needs.

DataSync

AWS DataSync is a newer service to AWS and a welcome addition. DataSync allows for the easy transfer of files between on-premises file servers and NAS devices to Amazon S3, Amazon FSx, and Amazon EFS. DataSync was released in late 2018; before DataSync, you would have to use third-party tooling and the AWS CLI tools to achieve the same data transfer. DataSync offers many additional features that make it much more desirable than using command-line tools or third-party software. DataSync works by deploying resources into AWS that receive data from agents you install that have access to the source data. DataSync can automatically scale the resources in the cloud to accommodate increased load during transfer.

When you migrate to AWS, you will want to move away from standalone NFS and Windows file servers. By running your conventional servers in AWS, you will not offload any of the management tasks associated with them. By using DataSync, you can transfer the data from those on-premises servers to the managed services in AWS and reduce your management overhead. If possible, transferring files to S3 object storage will be the cheapest option, with the largest number of storage tiering options available. However, to use S3, your application will need some code changes to shift from local files or shares to S3 locations.

Ultimately, DataSync will be your third most used AWS tooling for migrating.

DataSync can also be used for disaster recovery capabilities by replicating files to other locations.

Third-Party Tooling

AWS has done a pretty good job of providing the tool sets required to migrate your workloads into the cloud. With the three tools we discussed, 90% of companies will have everything that they need. However, some companies may need some additional capabilities that are not available in the native tooling.

When it comes to a block-copy tooling product like CloudEndure, few other options offer a significantly different feature set. You probably will not have to deviate from CloudEndure unless you want something that can upgrade your OS at the same time. For instance, Deloitte's ATADATA can perform an update of an older OS like Windows 2003 while it does the migration.[3] There are many tools in this space, and covering them is outside the scope of this book. My recommendation is to start with CloudEndure and then deviate if there is something you need to accomplish that is outside its feature set.

For database and file replication, there may be additional requirements for which you will need to use third-party tooling. For instance, if you want to split a data set into multiple regions based on country, this would need to be handled by something other than DMS, because it is outside its capabilities. Work like this would require something custom. Although DMS can change database engines, it still performs these conversions as a whole database. If you need to do anything more advanced, you will need to look elsewhere or build some custom scripting. We will touch on some examples of where you might need some additional tooling in Chapter 8, when we discuss application refactoring.

Building Your Plan

We have now looked at the tooling that you will use and your development methodologies. We also looked at how your business priorities might have shifted since you started your migration process. Now it is time to start building your plan. The good news is that about 80–90% of your migration plan has already been created for you. That's right, most of your migration plan is already done through application discovery mapping, which we discussed in "Dependency mapping" on page 82 in Chapter 3.

When you discovered your workloads, you should have obtained dependency mapping as well (if your selected tooling supported it). If you do have dependency data, your life will be much easier. I would estimate that 90% of a migration plan can be derived directly from the dependency mapping. The other 10% will have to be based on the availability of the business units. Their involvement will be necessary to do the

---

3 ATADATA can no longer be purchased by itself and comes as part of Deloitte services.

testing and any code modifications required to migrate the workloads. This effort is something that no tooling could know and requires manual planning. To solidify the concept of dependencies, let's review the next scenario.

Scenario 7-1

Hailey has an application (application A) that talks to the database (application B). Since application A is directly querying the database of application B, she cannot separate these two applications. By accessing the database directly over a chatty database protocol, she creates a latency dependency. When her users query a database through the application, they are often looking for many pieces of information from many tables. This querying creates many round trips from Hailey's application A server to the application B database server. In these applications, her users are not querying for a result like they would from a REST API, which would require one or a handful of round trips.

In Hailey's case, her applications are tightly coupled and have to be moved together. Figure 7-1 demonstrates the link between her application stacks visually. This will happen throughout your estate, which is why 80–90% of your plan will be completed for you through dependency mapping. Agility in migration is a function of the level of applications and several applications that are tightly coupled together. For most of the migrations I have been involved with, several blocks of applications are coupled. However, there is typically enough flexibility to create a viable plan without issue. Although it is a rare occurrence, you can get into trouble when you have a single application that is a linchpin in your entire infrastructure.

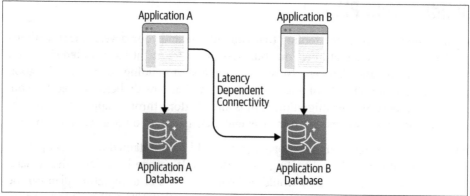

Figure 7-1. Application latency

In this instance, the company had a master database that was used by at least half of its applications. There was no way to create a migration wave that could contain half of those applications. It would be way too risky to attempt to move half of the infrastructure at once. To accommodate this migration, we needed to create two-way replicas of the database so that we could "move" a copy of the database to AWS. Once this database copy was in AWS and on-premises, we could create a migration plan based on the now smaller application blocks. Hopefully, you will not run into this kind of situation in your environment. They are not the easiest problems to solve and are very bespoke, based on your exact needs and technology.

Now that we have built some background on the level of effort required to create a migration plan, let us look at the steps required and how to go about the overall process. First, we will cover your migration timeline and planning tooling, because it is vitally important to streamline the process. Then we will cover planning the 90%, based on your discovery analysis and, finally, wrap up with the 10% refining process.

Creating a Migration Timeline

In Chapter 4, we talked about "Estimating Your Timeline" on page 102, which detailed how to ballpark your migration timeline. We are going to use this timeline as your starting point and apply any adjustments based on the priority shifts that we discussed earlier in this chapter. For instance, let us say that you had projected 13 months to migrate your infrastructure in your timeline estimate. However, a competitive situation has arisen that will block three of your major applications from getting migrated. That team needs three more months to complete the new features to compensate for the changes in the market. At this point, you will want to start with a timeline that is 16 months in total to compensate. When we get to planning, we can work on consolidating the timeline. However, it is best to start with a longer timeline and not attempt to squeeze everything into a shorter one.

In some instances, you might be constrained on how long your migration can take. You might not be able to extend your timeline because you must vacate your data center. In this instance, you will have to work around that timeline and instead compensate with resources. In this type of situation, I would start with the maximum number of months you have to vacate the on-premises data center and then subtract 20%. If you must be out of your data center in 10 months, then I would set the timeline at 8 months. This will give you a buffer to absorb things going wrong in your migration. The adage of hope for the best and plan for the worst is very prudent in migrating. If you want to be like Scotty, plan using the 80% and disclose the full time to everyone else; when you come in under time, you will be the hero.

Now that we have a revised timeline target, let us look at which tooling to use for building your migration plan.

Planning Tooling

There is a lot—actually, I need a better word. There is a *colossal* number of project management tools out in the world today: Microsoft Project, monday.com, Airtable, Trello, and Jira, just to name a few off the top of my head. However, I prefer to use tools you can get at your local grocery store: sticky notes and whiteboard markers. Yes, I am a very tech-centric guy, but it is hard to beat the collaboration that you can get with a team in front of a whiteboard moving around sticky notes. I will explain my method, which I have used on some very complex migration plans. You can make it your own or use a tool on the computer. The overall process will be the same, no matter which tool you decide to use. The reason I shy away from technology-based tooling for this aspect is that you will be working with a multitude of teams throughout the organization. These teams may or may not understand the tool that you decide to use, and that causes delays and frustration. Everyone can move a sticky note. You can always move your plan to another tool once it has been completed.

When I do migration planning, I start with a unit of migration. One sticky note equals one unit of migration. This sticky note represents the effort of one migration sprint. As we discussed previously, in "Agile, Waterfall, or Combination Plan" on page 188, a sprint is at least two weeks of effort. If you have a small application with no dependencies, then a single unit of migration should be enough to migrate the application. As the applications get more complex, you need more units and expand the application in question by using more sticky notes. For example, you have an application that will take four weeks to migrate due to its complexity, and you have two weeks in your sprints. You will need two sticky notes stuck together to represent that application. By using the sticky notes, you will be physically representing the level of effort for the application migration.

Obviously, having a bunch of sticky notes floating around will not help much for planning your migration. This is where the whiteboard comes into play. I start by marking an entire large whiteboard with threats of impending death if someone were to erase it. Once I protect it from would-be deletion, I draw out the migration timeline. The important part to capture here is that it must be drawn to scale, from both a timeline perspective and from the sticky note size. If you have sprints that are two weeks long and a six-month migration timeline, then you should have a line drawn out with 12 tick marks, with the names of the months on every second line. Figure 7-2 demonstrates what your whiteboard should look like at this point.

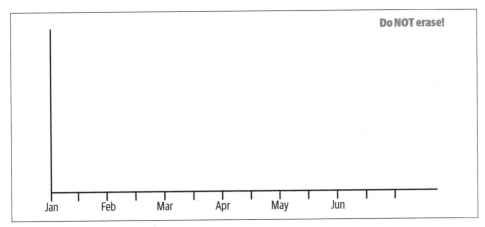

Figure 7-2. Migration timeline

Once you have your timeline drawn out, you need to draw in your workstreams. A *workstream* is a team or person who does the actual migration work. Typically, I would put two engineers on each workstream. Having two increases the probability of success and the ability to absorb staff outages due to vacations and sick days more effectively. Without two engineers, you would have to stop the migration work for that workstream when an engineer was out. If you have 10 engineers, then you would have 5 migration workstreams. To represent this in your migration plan, you need to draw in five additional horizontal lines, because we need to create spaces for the sticky notes to fit. Remember, we need to draw this to scale. Figure 7-3 shows what your migration plan should look like at this stage.

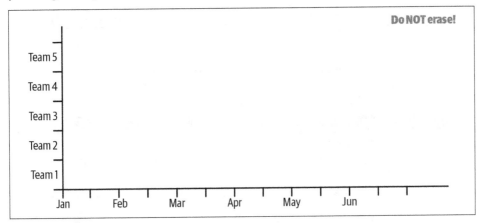

Figure 7-3. Migration workstreams

At this point, your migration plan is ready to be populated. I know it does not look or sound like much at this point, but the collaborative ability that this old-school method enables is pretty darn hard to beat. The worst thing that you could do at this point is single-thread the management of your migration plan. You will need to bring in key stakeholders to discuss the migration plan and their business units' capabilities, and you want to be able to change things on the fly easily for everyone to see immediately. The sense of collaboration that they will get from this experience will go a long way toward winning their hearts and minds.

Laying Down the 90%

Now that we have the migration plan on a whiteboard in a state that we can work with, we can start building out the plan with actual data. Before we get started, there are several things that we need from previous steps in the migration process. We will need:

- All of your application discovery information
- All the application dependency information
- The level of effort that your team can achieve

Once we have these pieces of information, we can start to calculate the level of effort to move each application. The level of complexity is a function of the number of servers an application has, the age of the deployment, whether code changes need to be made, the number of dependents, and the number of dependencies. Here is an equation to help you with the formula.

Equation 7-1. Timeline Equation

$$LOE = \frac{(servers \times code\ factor \times age\ factor) + (dependents + dependencies \times 0.1)}{team\ capabilities \times sprint\ days}$$

The components of the equation and potential values are shown in Table 7-1.

Table 7-1. Equation variables

Item	Value
Servers	The number of servers for the application
Code factor	The factor if code changes are required: 1 for no changes, 1.5 for moderate changes, and 2 for extensive changes
Age factor	The factor for the last time an application was updated: 1 for less than one year and 2 for one year or more
Dependents	The number of dependent applications
Dependencies	The number of applications that this application depends on
Team capabilities	The total number of servers per day for the *entire* migration team
Sprint days	The total number of business days in your sprints

I will start by saying that I am not a mathematician, and by no means is this formula the be all and end all when it comes to determining the level of the migration effort—but you must start somewhere, and this is the line I have drawn in the sand. It is effective at estimation and will be defendable to management. There are many variables in the migration of workloads, and humans are involved, which will always make things tricky. The amount of work that is completed per person will not be consistent across your whole team. A modicum of guesswork will always make its way into your planning and migration. There are too many items in motion to have a completely accurate number. If you were to try to get to complete certainty, you would spend way too much time in the weeds looking everywhere for variables to account for. In the end, you will not accomplish much.

Let us start your migration plan with an easy application. Look at your discovery information and find an application with no dependencies or dependents (outside of Active Directory). We will plug that information into the formula. For demonstration purposes, we will say that your application has one server, was updated in the past year, requires no code changes, and has no dependencies or dependents. Ultimately, you will end up with this equation:

Equation 7-2. Simple application equation

$$0.13 = \frac{(1 \times 1 \times 1) + (0 + 0 \times 0.1)}{1.5 \times 5}$$

When this equation is computed, you end up with a value of 0.13, which signifies the level of effort (LOE) to move this application. In this case, because the resulting value is less than one, the level of effort in sprints gets rounded up to one. At this point, we can write down the application name, the business unit, and the LOE on one sticky note, and add it to one of the workstreams. Since you will be working with many business units (BU) and applications, it helps to color-code the sticky notes by the BU so that BU leaders can see with one look the workstreams and applications that affect their teams.

That example was easy and gave you an idea of the process. Now let us look at an application that is a bit more complex. For demonstration purposes, let us say that the more complex application has 10 servers, was updated in the past year, requires no code changes, and has seven dependencies and no dependents. You will end up with this equation to denote its level of effort:

Equation 7-3. Semicomplex application equation

$$1.426 = \frac{(10 \times 1 \times 1) + (0 + 7 \times 0.1)}{1.5 \times 5}$$

For this application, you end up with a level of effort score of 1.426. This score indicates that you will need two sprints of effort. You can't really round down effort, only up, which might require more buffer time in your migration plan. Now you know that you will need two sticky notes to signify this application on your migration plan.

Before you can place this application on the plan, you will need to compute the complexity of its dependency applications as well. These seven applications will need to be part of the same sprint potentially. I say *potentially* because those seven dependencies will only need to be part of the same sprint if they are tightly coupled.

Before we get any deeper into planning, let us look at some scenarios of what is and what is not a tightly coupled application.

Scenario 7-2

Jim's company runs an application called Ariana Pequeño (AP). The AP application performs the credit card processing and invoicing for the company's online website that sells sheet music subscriptions. It has one server and depends on the database for website application. No applications depend on the AP application, because it performs a standalone operation. Jim's team needs to migrate the applications to the cloud, but they are running into some issues with the development team's time required for migrating the web application. Jim needs to determine whether the AP app and the web app are tightly coupled.

Jim's Ariana Pequeño application is, in fact, tightly coupled. The fact that the AP application uses the web application database directly creates this tight coupling. Unfortunately, in Jim's circumstance, he will have to move both applications at the same time, once the web app team is ready. Let us look at another and more complex example.

Scenario 7-3

The migration team at Kara's company, CamperSmiths, wants to move four applications into AWS that depend on the manufacturing system. The four applications perform operations for the website. One application queries the inventory number to update the website database. The second application is the website itself, which is not dependent on the manufacturing system but depends on the three other applications. The third application is a customer connectivity application that sends emails and contacts sales representatives. This application depends on the website database. The fourth and final application is a forecasting tool that uses the production line information from the manufacturing system to predict availability and updates the website database. Applications one and four communicate to the manufacturing system

---

through a REST API. Kara's team needs to fit these applications into the migration plan and figure out which ones are tightly coupled.

In Kara's scenario, five applications need to be evaluated to see how they move together, not four. Often, obvious connections can be missed when looking at your infrastructure. There are four applications, but we forgot the manufacturing system altogether, making five the total count. I know this seems obvious and common sense, but life happens, and simple mistakes arise. There are two major apps in Kara's environment: the website and the manufacturing system. She then has three minor systems left that provide ancillary services. The inventory application queries the manufacturing system, and it does this through a REST API, making it loosely coupled. However, the inventory application updates the website database directly. This connection will cause tight coupling between the website and inventory applications. These two applications will need to move together. Application three, the one that performs customer and sales interactions, works with the website database. In this circumstance, the application may or may not be tightly coupled, depending on the volume of interactions with the database. If their site is very popular and has thousands of sales requests a day, the applications would be tightly coupled. In the other case, with very few interactions, it would be safe to say that the applications are loosely coupled. The lower interaction and round-trip latency will not affect customers. The forecasting application, again, talks to the website database, making it tightly coupled, but the forecasting application also talks to the manufacturing system through the API, making that connection loosely coupled.

In the end, Kara's team will plan to move the website, forecasting application, inventory application, and possibly the customer connectivity application, based on the number of sales requests per day. The manufacturing system is loosely coupled and can be moved separately.

 REST APIs are considered loosely coupled because they are designed to be operated over the open internet. REST provides reduced round trips by providing more finalized data than direct database queries, thus reducing round-trip latency. These scenarios are to demonstrate how applications can be coupled and, being connected by database and API, were used because they are very common. Your applications might have different communications requirements that need to be evaluated based on your specific use case.

Finalizing the 90%

Now that you understand how to determine whether an application is tightly coupled, we can get back to our example application with seven dependencies. In this example, we will say that three of the applications are tightly coupled and the remaining four are not. For simplicity, we will also say that these seven applications only require one sprint to complete. Now that we have all the necessary information, we can place the sticky notes into our migration plan. The main application with two sprints needs to be placed first and occupies two sprint locations. The three tightly coupled applications need to occupy workstreams adjacent to the primary application. However, since the coupled applications only require one sprint of effort, they need to be placed in the second position to coincide with the cutover phase of the primary application migration.

If you were to place the three coupled applications in the first available sprint for the other workstreams, they would be migrated before the primary application and be decoupled accidentally. Once you place the coupled applications, you can backfill with the other four applications in any available position on the board. At this point, your migration plan should look like Figure 7-4.

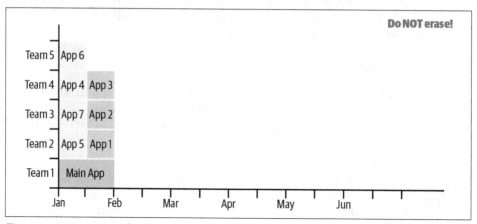

Figure 7-4. Migration plan

You can now continue putting all the applications and their dependencies into the plan, using the same process and level-of-effort calculations. For each application with dependencies, you need to evaluate the coupling to ensure that the tightly coupled applications are moved together. In the end, you should end up with a migration plan that looks like Figure 7-5.

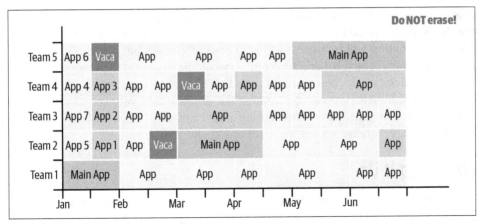

Figure 7-5. Primary migration plan

Once you reach this point, we need to work on the final phase of planning, which is to polish the last 10% of the plan.

Polishing the 10%

You might be wondering why I broke the planning phase into 90% and 10% blocks even though after the 90% phase, the whole migration plan is filled out. The 90% represents the amount of the plan that can be laid out without having to be manipulated. The discovery tooling that you used found the dependencies in your environment and the number of servers, but it has no idea what is going on in your business units. The last 10% is the massaging and polishing of the plan that occurs from good old-fashioned collaboration with the business units.

My preferred method of finalizing the plan is to invite the business unit stakeholders down to your conference room with your migration plan on the whiteboard and walk them through the migration. You are pointing out to them the key applications they own and when they will be migrated. If this process goes perfectly, they will say it sounds great and be on their merry way, but wouldn't you know it, life rarely works out that way. The accounting department might have issues around a month, quarter, or year-end close dates. Other teams might have issues with existing release dates or vacation schedules. These are the items that you need to address by moving the sticky notes around the board and working out the kinks in your plan. You may have to iterate this process more than once. Moving to accommodate team A may cause a new conflict in team B's schedule. Hopefully, you can get through the process with only two iterations to ensure that everything works for all teams.

You might find that you just cannot accommodate the needs of a particular team. I have run into this before, and there are three options to remedy it. The first option is to start their migration before the main migration during the landing zone build-out.

This option is not the most desirable, though, because some security and governance guardrails might not be in place. Your second option would be to add another workstream. This option will increase the cost of your migration, but it will allow for the greatest flexibility. The third and final option would be to extend the migration timeline to accommodate the business unit's needs. This option is not the most desirable either, because it increases costs by running the equipment in your on-premises data center longer than anticipated. This option might not even be possible if you must vacate your data center.

Wrapping It Up

Your plan is done! It has probably been quite some time since you began your migration process, but you finally see the fruits of your labor. In this chapter, we converted the raw data from your discovery into a finely tuned plan that is refined and polished like fine silver. At this point, if your landing zone deployment is completed, you could start your migration process, which involves the application of deep dives and final prep and planning during the migration sprints. We will be covering this process in detail in Chapter 8. But before we get into that, I want to cover evaluating your workloads for refactoring.

Refactoring, Retooling, and Final Preparations

Change the way you look at things, and the things you look at change.

—Dr. Wayne Dyer, *A Conversation with Wayne Dyer*

With the bulk of your planning effort completed during Chapter 7, we will now move on to looking one last time at your applications for refactoring opportunities. To recap what we covered in Chapter 4, refactoring is making significant application design changes to adopt cloud-native technologies and services. I have been beating my drum about the power of lifting and shifting your infrastructure to AWS as fast as possible to help reduce your double spend during the process. It would be a huge disservice not to talk about refactoring your applications and gaining some benefit from those changes. We want to look for easy changes with maximum impact on your business but low impact on your timeline and budget.

Once we cover refactoring, we will move on to what I call retooling. Retooling isn't as drastic as refactoring. You will make changes to your application's code. However, there are capabilities in AWS that you can bolt onto existing applications to increase their availability and performance for your customers and decrease even more management overhead. Finally, we will cover the final preparations required for migrating applications, the application deep-dive analysis.

Refactoring

You will probably have no trouble getting your development teams onboard with refactoring your applications. It is new and interesting work, and developers love to tinker. However, it is critically important to use restraint at this point in the process. I have seen many refactoring efforts go off the rails and drive costs significantly higher.

The number one reason that refactoring efforts derail is due to continual refactoring. Once a refactoring effort starts, developers tend to continually refine the design as AWS releases new services and capabilities. Although more cloud capabilities are awesome and will probably drive your costs down and your capabilities up in the long run, this continued refactoring prolongs the development cycle. The longer your development cycle, the longer your migration, and that is something you want to avoid. The key is to develop a design and stick with it through to the completion of the refactoring. Your team will need to resist the urge to try out the next shiny object from AWS. Although there may be a good business reason to adopt a newly released technology, I would still exercise extreme caution while expanding your scope at this stage.

Another potential pattern that I want to shine a light on is when a company seeks to refactor on-premises before migrating the application to AWS. The reason I believe this occurs is that companies feel more comfortable in the on-premises space. Adding cloud to the mix might feel like an additional risk or introduce delays. I strongly caution against this tactic. If you were to refactor on-premises, your capabilities in non-cloud native tooling such as containers would be limited. Although you can change your database engine or even your file storage to S3 over the internet, it becomes much harder to adopt more cloud capabilities after these high-level services are implemented.

Another thing to consider is the fact that as you are refactoring on-premises, some of your equipment might age out and need to be replaced rather than decommissioned. At this point, you are effectively buying food for a dead horse. You will end up migrating, and that new hardware will not be used or used to its full potential. Refactoring during or after the migration is a better and more cost-effective course of action than doing so while still on-premises.

Everyone knows the Pareto principle, but you might recognize it by its more common name, the 80/20 rule. By this principle, 20% of something (the cause) accounts for 80% of something else (the effect). You can see this principle in many places in business and life. It is not uncommon to see a company where 20% of its customers account for 80% of its sales, which means that by focusing on the most effective 20%, you can gain 80% of the benefit. This principle also holds for migration to AWS and refactoring.

When we defined refactoring, the word *major* was used to describe the changes. To me, *major* can mean many changes to the design or a significant impact on the business. It is this latter statement that we want to focus on. The key takeaway from this exercise is to be able to determine which changes could be made to your applications in the smallest way possible yet still have a significant impact on your business. This impact might not just be from a cost perspective, either. It is crucial to incorporate other potential business effects as well, such as better performance for customers, the ability to deliver new key functionality, reduced management overhead, or increased processing performance.

Now that we have covered the type of refactoring and impact we are looking to achieve with the 80/20 rule, let us take a look at what some potential targets look like.

 Just to be clear, we are not looking for mathematical precision here. The 80/20 rule is more of a metaphor for the type of impact and level of effort we are seeking.

Potential Refactoring Targets

These two criteria are quite important when looking at targets for a refactoring effort. We need to target services that will make a big enough dent in a business or cost issue, and we need to find the right applications to target. Together, these ingredients make the special sauce for your refactoring efforts, and we didn't even need mayonnaise. In the next two sections, we will cover some key points to look for and avoid when selecting applications and services. From there, we will dive into some suggestions of which services to look at for targets. We will cover some very specific information on those services and why they make good candidates.

Applications to target

When you start looking at your applications for refactoring, you can eliminate a few types right from the start. For one, you cannot refactor any COTS applications since you do not have access to the source code. You can adopt some AWS services with COTS, but only if the vendor supports them in the first place. There are a few instances of this kind of support. However, there has not been much traction in the marketplace. Many COTS vendors are instead focusing on driving hosted solutions in an SaaS model instead. You cannot fault them for this decision; it makes good business sense, because they can deliver customer value faster in this model than contemporary on-premises deployment. If your COTS vendor did add support for AWS services, the most common implementations I've seen are for S3 and additional support for PostgreSQL and MySQL (which are not AWS specific but make adopting Amazon Aurora possible). Vendors implement these two capabilities because they can be used on-premises and in the cloud. Implementing these capabilities is not technically a refactoring, but I would encourage you to take advantage of them nonetheless to keep driving your hard and soft costs lower.

Although COTS applications should be avoided during this stage, several types of internally developed applications make good targets for refactoring. I would avoid Visual Basic applications and those that are written in C. Visual Basic is a dated language and will not have the level of support needed to adapt to the cloud effectively.

In addition, since C is a lower-level language, it takes more coding effort to make the necessary changes than higher-level languages do. Instead, start with applications that are written in Java and .NET (preferably .NET Core). These languages also account for the largest number of enterprise applications, so they will give you the biggest pool to choose from.

In addition to the language used, it would be wise to target applications that are under active development and that have not become stagnant. As we discussed in Chapter 2, tribal knowledge loss can be a real problem for a company. The longer an application has not been under development, the greater the risk that some of that tribal knowledge has been lost. If you were to refactor an application that has not been updated in a year or two, you could increase your risk significantly. Injecting any more risk into your refactoring effort is not something that we want to do. Increased timelines mean increased migration costs, and we are trying to minimize that as much as possible. Now that we know what applications we should be looking at, let us look at which services make good targets.

Services to target

AWS has several services that would be great candidates for refactoring your applications. Unfortunately, many of them do not fall into the realm of our 80/20 rule. For instance, AWS has a service called Simple Notification Service (SNS), which provides a notification service. Although a great service that removes a lot of management overhead from staff, it will not make a significant impact on your business. Another service that has a lot of potential is a queuing service called Simple Queuing Service (SQS), which is a fully managed serverless service that provides a lot of capabilities at a very low cost. However, again, it won't move the needle enough for the kind of impact that we are looking for, so it should not be considered during refactoring.

In the next sections, we will cover the services that make good targets. We won't take a technical deep dive, but we will cover some high-level points around refactoring requirements, which will give you a good understanding and starting point. The reason I chose these services is that they are highly applicable and effective for a large number of companies. Many books are available that dive into refactoring and application redesign, and can assist you with major refactoring efforts and those technical deep dives.[1] Remember, we are looking for low-impact, high-return changes within our business and management scope.

---

[1] Some of these books include *Cloud Native Architectures: Design High-Availability and Cost-Effective Applications for the Cloud* by Farr et al. (Packt Publishing); *Cloud Native Transformation: Practical Patterns for Innovation* by Dobson et al. (O'Reilly) (*https://oreil.ly/cloud-nat-tr*); and *Cloud Native* by Scholl et al. (O'Reilly) (*http://bit.ly/cloud-native-1e*).

Database engine change. One of the refactors that we will look at as a potential target is changing your database engine so you can adopt newer technologies and/or drive down licensing costs. For much of IT's history, very few database options were available. Oracle, DB2, Microsoft SQL—and relational database technology in general—have reigned supreme in the database space. Since these were the only commercially available options, virtually all applications shoehorned their capabilities into the relational model and these vendors. Over time, with the expansion of the internet and online companies, additional open source options arrived, such as MySQL and PostgreSQL. Although startups were eager to adopt these new database engines, by and large, most software vendors have not due to lack of commercial support and industry stigma.

Over time, a few factors have made what CEO of AWS Andy Jassy calls *the old-guard databases* less and less attractive. One of the reasons for the decrease in attractiveness is that the relational database is no longer the only option. AWS offers several database services that offer NoSQL, blockchain, data warehouse, and graph databases. These options mean that you no longer need to shoehorn your application into a relational model when others would be better suited. The second reason that these database engines have become less attractive is that the vendors continue to increase the pricing on the licenses. Unfortunately, it is hard to track the cost increases over time due to technology changes such as multiple CPUs and multiple cores and the subsequent license changes around them. I can tell you from personal experience that the difference between Microsoft SQL Server 2008 and SQL Server 2012 rose around $100,000 between the two versions. These versions shifted from per-CPU licensing to per-core licensing, drastically increasing the cost. In my use case, the licensing changed from two CPUs to eight cores, and that caused a large spike in cost.

 Remember that changing the database engine is only possible if you have access to the application source code. You cannot change the database engine for COTS software unless the vendor supports it.

Now that we understand why changing the database engine makes sense, let's look at some specifics that ensure that refactoring your application will meet the 80/20 rule. The main thing we need to look at is the reason for changing your database. Changing your database to another type, such as NoSQL, would be a significant change to your codebase. That kind of change will push you outside of the 20% limit. However, keeping with the same database type and choosing another relational database engine could save you significant money. Before we can determine whether changing the database vendor will save you money, we have to determine the level of effort necessary to make the change. AWS provides a tool called the Schema Conversion Tool (SCT), which can analyze your current database structure and let you know how much of it can be converted automatically between engines. The SCT will generate a detailed report of your schema and stored procedures and let you know if items cannot be converted automatically, providing detail of what needs to be addressed by your developers. To meet our requirement of low level of effort, I would suggest that all items show an automated conversion of at least 95% in the SCT report. Anything more would slow down your migration, and I would recommend that the conversion be saved for postmigration.

Once you have identified an application that can benefit from a database engine change and meets the 80/20 criteria, you will need to make an adjustment to your migration timeline. The process you will need to mimic is the same as we talked about in "Polishing the 10%" on page 213. Your timeline will need to be adjusted to account for the addition of engineering and testing time required to change the database engine.

S3 object storage. Another possible refactoring change that can meet our 80/20 rule is moving file storage from a Windows or Linux file share or local storage to Amazon S3. Moving files to S3 offers better availability (multi-AZ), advanced functionality (signed URLs, requester pays), and reduced hard and soft costs. To recap what we have covered before, S3 is object-based storage rather than block-type storage used for a local file system. The beauty of S3 is that it is multi-AZ, highly performant, and takes all the management overhead off your teams. The other benefit is that S3 is very cost-effective when compared to EBS and EFS storage costs. At the time of writing, S3 has multiple storage tiers with costs of $0.023 per GB in the us-east-1 region, and can go down to as little as $0.004 per GB for the S3 Glacier storage tier. When compared to the $0.10 per GB cost of EBS, you can quickly see how S3 can meet your 80% effect target, because storage can be a large portion of your AWS spend.

In addition to being low cost and having multiple storage tiers, S3 also offers life cycle management and intelligent tiering. All of these capabilities create a significant effect on your business and can qualify for the 80% criteria. With intelligent tiering, S3 uses AI to determine usage patterns for your data in S3 and automatically life-cycles data between tiers for you. The life cycle management capability allows you to establish rules for migrating data between storage tiers manually, based on hard timelines. As an example, we can state that you allow customers to upload files to your web server, and they typically use them within the first day, but sometimes it could take a month. Your customers will sometimes access these files within the next six months, and rarely within the year. In this instance, both the life cycle and intelligent tier capabilities would allow you to keep data in the standard S3 tier for the first month, move the files to infrequent access after the first month, and finally move them to the glacier tier after six months. This tiering provides you with very effective cost control that wouldn't be available to you using standard server storage.

Now that we have established how S3 can meet your 80% goal, let us take a look at what it would take to convert from standard storage such as EBS volumes. We will do this to establish whether moving the data to S3 meets our 20% level-of-effort target. We need to look at two pieces when determining the level of effort needed to make this kind of change. We need to know how hard it will be to migrate the data, and we need to know how much engineering effort will be needed to make the required code changes.

AWS has a newer service called DataSync that allows you to migrate data from on-premises to S3 directly. The service is a better choice than building any internal scripting or using third-party tools, due to its deduplication and compression capabilities. Simply put, DataSync allows you to transfer more data faster. The service is agent-based and very easy to set up, lowering the level of effort needed to start the process. The remaining question to answer is how much time it will take to transfer the data and how that changes your timeline. Since you were planning to move this data anyway by lifting the server into AWS, you have already established a timeline for this data transfer, so it is included in your plan. A block-level replication tool like CloudEndure does not have the ability to do compression and deduplication like DataSync. In effect, by using DataSync, you may actually decrease your timeline to move the data. Now that we have established that the data moving will meet your requirements, let us take a look at the code changes required.

Typically when you are talking about making a code change from a local file API call to an S3 API call, the code change is not difficult. The complexity comes in how many places those API calls are made in your code. The more places to change, the more the refactoring will add to your timeline. Sure, you can search and replace to make all the code changes at once. However, the bulk of the workload and considerable effort comes with the regression testing required. Every function that reads or writes to S3 will need to be tested and verified that it still works as intended. Unfortunately, I cannot provide any guidance on what would be considered acceptable, because refactoring is highly dependent on your engineering and testing teams' capabilities and size. You will have to review this information and make a judgment call based on your company's specific situation.

Just like changing database engines, once you have committed to making an S3 application refactor, you will use the process we talked about in "Polishing the 10%" on page 213. You will want to account for the changes in your timeline required to make the necessary code changes and testing.

Containerization.   Containerizing applications is another refactoring effort that could meet our 20% target. Containerization is a form of virtualization to extract the applications and their components into a virtualized layer rather than into the whole OS, like a VMware or Hyper-V virtual machine. Containerization is beneficial because it lets you eke out a bit more economy of scale by running a bunch of containers on a cluster rather than on individual machines. The individual servers with full operating systems create additional overhead. You can gain further benefits by using the AWS Fargate service that manages the container subsystems for you, further decreasing your soft costs for the management overhead.

Three questions come into play when thinking about refactoring into containers. The first is whether it will make enough of an impact to meet our 80% impact target. The second is whether you can even containerize your applications. Last, what would good targets look like? For the first, I have seen containerization save a significant amount of money when an application has very disparate operations on a single server. For example, let us say that you have an application that imports files. The files are very large and require a lot of processing power when they arrive. They also arrive inconsistently throughout the day. In addition, the application has many other components that do not use nearly the same amount of processing power. In a conventional design, you would have to configure your server to accommodate the largest amount of load that would come from importing the files, even though most of the time the system is nearly idle. You have a lot of wasted capacity in this situation. The situation is further exacerbated when you have a cluster of these servers running to meet customer demand and redundancy targets.

If you split this application into containers, you could scale the individual components based on their individual need rather than on the whole. When new files came in, that process could scale to meet the need and scale back down to near zero for the rest of the time. You can potentially save thousands in this situation, depending on the overall scale of your application. What you would want to avoid during refactoring is looking at applications that would not yield this kind of benefit. Containerizing a constant usage application that runs on one server would not be a good choice.

To answer the third question—what kind of applications make good targets?—it is easier if we look at which applications *will not* make a good choice. Since we want to convert these applications quickly, we can eliminate some immediately, such as .NET applications. If you are not running .NET Core today, the likelihood of converting to .NET Core to run in containers is lower. This likelihood is especially true if you are using WinForms, which is only supported on Windows and, therefore, will require quite a bit of retooling. The same holds for the Windows Communication Foundation (WCF) technology, another Windows-only capability that needs to be replaced when moving to .NET Core. Any applications that predate .NET are also poor choices, such as Visual Basic (VB). In the case of VB, most of those applications are small, client-based apps that do not make sense for our 80% impact rule, either. They would require a new web-based interface to be created to gain any benefit.

Applications that make good targets are applications that are already running in .NET Core and Java. .NET Core can run on Linux, making it a good choice as the back end to the containerization services on AWS. Java is a virtualized language already, running in the Java Virtual Machine (JVM), also making it a good choice. With Java, the code needs to be Java-native, which allows you to port an application from AIX to containers running on AWS on x86 equipment and expand your migration capabilities.

Asking these questions will ensure that you are selecting a good potential candidate for refactoring into containers. Once you find a suitable target, the next question that you must ask is how easily you can split out the individual components based on the code structure. At this point, things can get tricky. Many business processes in applications do not align with the underlying code. Look back at the earlier example with the file import process. Although the file import is a separate business process, the application code might be shared among other processes. This intermingling of code makes it very difficult to split the application apart. Unfortunately, you will have to communicate with the engineers of the application and see whether the processes that you have in mind can be easily extracted out of the application.

Although I haven't seen this kind of benefit come up much in the migrations that I have done, when things do align, it has a potential for significant impact, which is why we have covered it here. Remember, if you do locate an application that fits these criteria, you will again have to adjust your timeline to compensate.

Redshift data warehouse. Changing a data warehouse is another service that would make a good target for refactoring. AWS has a service called Redshift that can significantly reduce costs while providing more capabilities for scaling. If you are running a data warehouse on-premises, you are probably running it on Oracle or Microsoft SQL Server. I have seen quite a few Microsoft SQL database servers running a data warehouse, and I can tell you they can end up being very large instances. For one company, I specifically remember the instances were somewhere around $16,000 per month, each. With contemporary databases, you usually end up scaling vertically instead of horizontally, and this leads to high costs. It is far cheaper to use a few smaller instances than one gargantuan one.

You are probably using a business intelligence (BI) tool as well to consume the data in a more usable format. This tooling will also use at least one server to run, although the cost of that server is probably not significant enough to meet your 80% impact target. The licensing of your BI tool, on the other hand, is a different story. During refactoring, I recommend you compare the cost of your current BI license to Amazon QuickSight, which offers a fully serverless managed BI tool at a significantly lower price point. I was able to save one company over $800,000 a year by converting it to Redshift and QuickSight from Microsoft SQL and Tableau. With savings like that, it is easy to see how moving your data warehouse can meet your 80% target.

The question left to answer is whether moving the data warehouse will meet the 20% target with the level of effort required to refactor. There are three major components to a data warehouse refactoring to look at to determine the level of effort needed. These are: (1) How will the data be moved into the new data warehouse? (2) How many queries need to be rewritten? (3) How many reports need to be re-created in the BI tooling?

Moving the data

When it comes to moving your data from a legacy database platform to Redshift, you will want to use the DMS service that we discussed in "Database Migration Service" on page 201. You would use a similar process to the one we just talked about in "Database engine change" on page 219. You first need to identify that the schema can easily be converted using the SCT. You will want to verify that the schema has a very large automatic conversion rate to keep the level of effort on the refactor low. Then you would move the data between the old on-premises server and the new Redshift cluster in AWS, using DMS.

Query rewrites

When it comes to rewriting your queries, Redshift does not have the same internal structure that conventional relational database engines have. Redshift is a columnar database instead of a row-based database. This design makes it very fast for looking up data for analytics but slow for individual row updates. Redshift also does not enforce primary and foreign key constraints, so your application must handle that. Ultimately, the queries you used for your conventional row-based system will not be appropriate for Redshift, and you will need to rewrite your queries for them to work properly. If your application needs a significant number of queries, it might push the level of effort past our 20% target.

Report rewrites

Although converting your BI tooling is a great way to save soft and hard costs, unfortunately, there is no way today to transfer your reports out of your old system and into Amazon QuickSight. Therefore, you will need to evaluate how much effort would be needed to re-create these reports. Your timeline delta boils down to the number of reports that you *need*. I was tempted to say the number of reports that you have, but let's face it, several reports are probably no longer needed that you can skip altogether.

Once you have evaluated these three items for the level of effort required, you can determine whether changing your data warehouse is indeed a viable 80/20 target. Once you make this decision, you can look at adjusting your timeline accordingly to compensate.

Static website. One of the capabilities that AWS offers that isn't looked at often from the aspect of refactoring is moving your website (or part of it) to a static site. A static website is one in which you do not use a server to generate the web pages but use static HTML files that are served to your customers instead. Many websites can benefit from moving some or all capabilities to static files. One of the best use cases is your company's landing page. Typically, the landing page does not have a lot of dynamic content on it because the user has not logged on or selected anything yet. This page is also the one in which you have the greatest number of users that do not follow through with other activities. A user will visit your site to check out what your company is about and leave. It makes sense to refactor this content to static pages and let AWS do most of the heavy lifting. This offloading allows your servers to do the more important work for real visitors while having more resources available to them.

A common misnomer is that a static site cannot have dynamic *content*, but this is not true. The important differentiation to make is that a dynamic site creates each web page for every visit and every user, whereas a static site pulls the pages from static files and receives dynamic data from an API. Many new single-page applications (SPA) commonly written in the React or Angular frameworks operate in this model. The pages, images, and JavaScript are all loaded out of an S3 bucket, and the data is retrieved from another AWS service called Amazon API Gateway. API Gateway provides the serverless API resources to connect to AWS Lambda or Amazon EC2 compute resources to return dynamic data. The SPA then renders the data on the client side, rather than the server side. Based on this model, you can see how it can significantly reduce the overhead on your servers as it offloads it to the AWS services and the clients themselves.

The question of whether this meets our 80% target rests solely on the level of load that your website gets. If your website runs an online application, the probability is high that moving some of it to a static type of hosting makes sense. It is important to highlight the word *some*. Because you are running an application, there is no way for you to convert it to static and meet the 20% effort target. This would require far too much testing and engineering.

If your website does not get a lot of traffic, then it probably won't make much sense to convert it to static files as part of the migration. With little load, it probably runs on a single server, or potentially a small cluster fronted with a load balancer for redundancy. The spend for these items, even on an annualized basis, probably does not make sense to include at this stage of the process. It would be better to leave the site refactoring for postmigration as an ongoing effort to reduce costs, using AWS capabilities. I would recommend this type of refactoring to be done as part of a website redesign to optimize your company's expenditures.

Mail server. Mail relay servers used for sending outbound mail from your applications are one potential item you can easily remove from your infrastructure as part of a refactoring. For smaller companies, this probably is not relevant, but medium-sized businesses or enterprises can save a decent amount of cash. Amazon has a service called Simple Email Service (SES) that allows you to send and receive email for applications. It is not a replacement for your actual email server, which collects your users' email, but it is best used for relay servers. Typically, you see these attached to web applications that send large amounts of email that you don't want disrupting your primary employee email server.

The primary benefit of using SES is that it's a fully managed service, and you don't have to worry about maintaining highly available email servers.

I often feel like a broken record, saying that because a service is managed it reduces your soft costs. Hopefully, I am driving home the point that AWS takes a lot of burden off your staff.

As with other AWS services, SES saves you the cost of the servers themselves as well as a load balancer and the soft costs that go along with patching and maintaining that server. You might be surprised to learn that an enterprise could have a dozen or so of these email servers strewn through its infrastructure.

The best and most attractive part of refactoring to use SES is that it requires an extremely low level of effort. If you can, I would suggest that you implement SES using the AWS API. Refactoring your application a little more deeply to use SES through the AWS API with a software development kit (SDK) will require a little more effort to implement. You can also implement SES using an SMTP connection, as you have for your existing mail server. However, using an SDK allows you greater control over access, by using IAM roles versus the username and password of the SMTP connection. Using IAM is not only more secure, but you have less configuration overhead for your application, because access will be granted to an EC2 instance through an IAM instance role that grants access to send email. This design alleviates manual mail server configuration from your application.

You can choose to use the SMTP method initially; this will prevent you from having to make modifications to your migration timeline. I would suggest you use this configuration method during migration. You can come back and make code changes to use the API later after you have migrated.

AWS offers several other capabilities for refactoring that we could discuss. However, those that we have covered should give you a strong foundation for refactoring, and that applies to many companies. You can take a look at the AWS website (*https:// aws.amazon.com*) to see whether there are any other services your company can implement to address other major pain points.

Before we finish up your migration plan with all of your refactoring efforts, we first need to double-check the math on run rates for these changes. In addition, we will also want to put together a business case for the refactoring efforts by application, so that you can easily convey the benefit to the necessary stakeholders. In the next two sections, we will cover how to address these two items.

Estimating Run Rate After Refactoring

There is a high probability that the biggest driver in refactoring your application is cost. It might not be directly related to EC2 compute costs, but it will be costs nonetheless. In the following sections, we will focus on the changes in the run rate by refactoring your application. We will discuss other potential savings in the follow-on section on business cases.

When it comes down to it, migrating to the cloud always seems to default to talking about the run rate and savings, even though this is not the compelling business story for migrating to AWS. The good news is that calculating run rates are a well-trodden path, and we can calculate your numbers and craft a compelling story to drive the refactoring. Refactoring causes a unique problem in that it can become difficult to calculate the differences in run rate between the contemporary design and the refactored one. Some of the types of refactoring that we discussed, such as containerization, don't paint a very clear picture, since the savings depend on your code and how the individual components of your application are laid out.

To highlight how your costs might look, we don't want to talk in generalizations about costs and AWS services. Instead, it is better to cover in detail each of the refactoring items that we just discussed and highlight how the run rates would be affected directly. The following walkthroughs will help you draw similarities and conclusions about the run rates in your environment and allow you to craft your run rates.

Database engine change

When it comes to changing database engines, not much adjustment might be required to run rates. It all depends on whether you selected Amazon RDS or Aurora as the database endpoint. Both RDS and Aurora support the MySQL and PostgreSQL engines, but they have vastly different capabilities. In the case of RDS, you most likely will not have any difference in run rates. RDS supports a single or failover multi-AZ deployment. In most cases, this will mimic your current environment exactly. You will have a single server that supports the entire load of your application and a second to take over in case of primary failure. This lack of change makes me hesitate to say that changing the engine will reduce your compute requirements. Instead, changing the database engine will mostly affect your licensing costs.

If you have selected Aurora as the destination, some additional capabilities might change your costs. Aurora has two capabilities that reduce costs. The first is that you can scale Aurora horizontally with read-only servers for read queries, which will allow you to use a number of smaller servers to meet your requirements. Typically, many smaller servers are more cost-effective than single large ones. The second capability that Aurora offers for driving down costs is Aurora Serverless. In this configuration, Aurora will scale up and down to meet your load, so you only pay for what you use. In addition, Aurora Serverless has the capability of turning off completely while not in use to save you additional cash.

To address these changes in compute spend, you will have to extract the size and count of instances that your discovery tool suggested for your selected application. You can add these up separately to get your original run rate. If you will use read replicas to spread the load moving your database servers into Aurora, you will need to look at the percentage of read queries versus the write queries that are being run against your current server. Once you determine those percentages, you can estimate how you can break up the server. For simplicity, let us use the 80/20 rule again. We will state that 20% of your queries are write and 80% are read. In this instance, you can split your single large server into five smaller servers. Your write node services the 20% of write requests, and your 80% of read requests is serviced by the 4 other nodes, with 20% of the read load each. If you had a monster database server that was running a 32xlarge instance type, you could change this single server instance into five 8xlarge servers and still have a little room to spare.

If you are planning to run Aurora Serverless, it could be tricky to calculate the difference in spend since you have both the ability to scale and the ability to turn off. At this point in the process, I do not think it is worthwhile for you to go down the rabbit hole, trying to calculate the difference to that level of minutia. Instead, you should take the average server capacity that you have and then calculate the run rate for that capacity. Once you have that cost, you would then divide it by the number of hours in a week and determine how many hours you *will not* need it running. Then subtract those hours from the weekly rate. From there, you can easily calculate the annual cost by multiplying by the 52 weeks in a year.

S3 object storage

Luckily, calculating the cost difference in S3 over EBS is much easier than calculating the database engine change we just covered. When you move your data from S3, you are most likely substituting EBS costs. To calculate the run rate, you can simply multiply the number of gigabytes of data that you are refactoring in your application by the S3 storage rate for your chosen AWS region. If you are using tiering, you can further refine this cost by estimating the percentage of S3 standard storage and S3 infrequent access storage and calculate the new storage costs.

To refine the EBS costs that are in your current estimate, you will need to take the gigabytes that you are refactoring plus the 30% storage buffer. Remember, I recommend a buffer to be added to your used disk capacity so that you will not run out of space. When you use S3, you do not need this space, because you can continually expand your footprint without running out of capacity.

Containerization

Computing savings based on containerization is probably the hardest of all the items that we have discussed. Multiple levels of complexity need to be considered. You have a shared operating system container, shared subsystem and library containers, and individual container scales based on usage independently. To make matters a bit more complicated, you might not have been able to split your application into as many microservices as you had hoped. If you want, you can get into the gritty details of how much CPU power is required by each process and create a detailed spreadsheet of your expected load. The other option is putting your finger in the air and creating a SWAG of how much savings you will have. The latter is usually how I end up coming up with a number to estimate savings.

Data warehouse

Computing the changes in cost between Redshift and your conventional database looks very similar to Amazon Aurora. Redshift also switches from a single-node database to a multinode deployment. In the case of Redshift, we need to divide the total compute capacity by the number of nodes needed. The major difference that Redshift has from other compute resources in AWS is that the disk capacity is tied to the instance type. There are two classes of instances in Redshift: a compute preference class and a disk preference class. The first step is to determine whether you need the compute preference instance class. You can determine the required capacity by looking at the load of your queries. Once you determine which class you need, you can divide your data storage requirements by the amount of available storage for the selected instance. For example, a ds2.8xlarge instance is a dense storage instance that supports 16 TB of storage. If you had 28 TB of data, you would need two nodes to meet your storage requirement. This example might not be the best, because you might be out of storage in short order, depending on your capacity expansion. Once you know how many Redshift nodes you will need, you can calculate out your new run rate on an annualized basis, using the one-year RI pricing. I recommend using the RI pricing because data warehouse capacity does not change and is consistent. Using RIs ensures your lowest cost option.

Like changing your database engine, most of the savings will be licensing savings. You will be replacing your expensive engine license and potentially saving the expense of your visualization software such as Tableau. We will address items like this in "Building the Business Case for Refactoring" on page 230.

Static website

If you are refactoring your website to use static hosting capabilities in AWS, you will need to adjust the run rate of your web servers and EBS storage. Before we can calculate your new run rate, we need to determine what percentage of your site is being converted. Once we have that number, we can take that cost from your EC2 spend to get the new run rate. Let us say that your website allows for the refactoring of 10% of its content. Using this information, we can look at the EC2 spend on your web server farm. We will use the spend that was determined by your discovery tooling. To find your new run rate, you would simply multiply the total EC2 cost by the remaining required capacity. If your EC2 spend was estimated at $500 a month, you would multiply that by 0.9 to get a result of $450 per month in new spend. Spending on web servers becomes a bit of a moving target with load balancers and auto scaling. This situation is yet another example of when simplicity is probably your best course of action.

Once you compute your EC2 costs, you can do the same for your EBS storage costs. When you move to a static hosting situation, you store your data in S3. You would mimic the process that we just discussed to estimate S3 object storage costs. You need to find the total storage your static content will use and then divide that up using your estimates of how much data will be used all the time in S3 standard, and how much will be used infrequently. You will then be able to calculate the combined total cost of your website storage. On the reverse side, you can also back out the storage from the EBS cost, using the same method as for your S3 storage in GBs plus your EBS storage buffer.

Mail server

Finally, we come to the last refactoring that we discussed with the mail server change, using SES. In the grand scheme of your migration, the run cost for SES probably does not matter. AWS gives you 62,000 email messages for free each month (no idea why it is 62K; it seems to be a very odd number to me), and then they charge $0.10 for every 1,000 email messages you send after that. Even if you send a million email messages, it will only cost you less than $100. You can easily cover the cost of SES in the uplifts that we talked about in "Run Rate Modeling" on page 114. The important item to address with mail server refactoring is the removal of the run rate for your mail servers from your forecast, because this can be a large number.

Unfortunately, you can probably see that some run rate modeling isn't very easy to calculate, and we end up performing some SWAG calculations. I do not *hate* SWAG numbers, but I see them as unavoidable. I do try to limit them to the lowest number in my calculations as possible. With the addition of each one, you potentially move further and further away from reality. Now that we have these numbers nailed down, we can move on to building the business case for refactoring.

Building the Business Case for Refactoring

Now that we have covered how you can calculate changes in run rates, it's time to create your business case, which justifies the refactoring of the application, the additional timeline, and the efforts involved. There may be some preexisting negativity toward refactoring, and it's important to demonstrate that you are not just chasing a new shiny object.

 The tendency to want to implement the newest thing is not only an engineering issue. I have run into plenty of what I call *magazine managers* who want the latest thing they read about in a magazine to be implemented as soon as possible, the technical limitations be damned.

We will be following the same path as we did for the migration business case. In Chapter 3, you performed your discovery, which gave you the run rate for your whole migration. Then in Chapter 4, we created the migration business case. We will be doing the same here now that you have your refactored run rates. Making a business case for refactoring isn't anywhere near as complex as the business case you worked on for the migration itself. Unlike your migration business case that had a narrative, an FAQ, and a closing, we will just focus on the closing for the refactoring effort.

For each application that you are refactoring, I would recommend at most a one-page narrative that explains the refactoring effort. Avoid getting too burdened with justification at this point in your migration, and remember that the purpose of your refactoring is to target the easy wins for migration that will not significantly affect your timeline or costs in a negative way. If you were justifying a large refactoring postmigration, such as redesigning a major application into a serverless model that could cost months of engineering time, then a more elaborate justification would be appropriate.

When writing the narrative, focus your argument on the 80/20 rule and how you used that to target the application and services. This elaboration on your process will set the tone for the rest of the document by establishing that your method focuses on driving high-value changes to the application. By setting this tone, you will supplant any negativity that likely started to hatch the second you mentioned making application changes.

After you go over the selection methodology, move on to discussing the downfalls of the current technology in use. The refactored items that we talked about mostly focus on costs (agility items tend to take longer to refactor that are outside our 20% target), so feel free to center your story on that.

In addition to the run rate savings, we don't want to leave out the significant cost savings that can be had if you refactor your database engine or data warehouse. In the previous section, we just talked about the run rate modeling in the refactored mode. Those costs did not include the savings that you get by cutting out your high licensing costs. Oracle and Microsoft SQL licensing adds up to some pretty significant numbers, and you will want to make sure that you include those savings as well. In the end, items such as license cost savings make up the greatest business drivers. It is important not to dismiss license costs savings. For instance, a company that I was working with intended to see three-million-dollar annual savings by getting rid of their Oracle databases. A story like that can make a career in very short order, and that is why it is so important to investigate license costs thoroughly.

The last item that I would suggest putting into your narrative is a short list of risks. Let's be honest. Nothing is risk free. Getting your risks out in the open right away rather than trying to sweep them under the carpet shows that you are a stronger manager. When I was in management, and someone on my team brought me a proposal that did not have any risks or potential negatives in it, I would immediately ask them to add them before we would continue discussions. I wanted them to provide an honest, unbiased view.

Final Thoughts on Refactoring

One important thing to remember is that it's OK if you couldn't find any applications to refactor at this point in the process. You might just have a lot of COTS applications that limit your capabilities to change. On the other hand, you might be working with older technology that would not fit into our target for low-hanging fruit. Maybe the changes you want to make will extend your timeline longer than you can accommodate. Whatever the reason, there is always the day after your migration to come back and take a new look at what you can do with AWS. Now that we have looked at refactoring, I wanted to touch on what I call *retooling*.

Retooling

There are always some new capabilities that you can easily add using AWS services that were not available to you on-premises. I do not consider these to be refactoring per se, but rather net new additions to your capabilities. These items often add a lot of value for companies and do not have a very high price point, but they don't require changes to your application itself. It is true that they will increase your costs above what you had on-premises, but the value that they add to your business is well worth the expense. The three items that we will cover in the next sections are the AWS Web Application Firewall (WAF), AWS Systems Manager, and Amazon CloudFront. These specific services have been chosen because they increase your collective security posture and improve your customer experience.

Retooling typically happens as part of your individual application migrations. However, it makes sense to create a guiding principle on their use prior to getting into the application deep-dive analysis. During that analysis, your team can determine whether their implementation is appropriate for the application.

Web Application Firewall

The Web Application Firewall (WAF) is a network Layer 7 firewall service, which means that this firewall can understand protocols and not just IP addresses and ports. This additional capability allows it to see inside the HTTPS and HTTP protocols and look for malicious attacks. The WAF service is also serverless, so there are no servers to maintain and patch and no capacity and scaling to worry about. Basically, the WAF enables you to apply a significant level of protection to your web servers with nearly zero effort. In addition, AWS released a new version of WAF that includes redefined rulesets that detect such attacks as cross-site scripting and SQL injection attacks.

The WAF is also extremely cost-effective compared to on-premises capabilities. The WAF charges $5 for a web access control list (ACL) and $1 per rule (at the time of writing). One of the best parts of how AWS has set pricing for WAF is that managed rulesets only count for one rule. For example, the AWS SQL injection managed ruleset has five rules but only costs $1 because it is managed. If you were to write your own rules, you would be charged $1 *per* rule. That is still a great deal considering the costs that you would have to endure on-premises.

I would consider running WAF on all web-facing applications to add another layer of inexpensive security protection. AWS WAF can secure Amazon CloudFront, Amazon API Gateway, and the Application Load Balancer.

Systems Manager

AWS Systems Manager is a tool that, like most others I've suggested, is serverless and offers your company the ability to manage your instances and apply patches. If you are running Chef, Puppet, Salt, or Ansible on-premises, then using Systems Manager Service (SSM, not to be confused with Server Migration Service, SMS) would be considered a refactoring instead of an additional capability. If this is the case, I suggest that you do not convert to Systems Manager during the migration. However, if you are not running any of these capabilities, then I suggest that you implement SSM during migration. SSM has many capabilities, but the most relevant ones are the ability to control instance state and apply instance patches.

The ability to control instance state allows you to ensure that the configuration you deploy to your instances stays in compliance. Using SSM state manager allows you to control Windows settings as well as install Windows features. You can also use the state manager to install software. These capabilities allow you to add a high level of automation to your environment and save your company a significant amount of soft costs. During migration, you will want to automate as many security-related controls as possible to ensure continued security compliance. These controls might look like firewall rules that are deployed to instances.

The second highly effective feature of SSM is the Patch Manager. Patch Manager allows you to deploy patches to your instances automatically for both Linux and Windows during a maintenance window. In addition to rolling out patches on a schedule, the patch manager can deploy patches based on the release date. This feature comes in very handy by allowing you to test patches before you roll them out to your production environment. For instance, you can allow patches to be deployed to development immediately when they are released. You can follow this up with the testing environment to be deployed after seven days. Finally, you can configure your production environment to roll patches out after 14 days. These delays ensure that the patches that roll out to production have had at least 14 days to incubate and be tested prior to deployment. These delays ensure that your customers never experience an outage due to a patch that affects the operations of your application.

CloudFront

The last service to consider adding to your infrastructure is Amazon CloudFront. We touched on CloudFront in Chapter 1, but to recap, CloudFront is a content delivery network that brings your data closer to your end users through caching. Not only can CloudFront increase your customers' satisfaction, but it can also increase your web server security by providing another abstraction layer before your servers. CloudFront will be your first line of defense in the event of a denial of service attack before it hits your web servers. It would be advantageous to put CloudFront in front of all your web servers. The cost of CloudFront can actually reduce your data transmission rates because it is cheaper to send data out of CloudFront than from standard AWS.

When you couple CloudFront with AWS WAF, you create a layered security that greatly increases your ability to absorb and defend from various types of attacks. Like most AWS services, CloudFront is completely serverless and offers you these capabilities without the need for managing and patching. You could replicate some of the capabilities of CloudFront on your own by using proxy servers, but that won't offer you the security or global scale that is available using CloudFront.

Final Preparations

Now that we have covered the additional features that you can add to your environment to boost your capabilities for a small incremental cost, it is time to move to the final phase and prepare for application migration. At this point, you have discovered your workloads, created your business case, worked through creating your migration plan, and figured out what applications you can refactor to maximize your cost optimizations in AWS. You are now ready to start your migration process. Although this book does not include the technical documentation to use the tools that we talked about, there are several resources on the web such as A Cloud Guru (*https://acloud.guru*), which we discussed before, as well as AWS Support YouTube (*https://*

oreil.ly/m6fzB), AWS blogs (*https://aws.amazon.com/blogs*), and online learning from O'Reilly (*https://www.oreilly.com/online-learning*). The last item that we will cover is application deep dive and planning, in which we will discuss the various pieces of an application-level migration plan.

Application Deep Dive and Planning

In Chapter 3, we covered discovering your workloads in a broader sense. Now, we will cover the detailed discovery you'll need to perform for each application in your portfolio just before migration. This discovery may sound like a lot of work, but much of the information among your applications will be the same. The process will get faster as you progress through your applications. I will detail the critical items to cover here, but there are many more that are important to your success.

Application Status

When you are assessing for migration, you will want to know the current status of your application. Look for the following things: when the application was last updated, whether the application version is current, and whether there any pending updates, to name a few. You are looking for this information because it gives you a good indication of the level of knowledge the stakeholders have regarding the operations of the application. An application that has not been updated in a long time or is one or more releases behind is an indication of poor knowledge. As we discussed before in "Staffing and Expertise Loss" on page 65, turnover and the loss of tribal knowledge in IT is an issue. When an application has not been updated in quite some time, the probability that the tribal knowledge has left the building with Elvis is higher. Why is this important? The tribal knowledge in question is the nitty-gritty details about what broke and how to fix it that are not in any instructions. During your migration, these small pieces of information are critical to meeting your timeline and quality goals. The perfect situation for migration is when the application has been recently updated and is on the latest version.

Application version currency is not a huge issue in migrating to AWS from a technical perspective. Version currency becomes an issue about what version the vendor supports in the cloud. It is common for vendors not to certify older versions to run in AWS, which can create an issue when you call support. From a technical perspective, EC2 is just another form of virtualization, and today's operating systems are abstracted from the application layer. These abstractions mitigate any issues with changing drivers for network cards and so on. Therefore, application currency is purely a business problem.

Team Bandwidth

Sometimes internally developed applications need slight modification to make them work in AWS, and some developer time is necessary. Another common occurrence is when the application could benefit from a slight refactoring that significantly reduces costs. In either of these situations, you need to make sure prior to migration that the development team performing the work has the necessary bandwidth, and that the refactoring does not overlap with other migrations taking place that need the same development team. Team contention like this can lead to delays in migration that drive up costs or, worse, rushed work that ends up in downtime. Either of these scenarios results in business repercussions that you want to avoid.

Another issue that you will want to query from the business unit is the amount of testing required and the number of staff members available to complete the testing. From there, you can assess how long you will need the testing staff and can determine whether they have the available bandwidth to complete the testing within the migration timelines. If there is a discrepancy, you may need to bring in outside help for the business unit or adjust your migration timeline to compensate. Failing to address the testing bandwidth leads to inadequate testing or program delays. Either of these scenarios drives up costs unnecessarily.

Technical Details

Some technical details need to be captured during application discovery as well. Some technical constraints have a large business impact that need to be considered for migration timelines and risk. For instance, I worked for companies that still used FTP as a mode of transferring files between themselves and customers. Since FTP is an insecure protocol, many customers block it on their firewalls to prevent their users and servers from using it. To be able to connect to our FTP server, many of the customers would have to put exception rules in their firewalls to allow their servers to communicate. We had nearly one thousand customers connecting to this server. As you can imagine, moving this type of server could have a substantial impact on your migration effort and migration timeline, in addition to the reputational risk associated with it.

If you were to migrate this server without prior knowledge of how it operated, it could have a potentially negative effect on hundreds of customers, which could affect revenue and the company's reputation. Because of this risk, it is vital to capture technical details. Unfortunately, it is impossible to cover all of the potential technical items that might come up, but here is a list of a few to give you an idea of what to look out for:

- Permissible IP addresses
- Nonstandard TCP ports for protocols

- Permissible domains in proxy servers and firewalls
- License keys tied to server network card MAC addresses

Technical Migration Plan

The technical migration plan details the types of technologies that will be used to perform the migration. There are multiple AWS services available for migrating servers and data based on your use case. For migrating substantial amounts of older static data, there are Snowball and Snowmobile physical devices. These devices are sent to you, either by truck or UPS/FedEx. Once you have the device, you can copy data over to it and then send the device back to AWS, which loads the data into S3.

For databases, there is the Database Migration Service (DMS). For migrating servers, there is CloudEndure. Which of the technologies you use is based on volume and the acceptable age of the data. For instance, the Snowball device takes about seven days to ship and load the data into S3 and become available for use. If your application has a 10-minute cutover time and you need data that is current up to the second, Snowball would not be a desirable choice for this application. Your technical migration plan should detail these typologies and how they will be represented for each component of your application.

Testing Process

One place that you do not want to overlook is the testing process. The testing process details the testing that needs to happen pre- and postcutover. Typically, I like to see a significant amount of precutover testing, because this leads to less testing later in the process during cutover when stress is high and time is short. Testing is such an important part of the migration because of the changes to infrastructure that might be necessary to take full advantage of the benefits of AWS. Enhanced HA, better DR, and dynamic scaling all implement some amount of change to your environment and could cause issues that lead to poor customer satisfaction. Let us look at an example of how you might encounter risk related to testing.

Scenario 8-1

Bethany is migrating her three-tier web application from her colocation data center into AWS. As part of the migration, she wants to take advantage of making her web servers highly available. She wants to put a load balancer and an auto scaling group in to maintain the lowest cost possible. Bethany failed to create a testing plan for the application. Since it was a simple web application, she figured she would have one of the engineers log on to the application and make sure that everything was online, and that they could log on. During the cutover, everything worked great. The next

---

> Monday, when customers started logging on to the application, they started to experience all sorts of problems with the site, and they kept getting logged out randomly.

Bethany's story is a good example of why you want to thoroughly test your application ahead of time. In her case, she had performed a smoke test during the migration, which is OK only when you have done robust testing ahead of time. Her web application was stateful, and by using auto scaling and a load balancer without sticky sessions, her users had a poor experience. If she had performed proper testing ahead of time, they would have run into this issue and identified the need for the sticky session configuration on the load balancer before customers experienced the problem. Sticky sessions ensure that the same user lands on the same server every time. The load balancer maintains the connection for the duration of the session rather than for the server with the least load. By only performing a smoke test to ensure that the servers were online, they did not increase the load enough or cause a scaling action to expose the problem. Adequate testing is a vital step in migration.

Cutover Process

It is common for migrations to focus solely on the technical aspects of migration and completely forget about the organization of the cutover. In migration terms, the *cutover* is the process of changing the application from running on-premises to running in AWS. The technology used for the migration influences how long cutover can take, but there might be additional business items to be aware of. Obviously, knowing when you need to cut over is an important item. Whether the cutover needs to be on the weekend or needs to have a data validation are also important questions to ask. The idea is to capture as many caveats as possible that the business unit knows prior to the migration.

By documenting the cutover process, you minimize the time needed for cutover and ensure that all necessary steps have been addressed. Typically, the issues that I have seen during cutover are due to sequencing problems. Here is a scenario that details how a sequencing problem can derail your cutover due to poor preparation.

Scenario 8-2

Kurt's team is performing a cutover of their global accounting application from their in-house data center to AWS. They did not create a cutover plan because the application is simple, with only an application server and database server. The team is using the CloudEndure tool from AWS, which performs ongoing block-level disk replication to copy the application server into AWS. For the database server, they decided to set up a new RDS instance in AWS and restore a backup of the on-premises database. During the cutover, they took a backup of the database and restored it to the RDS instance in AWS. Once they had completed that, they used CloudEndure to deploy

---

the application server in AWS and shut down the one on-premises. After the migration, an accountant in Singapore opened an IT support ticket stating that their work had been lost and asking what happened.

Kurt has experienced a classic case of a cutover sequencing issue. During the cutover, the team failed to stop the application prior to the database backup. This timing allowed an employee who was not aware of the intended outage to access the system and do work between the database backup and the application server being shut down. This discrepancy in timing allowed the database to get out of sync with the last backup. In this scenario, Kurt would have performed some diagnostics to find out what happened. Once it was discovered, there would have to be another database backup and restoration along with another application outage. Kurt's simple application migration ended up costing the company hundreds or thousands of dollars more than it should have due to poor cutover planning.

Rollback Process

In migrations as well as in life, we always plan on things going correctly, but we do not always plan for when they don't. When planning for migration, you want to ensure that you have created a rollback plan so that if something does go wrong, you can revert to the previous on-premises version. The processes of cutover and rollback are not necessarily done in the same order; they can even be a different process altogether. Often rollback consists of destroying or stopping the new AWS version of the servers and reactivating the on-premises version. Other issues that might arise concern DNS changes, specifically the time-to-live values that might cause issues for customers trying to access your site. I have found that performing a mental exercise of walking through the rollback with business stakeholders, developers, and your engineering staff will flush out much of the process and caveats. A rollback is easier than a cutover because the original state of the application is not destroyed and can be made functional with minimal effort.

Closing

Sam's chair creaks as she leans back. She just checked her project management software, and everything is on track for the cutover Sunday evening. Not bad, she thinks. It's two p.m. on Friday, and everything is on schedule. Feeling the warmth on her arm, she turns her attention to the kids in the park across the street. The blue of the sky is inviting, and the leaves dance gently. She decides to pack up her things and head home to spend some time with her kids. On the way out, she stops by the vice president's office.

"Tom, just wanted to let you know that we are all set for our production cutover of the accounting system this weekend," she says from the doorway. She is a little anxious holding her laptop bag, wondering if he will notice.

"That's great, Samantha, everyone is impressed with the progress that has been made with the migration so far." The corners of her mouth turn up, even though she's trying to be humble. "I see you have your laptop, why don't you just put that back on your desk?" Tom suggests. "You have earned some free time." Sam gives a gentle nod and walks back to her desk to leave her laptop behind.

When it comes to migration, Benjamin Franklin had it right with "an ounce of prevention is worth a pound of cure." Hopefully, this book has demonstrated how short-sightedness can cause you more issues, frustration, and, potentially, your future success. Most of the follies in migration can be prevented with proper research and planning, items that are so often passed over in an attempt to reduce timelines and cost.

At this point in the process, you've done the research and planning and are ready to begin your migration. Since this book is focused on the managerial aspects and not on the technical implementation of migration, here is where we must part ways. I wish you good luck on your migration—though if you made it here, luck isn't necessary.

Index

notifications, 44

O

object storage, 220-221, 228
Okta, 180
online learning, 235
operating systems (OS)
    recommended tagging, 70
    unsupported and outdated, 190-191
operational expenditures, 35-37
operational pyramid, 144
    apex, 155-156
    base, 145-153
    building, 144-156
    expansion layer, 154-155
    foundation, 144-145
operational readiness, 74, 141-161
Optimize CPUs function, 6
Oracle, 201, 219, 223, 231
Organizations service, 43
OS (see operating system)
outbound bandwidth, 93-94
owner tags, 70
O'Reilly online learning, 235

P

Pareto principle, 216
partial run rate, 86
Patch Manager, 234
patch tags, 70
pay-as-you-go model, 37
Payment Card Industry Data Security Standard
    (PCI-DSS, or PCI), 142, 170, 182
percentage migrations, 127-128
performance monitoring, 50
personally identifiable information (PII), 166
physical MFA devices, 177
PII (personally identifiable information), 166
pipelines, 158
planning
    agile, 188-189
    building your plan, 203-214
    combination, 188-189
    finalizing the 90%, 212-213
    laying down the 90%, 208-211
    migration, 64, 74, 187-214
    needs for, 187-188
    polishing the 10%, 213-214
    preplanning, 189

rollback plans, 149
    technical migration plan, 237
    testing, 64
    tooling for, 206-208
    waterfall, 188-189
platinum tier, 185
PostgreSQL, 217, 219
preplanning, 189
pricing, 2, 175
    on instances, 125
    Reserved Instance, 229
    URLs for, 2
Pricing Calculator, 25
priority shifts, 196
privacy regulations, 13
process management, 153-153
progress measurement, 199
project management, 152, 206
prototyping, 145-153
Puppet, 233
pyramid building (see operational pyramid)
Python, 59

Q

quality of service (QoS), 54
query rewrites, 224
QuickSight, 17, 168, 223, 224

R

R factors, 111, 189
RAID (Redundant Array of Inexpensive Disks),
    90
RDP (Remote Desktop protocol), 55, 167
RDS (see Relational Database Service)
re-platforming, 113
React, 225
read-only role, 45
recommended accounts, 167-171
recovery point objective (RPO), 32
recovery time objective (RTO), 32
Red Hat, 191
redeployment, 112
Redshift, 223-224, 229
Redundant Array of Inexpensive Disks (RAID),
    90
refactoring, 112, 215-232
    business case for, 230-232
    potential targets, 217-227
region management, 173-174

About the Author

Jeff Armstrong has 25 years of information technology experience, working in several industry verticals for startups and Fortune 100 companies alike. For the past six years, he has been working as an architect in the mass migration space, four of which have been exclusively cloud migrations to AWS. He has evaluated, designed, or migrated more than 150,000 workloads in that time. Jeff is also an avid programmer, having worked in nine different languages throughout his career. He has obtained nine AWS certifications, is CISSP certified, and also holds the Certified Ethical Hacker (CEH) and Computer Hacking Forensic Investigator (CHFI) security certifications.

Jeff believes in self-innovation and continued education. He holds a bachelor's degree in business administration, a master's degree in information technology and assurance, and is pursuing his doctorate in business administration. He also holds a certificate in strategy and innovation from MIT Sloan and a certificate in executive leadership from Cornell.

Colophon

The animal on the cover of *Migrating to AWS: A Manager's Guide* is an upland sandpiper (*Bartramia longicauda*), a species of migratory shorebird also known as the upland plover or grass plover. Unlike other North American shorebirds, the upland sandpiper does not inhabit wetlands or mudflats and instead prefers grasslands, meadows, dry tundras, and prairies. Their native breeding habit covers parts of Alaska, Canada, the Midwest, and New England, but they are most commonly found in the Great Plains region.

Upland sandpipers are large birds (about 12 inches long) with small, distinctive round heads, large eyes, and long legs and necks. Their bodies and wings are speckled brown with white around the eyes and along the throat and belly. They forage for food by walking quickly through short grass and pecking at various seeds and insects, including grasshoppers, crickets, beetles, ants, and fly larvae. During mating season the males perform aerial displays and flight calls as they circle the breeding territory. These birds are not particularly territorial, so while they do mate and tend their young in pairs, some breeding adults will forage and rest together in small groups. Baby sandpipers are downy and active from the time they hatch, and can leave the nest and feed themselves almost immediately.

While migrating to South American grasslands for the winter, upland sandpipers have been known to nest in unusual places such as beaches, airports, pastures, and even ballfields. These birds are so closely associated with native prairies that they are considered an *indicator species* whose absence would signal a problem with the habitat. Though they are considered threatened in many parts of the US due to loss of habitat and declining numbers, the International Union for Conservation of Nature considers the upland sandpiper a species of "Least Concern" because the global population is still trending upward. Many of the animals on O'Reilly covers are endangered; all of them are important to the world.

The cover illustration is by Karen Montgomery, based on a black and white engraving from *British Birds*. The cover fonts are Gilroy Semibold and Guardian Sans. The text font is Adobe Minion Pro; the heading font is Adobe Myriad Condensed; and the code font is Dalton Maag's Ubuntu Mono.

O'REILLY®

There's much more
where this came from.

Experience books, videos, live online
training courses, and more from O'Reilly
and our 200+ partners—all in one place.

Learn more at oreilly.com/online-learning

CPSIA information can be obtained
at www.ICGtesting.com
Printed in the USA
FSHW011742090720
71721FS

9 781492 074243